RETHINKING THE FRANKFURT SCHOOL

RETHINKING THE FRANKFURT SCHOOL

Alternative Legacies of Cultural Critique

Edited by
Jeffrey T. Nealon and Caren Irr

State University of New York Press

Cover illustration: Andy Warhol, "Soup Can with Dollar Bills"
© 2002 Andy Warhol Foundation for the Visual Arts/ARS, New York

Published by
State University of New York Press, Albany

© 2002 State University of New York

For information, address State University of New York Press,
90 State Street, Suite 700, Albany, NY 12207

Production by Dana Foote
Marketing by Patrick J. Durocher

Library of Congress Cataloging-in-Publication Data

Rethinking the Frankfurt School : alternative legacies of cultural critique / edited by
Jeffrey T. Nealon and Caren Irr.
     p. cm.
   Includes bibliographical references and index.
     ISBN 0-7914-5491-6 (alk. paper) — ISBN 0-7914-5492-2 (pbk. : alk. paper)
     1. Frankfurt school of sociology. 2. Culture—Philosophy. 3. Culture—Study and
teaching. I. Nealon, Jeffrey T. (Jeffrey Thomas) II. Irr, Caren.

   HM467 .R48 2002
   306'.01—dc21   2002070658

10 9 8 7 6 5 4 3 2 1

CONTENTS

III BENJAMIN, HORKHEIMER, MARCUSE, HABERMAS

IV CONCLUSION

ACKNOWLEDGMENTS

The editors are grateful for permission to reproduce the following essays:

Fredric Jameson, Winter 1994, "The Theoretical Hesitation: Benjamin's Sociological Predecessor," *Critical Inquiry* 25, 267–88.

Douglas Kellner, 1997, "The Frankfurt School and British Cultural Studies: The Missed Articulation" in *Cultural Methodologies,* ed. Jim McGuigan (London: Sage): 12–41.

Andreas Huyssen, Fall 2000, "Of Mice and Mimesis: Reading Spiegelman with Adorno," *New German Critique* 81.

The online journal *Theory & Event* published earlier versions of the essays by Nancy Love (volume 3.1, 1999) and Jeffrey T. Nealon (volume 4.3, 2000).

We would also like to thank the Department of English at the Pennsylvania State University and the provost's office of Brandeis University for their support of this project.

Introduction
Rethinking the Frankfurt School

Jeffrey T. Nealon and Caren Irr

The essays in this volume "rethink" the relationship between the Frankfurt School and theoretical scholarship on contemporary culture, asking what consequences such a rethinking might have for study of the Frankfurt School on its own terms. This question arises because of the paradoxical situation of the Frankfurt School in relation to the humanistic interdiscipline known as "Theory." On the one hand, in the humanities, the Frankfurt School is often taught as an approach that can and is studied alongside other "approaches" (such as poststructuralism, feminism, deconstruction, and cultural studies). On the other hand, the critical theory of the Frankfurt School is also treated as a somewhat dated, slightly ossified predecessor to theory per se. As both contemporary and antecedent to theoretical approaches to culture, then, the Frankfurt School as a topic urges a retrospective reconsideration of the pedigree and genealogy of Theory itself.

In recent literature devoted to the Frankfurt School, such a retrospective view is prominent, and in this project three major trends emerge. First, we find numerous commentators situating the Frankfurt School in relation to problems or themes that have preoccupied the American academy generally. Postmodernism, feminism, sexuality: these and other topics are addressed generally with the sense that they have emerged "after" the Frankfurt School's heyday and thus introduce concerns addressed only partially or as latent issues. It is not uncommon to find essays that look back to the Frankfurt School with a desire to make use of underappreciated resources. For instance, Randall Halle locates tensions between Erich Fromm and Herbert Marcuse's theories of sexuality, locating in the latter means for dissociating the former's metaphorical linkage of homosexuality and fascism.

A second major trend in recent Frankfurt School scholarship involves reading the school internally whether by means of biographical or textual criticism on individual figures, rescuing the reputations of minor contributors, revisiting debates or theses of major figures, or identifying various heirs to the first generation of critical theorists. The first two of these tasks have been, of course, greatly facilitated by the republication and translation into English of major works of Theodor Adorno, Walter Benjamin, and Marcuse. For instance, a significant number of pieces reconsidering critical theories of technology have recently appeared perhaps in response to massive technological transformations in cybernetics over the past twenty-odd years. On the question of heirs, an enormous body of scholarship has of course been devoted to discussion of Jürgen Habermas's work, and a smaller body to the work of Axel Honneth and Alexander Kluge; but a major reevaluation of Adorno and Adornian-influenced scholars also seems to be underway. With substantial recent works on Adorno from Martin Jay, Peter Uwe Hohendahl, Fredric Jameson, Shierry

Weber Nicholson, and Lambert Zuidervaart, Adorno's centrality to any culturalist interpretation of the Frankfurt School seems assured. It might even be said that reconsiderations of Adorno have proceeded at such a pace that a renovated, re-published, and poststructuralist-friendly Adorno (as opposed to the cranky modernist of *Dialectic of Enlightenment*) has become the leading figure of the second-generation Frankfurt School.

The third major trend in recent treatments of the Frankfurt School comple-ments these "internal" approaches with "external" ones. Perhaps the liveliest area of scholarship during the 1990s (after explications of individual figures' major works) was populated by efforts to consider the Frankfurt School as a whole in relation to other schools or approaches. Comparative and/or historical work has situated the Frankfurt School in relation to Martin Heidegger, Friedrich Nietzsche, pragmatism, Michel Foucault, Paul Tillich, Wilhelm von Humboldt, rational choice theory, pre-fascist social thought, Thorstein Veblen, liberal democratic theory, Jerzy Kmita, existentialism, and poststructuralism generally. In addition to illustrating the ten-dency to see critical theory as offering a distinctive and relatively coherent "ap-proach," this body of work also usefully draws attention to the historically situated character of the Frankfurt School (see especially Agger, Dallmayr, and Wolin). Once critical theory acquires a definite set of parameters, then it can be read symptomat-ically in relation to specific cultural situations. In the spirit of a dialectical intellectual history, then, we find a number of scholars reading the Frankfurt School theses "externally" in relation to the politics of exile, the "decay of experience," transforma-tions in national culture industries, and the rise of mass media (see Israel 1997, Jay 1999, and Koepnick 1996). Complementing this trend toward sealing the Frankfurt School off from the present—by means of the tactic of situating—are various efforts to "extend" specific theses of critical theory to institutions, subjects, or themes not initially or entirely addressed by the first generation. Work on law, nature, education, and science appears in this vein.

If we understand cultural studies as an effort to identify determinate links between the "internal" and "external" elements of a cultural form, then clearly the impact of contemporary Theory on study of the Frankfurt School is likely to encour-age and build upon work in the both of the latter two trends. Understanding Theory as a new articulation of the particular in its social situations and a willful defamiliariz-ation of those particularizing theses by extending them to situations for which they were not developed—we might propose these activities as the hallmarks of a meeting of contemporary work on culture and the Frankfurt School. The Frankfurt School is Theory now, in part because it appears as the result of Theory's rereadings. Results of the theoretical reading of the Frankfurt School often involve reading the writings of the school architecturally (as a synchronic assembly of motifs, concepts, intellectual styles), rather than biographically or institutionally. Yet, broadly sketched historical approaches still appear. As essays in this collection illustrate, reconsidering the Frank-furt School in the light of contemporary, cross-disciplinary Theory will often, though not always, lead toward a renewed emphasis on Adorno and on the problems of the relationship of critical theory to poststructuralism, the American media industry, and the social determination of subjectivity and/or experience. Theory helps make the themes and methods of the Frankfurt School legible again.

The Frankfurt School and Cultural Studies

The Frankfurt School has had a particularly difficult relation to the myriad discourses and methodologies of contemporary Theory that travel under the name "Cultural Studies." On many accounts, in fact, Cultural Studies gets off the ground precisely by rejecting the Frankfurt School and its style of critical analysis. The litany of charges leveled against the Frankfurt School is almost too familiar to bear repeating: Frankfurt School theorists put forth a totalizing view of culture as somehow controlled by capitalist masters; they are far too sober, serious, and dire in their condemnations of everyday life and its pleasures; and the most serious and universal charge, Frankfurt School theorists are painted as cultural elitists who evidence little faith in the agency of the common person, and show no interest whatsoever in uncovering the hidden subversive codes seemingly buried in the rituals and products of popular culture. Adorno's work on jazz is routinely cited in this context as proof positive of the Frankfurt School's mandarin elitism.

Simon During's massively influential 1993 Routledge anthology *The Cultural Studies Reader* stands as a representative and powerful example of the Frankfurt School's traditional role within Cultural Studies. In During's collection, the Frankfurt School remains important to Cultural Studies primarily as a kind of negative or naïve moment, as that which has to be overcome for Cultural Studies to properly exist at all. An excerpt from Adorno and Horkheimer's "Culture Industry" essay opens the collection, but During's headnote carefully establishes the negative thesis that the essay is intended to convey for the collection's (largely student) audience: "Adorno and Horkheimer neglect what was to become central to cultural studies: the ways in which the culture industry, while in the service of organized capital, also provides the opportunities for all kinds of individual and collective creativity and decoding" (30). The Frankfurt School's dire determinism concerning "mass deception" has to be overcome, During argues, if Cultural Studies is to take up and valorize the central role of the subject and the subversive agency—the "creativity and decoding"—that she performs every day in the face of capital. On this reading, the Frankfurt School is dismissed for remaining territorialized on economic questions about unification or mass production, rather than exploring diversification or subversive consumption.

From its inception in England to its present configurations in North American and Australia, much (but certainly not all) English-language Cultural Studies has maintained a skeptical distance from the Frankfurt School, locating its genealogies and critical concepts elsewhere in modern Europe. From its engagement with theorists like Antonio Gramsci and Louis Althusser through Foucault and de Certeau, Cultural Studies has predominantly focused its intellectual and political energies on unleashing subjective resistance and "agency," the subversive multiple potentialities of the individual in his or her everyday life. And if Cultural Studies in the future is to remain territorialized on the insurgent agency of the consuming subject and the secretly transgressive qualities of cultural commodities, then the Frankfurt School will just as likely remain a merely negative or archaic moment in the ongoing study of the present.

Recently, however, Cultural Studies has been undergoing something of a crisis, as the "transgression" model has come increasingly under fire. As Tom Frank points out, after reading article after article about the hidden transgressive qualities of pornography or outlet shopping or soap operas, "one finds the cult-stud's particular species of transgression transgresses a lot less than all their talk of a 'radical politics of difference' would imply" (8). Frank continues his critique by pointing out the snug fit between notions of transgression in Cultural Studies and the contemporary right-wing ideology of consumer choice and niche marketing: "To an undeniable degree, the official narratives of American business—expressed in advertising, in management theory, in probusiness political and journalistic circles—largely share the cult-studs' oft-expressed desire to take on hierarchies, their tendency to find 'elitism' lurking behind any criticism of mass culture, and their pious esteem for audience agency. . . . It is a surprisingly short walk from the cult-studs' active-audience theorizing to the most undiluted sort of free-market orthodoxy" (8–9).

Given this unhappy state of affairs (where Cultural Theory finds itself in bed with the "Man" that it ostensibly wants to transgress or resist), scholars have recently been turning away from celebrations of subjective transgression and back toward trying to understand how subjects are produced by the canalization of desire on a "mass" scale. For many, this has entailed a rethinking of the Frankfurt School. Read in a certain way, the Frankfurt School shows you how the culture industry doesn't really produce products at all; rather it produces subjects. Adorno and Horkheimer's "Culture Industry," for example, argues that modern capitalist society is a kind of Fordist factory, but the assembly line finally yields only one product: consumers. And more specifically, this brand of cultural capitalism produces consumers who ideologically understand (or misunderstand) their own consumption practices as transgressive or authentic. "Something is provided for all," they intone, "so that none may escape" (During 34).

Historically, it is just such an emphasis on Fordist subject production—a very hard version of "interpellation"—that has caused many contemporary theorists to hesitate before Frankfurt School analyses. If "everyone, however powerful, is an object" (37)—as Adorno writes in *Minima Moralia*—then there would seem to be very little room for the individual or collective subject to resist this social reduction of us all to inert passivity. Cultural construction, in the world of the Frankfurt School, can all too often seem like cultural determination. But recent and continuing work on interpellation and subjection—work as diversified as Judith Butler's and Emmanuel Levinas's—has opened up new ways to conceptualize thoroughgoing cultural construction as other than ham-fisted cultural determination, and thereby has sent many thinkers back to the Frankfurt School with a fresh set of conceptual apparatuses and questions. Of course, one could easily argue that the Frankfurt School was there all along, informing contemporary work on subjectivity and interpellation; and perhaps only now can it be reexamined and affirmed as a crucial component in the toolkit for studying contemporary life.

There seems at least one other obvious historical reason for reemerging interest in the Frankfurt School. The "transgression" thesis in Cultural Studies was based on a parallel historical thesis about diversification in the culture industry's modes of production. As the argument goes, the Frankfurt School theorized in a much more hierarchized world of cultural products; their theses may have some relevance in the middle of the twentieth century, but at the dawning of the twenty-first, their analyses seem clumsily based on an outdated, paranoid, and totalizing model of increasing corporate control.

Looking again at the *Cultural Studies Reader,* During highlights this supposedly antiquated quality of Frankfurt School analysis, specifically referring to Adorno and Horkheimer's work on the culture industry: "when this essay was written," he argues, "the cultural industry was less variegated then it was to become, during the 1960s in particular. Hollywood, for instance, was still 'vertically integrated' so that the five major studios owned the production, distribution, and exhibition arms of the film business between them; television was still in its infancy; the LP and the single were unknown; the cultural market had not broken into various demographics sectors—of which, in the 1950s, the youth segment was to become the most energetic" (29–30). Ironically, During's 1993 charge that the Frankfurt School's moment is over (and his rather rosy version of diversification in the culture industry) seems itself rather dated less than a decade later: in the late 1990s, there was an unprecedented consolidation within the multinational "infotainment" industry—topped off at the end of the decade by the largest media merger in history, the AOL–Time Warner monopoly. And it seems like there are plenty of such megamergers yet to come. Mass media is, it seems, no longer just a convenient catch phrase.

Indeed, Frankfurt School attitudes toward cultural leveling (the dreaded "totalization" for which the Frankfurt School is commonly reproached) seem again to make very good sense in the twenty-first century—in the Disnified world where the corporate orthodoxy is local diversification, while the corporate reality is global consolidation. The Frankfurt School's theses on totalization and massification seem to have a new (or perhaps an enduring) relevance in the present economic climate of global corporatization—where not only individual cultures and indigenous practices, but public spheres on a global scale seem in danger of collapsing into a kind of corporate monoculture.

Indeed, as studies of the contemporary moment turn to concern themselves more with economic questions about production and multinational circulation, and less with subjective questions about transgression and recognition, the Frankfurt School is reemerging as a key site of historical and theoretical tools for today. Ironically, contemporary theorists find themselves turning back toward another reading of the Frankfurt School—that is, rethinking the Frankfurt School—precisely for the reasons it was once scorned: for notions of interpellated subjectivities whose desires are less liberated and multiplied than they are produced and canalized by a far-reaching, very nearly totalizing global culture industry. Indeed, as new questions concerning globalization and economic redistribution emerge, while analyses of identity politics and transgression become less central to contemporary theory, the future of the Frankfurt School looks at least as promising and productive as its past has proven to be. At least this is the theory and practice informing our collection, *Rethinking the Frankfurt School.*

Bibliography

Agger, Ben. 1992. *The Discourse of Domination: From the Frankfurt School to Postmodernism.* Evanston, Ill.: Northwestern University Press.

Alford, C. Fred. 1988. *Narcissism: Socrates, the Frankfurt School, and Psychoanalytic Theory.* New Haven: Yale University Press.

Anderson, Perry. 1976. *Considerations on Western Marxism.* New York: Verso.

Cadava, Eduardo. 1997. *Words of Light: Theses on the Photography of History.* Princeton: Princeton University Press.

Cohen, Margaret. 1995. *Profane Illumination, Walter Benjamin and the Paris of Surrealist Revolution.* Berkeley, Calif.: University of California Press.

Dallmayr, Fred R. 1991. *Between Freiburg and Frankfurt: Toward a Critical Ontology.* Amherst: University of Massachusetts Press.

Dews, Peter. 1987. *Logics of Disintegration: Post-Structuralist Thought and the Claims of Critical Theory.* New York: Verso.

During, Simon, ed. 1993. *The Cultural Studies Reader.* New York: Routledge.

Frank, Thomas. 1997. *The Conquest of Cool: Business Culture, Counterculture, and the Rise of Hip Consumerism.* Chicago: University of Chicago Press.

———. 1998. "CultStuds." *Baffler* 12:1–12.

Halle, Randall. 1995. "Between Marxism and Psychoanalysis: Antifascism and Antihomosexuality in the Frankfurt School." *Journal of Homosexuality* 29: 4: 295–317.

Hohendahl, Peter Uwe. 1991. *Reappraisals: Shifting Alignments in Postwar Critical Theory.* Ithaca, N.Y.: Cornell University Press.

Huyssen, Andreas. 1986. *After the Great Divide: Modernism, Mass Culture, Postmodernism.* Bloomington, Ind.: Indiana University Press.

Israel, Nico. 1997. "Damage Control: Adorno, Los Angeles, and the Dislocation of Culture." *Yale Journal of Criticism* 10 (Spring): 85–113.

Jameson, Fredric. 1990. *Late Marxism: Adorno, or, The Persistence of the Dialectic.* New York: Verso.

Jay, Martin. 1984. *Adorno.* Cambridge, Mass.: Harvard University Press.

———. 1999. "Is Experience Still in Crisis?: Reflections on a Frankfurt School Lament." *Kriterion.* 40: 9–25.

Kilminster, Richard. 1979. *Praxis and Method: A Sociological Dialogue with Lukacs, Gramsci and the Early Frankfurt School.* London: Routledge.

Koepnick, Lutz. 1996. "Negotiating Popular Culture: Wenders, Handke, and the Topographies of Cultural Studies." *The German Quarterly* 69 (Fall): 381–400.

McCarthy, Thomas. 1993. *Ideals and Illusions: On Reconstruction and Deconstruction in Contemporary Critical Theory.* Cambridge, Mass.: MIT Press.

McLaren, Peter L., ed. 1995. *Critical Theory and Educational Research.* Albany: State University of New York Press.

Mills, Patricia Jagentowicz. 1987. *Woman, Nature, and Psyche.* New Haven: Yale University Press.

Nicholsen, Shierry W. 1997. *Exact Imagination: Late Work, On Adorno's Aesthetics.*Cambridge: MIT, 1997.

Pensky, Max, ed. 1997. *The Actuality of Adorno: Critical Essays on Adorno and the Postmodern.* Albany: State University of New York Press.

Posnock, Ross. 1989. *Bourne, Dewey, Adorno: Reconciling Pragmatism and the Frankfurt School.* Milwaukee, Wisc.: Center for Twentieth Century Studies.

Scheuerman, William. 1994. *Between the Norm and the Exception: The Frankfurt School and the Rule of Law* Cambridge, Mass.: MIT Press.

Siebert, Rudolph. 1985. *The Critical Theory of Religion: The Frankfurt School: from the Universal Pragmatic to Political Theology.* New York: Mouton Press.

Watkins, Evan. 1993. *Throwaways: Work Culture and Consumer Education.* Stanford, Calif.: Stanford University Press.

Whitebrook, Joel. 1995. *Perversion and Utopia: A Study in Psychoanalysis and Critical Theory.* Cambridge, Mass.: MIT Press.

Wiggershaus, Rolf. 1994. *The Frankfurt School: Its History, Theories, and Political Significance.* Cambridge, Mass.: MIT Press.

Wolin, Richard. 1992. *The Terms of Cultural Criticism: The Frankfurt School, Existentialism, Poststructuralism.* New York: Columbia University Press.

———. 1994. *Walter Benjamin: An Aesthetic of Redemption.* Berkeley, Calif.: University of California Press.

Zuidervaart, Lambert. 1991. *Adorno's Aesthetic Theory: The Redemption of Illusion.* Cambridge, Mass.: MIT Press.

I

THE FRANKFURT SCHOOL TODAY

1

The Theoretical Hesitation: Benjamin's Sociological Predecessor

Fredric Jameson

Ours is an anti-theoretical time, which is to say an anti-intellectual time; the reasons for this are not far to seek. The system has always understood that ideas and analysis, along with the intellectuals who practice them, are its enemies and has evolved various ways of dealing with the situation, most notably—in the academic world—by railing against what it likes to call grand theory or master narratives at the same time that it fosters more comfortable and local positivisms and empiricisms in the various disciplines. If you attack the concept of totality, for example, you are less likely to confront embarrassing models and analyses of that totality called late capitalism or capitalist globalization; if you promote the local and the empirical, you are less likely to have to deal with the abstractions of class or value, without which the system cannot be understood. There are several famous precedents in the diagnosis of this antitheoretical strategy: I think, for example, of Perry Anderson's epoch-making "Origins of the Present Crisis" of 1964, in which he denounced the empiricisms of the Anglo-American tradition as so many defense mechanisms in the face of a world reality in full political and revolutionary upheaval; more recently, of Paul de Man's "The Resistance to Theory," which evokes the terror of the seam between meaning and matter; or of Theodor Adorno's late crusade against what he called positivism in general, in other words, the systematic elimination of the negative and the critical, of theory defined as negation, from modern thought and everyday life.

I want to make a much more modest contribution to that debate, one that raises the issue of the evasion of abstraction as such and that along the way also asks questions about the unexpected fortunes and prestige of Walter Benjamin, in a period that has seen the discounting of the stock of most of the other radical thinkers and litterateurs of our period. We may suppose, among other things, that Benjamin's good luck (in North America at least) was (like Gramsci's) to have never been fully translated into English until now and thus never to have been fully available as a coherent work, but rather to have offered the merest and most tantalizing, yet legendary, fragments. I've suggested elsewhere that Benjamin may uniquely fill a pressing need in the reunified Germany of today, which needs literary predecessors and canons not tainted by any of its earlier avatars (from the West German federal republic, through Hitler, back to Weimar or the Wilhelminian period). As something of a pre-Nazi-era exile, Benjamin has something to offer the gaps in the German tradition today that is only enhanced by his complex inner contradictions, whose various poles can be counted on to neutralize each other in an ideologically reassuring fashion.

In the anti-theoretical context I have been mentioning, however, a different kind of suspicion comes to mind. I don't fully endorse this doubt but feel it demands expression. For cannot Benjamin himself be enlisted among the ranks of those for whom theory and abstraction are pernicious? Are not the places of theory in Benjamin blinded by the transcendental glare of a whole range of mysticisms; while at its other reach, the passion for philosophy as such is replaced by the *fiches* of history, abstraction and concept by quotations and curious, stray facts? And does this movement away from theory not find its climactic expression in the great exchange of letters between Benjamin and Adorno on the form and staging of what I still prefer to call the *Passagenarbeit?* An exchange in which Adorno tells Benjamin, in effect, that if he wants his readers to draw dialectical conclusions from his various exhibits and montages, then he has to spell them out himself, to articulate his own interpretation and express the concept of his dialectic in conceptual language, something Benjamin was unwilling to do for reasons that may well have been aesthetic but that were surely also ideological (and even philosophical).

Alongside this Benjamin, who might, for example, serve as a precursor to the New Historicism, there are others who fit into the theory spectrum in rather different ways. It has always mildly surprised me, for instance, that in this time, which is supreme characterized by its resistance to any and all conceptions of an original or primordial human nature as such, the omnipresent traces of a seemingly humanist doctrine of experience—preserved within Benjamin's very interrogation of the consequences of its loss or breakdown—have not seemed in the least to discredit his work. Such a doctrine presumably lies as an amorphous concept somewhere in between psychology and metaphysics—neither of them very prestigious fields at the moment, and both very different from psychoanalysis, to which Benjamin's occasional appeals do not carry much conviction and scarcely suffice to undo the associations of the merely psychological. Indeed, in the great symbolic trilogy, which begins with "The Storyteller," passing through the essay on Baudelaire's "motifs," and concludes with "The Work of Art in the Age of Mechanical Reproduction," Benjamin evokes a no doubt socially grounded conception of the unity of experience in order to denounce modern psychic and experiential fragmentation, only to project some future utopian transformation of all this in forms that need not be thought to be organic. Still, it is the premise of some original unity of experience that is bound to arouse suspicions and hesitations, reservations, and perhaps even ideological critique in the present day and age of the nonfoundational and the anti-organic.

So we confront two antithetical yet evidently interrelated phenomena here: a resistance to theory and to the dialectic, accompanied by traces of the unexamined presuppositions of a kind of phenomenological or prephenomenological *Lebensphilosophie.* Both perhaps betray a resistance to the philosophical concept, the one in the name of an aesthetic refusal of abstraction, the other in that of a phenomenological commitment to the "concrete." In the present essay I will not go further with this in the work of Benjamin himself but have felt I could make a useful contribution to the problem by returning to the work of one of Benjamin's most important precursors and predecessors, in which both of these features are even more strongly marked. I refer, of course, to the work of Georg Simmel, who seems to be knowing something of a revival at the present time, when his incalculable but underground influence in previous intellectual generations of the last century (from the United States to Japan) has been altogether forgotten and obliterated.

I should add that I'm not interested in positing any direct influence, although Benjamin attended Simmel's seminar in 1912. He could later on be dismissive indeed in his reactions to Simmel's work (as in his letter to Gershom Scholem of 23 December 1917), but his own work on the city equally failed to escape the force field of Simmel's thought, and he was capable of observing—to Adorno, perhaps as a sly provocation—that it might well be time "to give him his due as one of the forefathers of cultural Bolshevism."[1] At any rate, it is a comparable rhythm of procedures I wish to draw attention to, a set of hesitations, evasions, theoretical decisions, a relationship to empiricity, that the two thinkers oddly seem to share. I only have space to refer to two texts by Simmel here, one small but classic—the famous essay, "The Metropolis and Mental Life," in which anticipations of an already rather Benjaminian *Lebensphilosophie* can be detected—the other an immense morass of a book, *The Philosophy of Money*, in which the very root of a dialectical reluctance that keeps the dialectic alive can be uncovered.

To evaluate Simmel is to measure the stimulation he afforded any number of very different people and thinkers (from the Chicago sociologist Robert Park to Georg Lukács, from Max Weber to Benjamin). He knew this himself: "My legacy will be like cash, distributed to many heirs, each transforming his part into use according to *his* nature."[2] I try to imagine this transmission of intellectual excitement, and even of intellectual productivity, on the order of the awakenings stimulated by French phenomenological existentialism, which showed so many people how to theorize about daily life and the most seemingly unphilosophical items and events. *The Philosophy of Money* thus contained a whole program within its provocative title, namely, that things are already philosophical in and of themselves. They (and we leave "their" contents open: a walk in the city for De Certeau; Raymond Aron's famous glass of beer, which has evidently been reidentified as a crème de menthe; Jean-Paul Sartre's "look"; Edmund Husserl's mathematical operations; an automotive directional signal in Martin Heidegger; prostitution for Simmel himself) do not require the massive application of external philosophical and interpretive machinery, already bearing as they do an intellectual and philosophical meaningfulness within themselves.

But Simmel must pay a heavy price for this generalized suggestiveness, and it is a toll that contemporary *doxa* has generally been unwilling to identify as such, namely, the refusal of the philosophical system and, in the textual detail of the writing itself, of the jargon and neologisms with which most powerful contemporary philosophies or theories have violently displaced everyday speech and made it over into so many charged names that signify the operation of a specific idiolect. For it is only at this price that theory today marks its commodities with so many logos, and packages its distinctive wares in the strident bazaar of the contemporary public sphere.

But it would be wrong to interpret Simmel's elaborate qualifications in terms of the familiar liberal mean: neither this nor that, somewhere in between too much and too little. Rather, I think that it is his commitment to the particular that strategically interrupts a traditional philosophical movement toward the absolute of universal or abstract ideas. Unlike empiricism, it does not seek to replace that movement with some radically different positivist orientation; rather, it identifies this movement as a process that it wishes to assign to one specific moment of the inquiry in order to set in place a change of direction and a new kind of movement in some second moment, which will have been motivated by some new acknowledgment of the rights of the particular. We have here, then, a combination of two distinct thought modes, without synthesis: a mechanical wiring together of two kinds of conceptual machinery; a careful and inveterate yet provisional splicing together of two radically different conceptual processes. It is a distinctive way of thinking that can no doubt be clarified by its distinctive historical context, but which, if it does not altogether explain Simmel's originality, it at least lends that originality its unique style.

What is more old-fashioned in Simmel's sociology can then be identified as a breach in this systematic procedure, a kind of unwitting violation of his own method—even though it is a category mistake he shares with the whole first generation of the theorists of the entity called society, one that persists well on into the canonical Parsonian synthesis itself. This is the insistent effort—not yet present at all in Hegel, for example, and renounced by all the sociology we think of as contemporary—to deduce the larger social forms from the smaller ones and to build up notions and models of the collective out of primary accounts of individual actions and immediate face-to-face encounters, as though these "simple" elements and forms, added together and combined in more elaborate ways, would somehow directly yield the forms of the "complex." But the dialectic already knew, and contemporary thought has rediscovered, some fundamental incommensurability between the individual and the collective—that there was a gap and a leap between the two; that no careful Cartesian procedures could ever build the bridge from the logic of individual experience to that very different logic of the collective and the social; that no ingenious analysis of the social back into its individual components could ever conceptually master the properly dialectical paradox whereby the whole is always more (or less) than its individual parts. The category mistake—the will to maintain a continuity between these two incommensurable dimensions—does not often vitiate the striking power of Simmel's insights into their concrete and provisional relationships; perhaps, indeed, it was the condition of possibility of such insights and such discoveries. But it envelops his work as a whole with an anthropology and a metaphysic that draw a historically outmoded veil between the contemporary reader and Simmel's discrete analysis, something his editors have sometimes dealt with by breaking up the longer works into the essay forms he also practiced, as though in untheorized awareness of his own problems and real strengths.

Indeed, one may even see these anthropological underpinnings as a kind of allegory of their own content: "The deepest problems of modern life flow from the attempt of the individual to maintain the independence and individuality of his existence against the sovereign powers of society."[3] The inscription of individual psychology, then, into the collective system modeled by a nascent sociology is itself a figure for this attempt and this struggle, which is no longer grasped objectively as the banal tension between this or that real individual and this or that real society but rather as the incommensurability of theories, of those individual phenomenologies of individual experience whose discursive and theoretical fabric it proves difficult to weave into the greater collective structural and theoretical system.

Yet even as an anthropology—which Simmel's thought sometimes is—the balance struck between these two poles is less banal than one might expect, for the poles are themselves immediately rethematized in the one place in which Simmel's work does take on the appearance of something like a system, namely, in that well-nigh metaphysical opposition between life and form (which afforded his student Lukács the title of one of his most significant early works). In those places in which Simmel is willing to spell this thematic out in the form of a philosophical position, if not a system—and it is characteristic of him that he is generally unwilling to do this, so that the untheorized thematic opposition seeps out laterally and, omnipresent, informs much of the texture of his other work—this is something like a dialectic of objectification, in which the life process requires externalization in order to come to its fullest expression. It thereby objectifies itself in a series of forms, which then begin to constrict it in their increasing rigidity. As they approach most closely to their condition as delimited form, the living impulses that gave rise to them are increasingly stifled. Form must therefore now be opened up and broken in order for some new life creativity to emerge in its turn (and produce a new form). One remembers the shift of registers in Lukács's climactic outcry in *History and Class Consciousness*: "*history is the history of the unceasing overthrow of the objective forms that shape the life of man.*"[4] If Simmel was never willing to go so far as this, at least we have an acknowledgment, in other cultural essays, that the form modern life strives for may even be an absence of form: "a struggle of life against the form *as such,* against the *principle* of form";[5] but I think such cultural anarchism was not really acceptable to any of the members of this generation—not to Lukács or to Benjamin, finally, and certainly not to Simmel himself.

I take it that the passage of time has allowed such ideas to congeal into what they visibly were all along, namely, so many ideologies. Vitalism itself is, of course, the strong form of the *doxa* of the period, less a philosophy in its own right, perhaps, than the aesthetic solution to intractable philosophical contradictions, and this whether it takes the form of psychology or expressivism, evolutionism or spiritualism or primitivism. Thus one of the interesting stories of this turn of the last century is the way in which modern thinkers like Lukács and Benjamin—in their very different ways—managed to extricate themselves from a vitalism that they could not but breathe in everywhere during their formative years. Vitalism produced magnificent aesthetic expressions in its day, neither did it preclude the subtlest philosophical reflections of a Bergson. I think it is no longer a current temptation (save perhaps in Deleuze and in the Bergsonian revivals inspired by him); contemporary ecology, for instance, does not seem to need to appeal to the rich orchestral resonance and excitement of the vitalistic for its effects.

But it is not only vitalism as such that I have in mind at this point in the analysis; rather, I want to imply that contemporary anti-essentialisms and anti-foundationalisms—with which one must have all kinds of sympathy and which my diagnosis of Simmel clearly leans on here—all miss the mark insofar as they are themselves framed in the form of so many philosophical essentialisms and founda-

tionalisms. What is more satisfactory philosophically, I want to suggest, is a repudiation of all forms of ontology and all hypotheses about human nature and human
psychology, let alone about metaphysics, in the name of a conception of philosophical
language as such. For it suffices to grasp all philosophical propositions (particular
ones, I hasten to add, fully as much as universal ones) as *ideologies* for the analytic
perspective to be utterly modified. It is clear enough to me that the repudiation of the
term and concept of ideology was not only itself ideological but also premature, for, as
we shall see in this reading of Simmel, we will not be able to identify and characterize
what is truly original and energizing in his theoretical production without first being
in a position to isolate its ideological elements, whose immobilities and static or
ontological natures or essences it is precisely the mission of this discourse to set in
motion and to redynamize.

Let me give a first illustration of all this by way of a reading of his great essay
"The Metropolis and Modern Life" (1903), whose kinship with some of Benjamin's
most famous essays will readily be apparent. The essay begins with a series of what I
have called ideological propositions, and in particular with a juxtaposition of the
mental state of the city dweller with that of a rural or small-town life. The social
situation of the latter is characterized by "lasting impressions, the slightness in their
differences, the habituated regularity of their course and contrasts between them," all
of which develop a social life based "more on feelings and emotional relationships"
("MM" 325; "GG" 1902–1903, 188); in contrast, Simmel identifies big-city life
with the mental function of Reason, and even of calculation in all its forms, and it
should be clear enough even at the outset how profoundly ideological any such
allegory of the mental functions and faculties must necessarily be.

On the other hand, everyone will also recognize in this initial characterization
the crucial theme of Benjamin's essay "The Storyteller," as well as that of "On Some
Motifs in Baudelaire": the historicist proposition—a simpler kind of social life, to
which a specific *mentalité* corresponds, alongside a far more complex one, later in
chronological and developmental time, to which a radically different constellation of
mental properties may be ascribed. Thus, for both Benjamin and Simmel ideology is
compounded, for to one profoundly historicist level is added another psychologizing
or essentialist one, which we must now examine.

What we find—and what plays a far greater role in late nineteenth-century
culture in general than scholars have been willing to investigate—is a whole iconog-
raphy of nascent laboratory science and in particular, of experimental psychology.
The role of this weird and wholly outdated machinery in the theory and practice of
the Impressionist painters is well-known; meanwhile, Bergson's own work is suffused
with the imagery of all these experimental materialisms he so fiercely attacked and
analytically undermined—rods, cones, stimuli, irritation, nerves and their movements, attraction and repulsion, magnetisms, light waves, intensities, synapses. Such
is the bristling panoply of the nineteenth-century psychological laboratory, whose
poetry, often remastered by even more energetic vitalisms, reaches out even into those
modernisms that wish most violently to shake loose its cumbersome baggage. So also
in Simmel himself, who characterizes big-city life as an "intensification of emotional
life due to the swift and continuous shift of external and internal stimuli" ("MM"

325; "GG" 188). Nor is this a merely incidental figure; the whole analysis is intri-
cately indebted to the concept of the stimulus, as we shall see. Much the same could
obviously be said of Benjamin, except that the latter had a signal literary advantage
over Simmel, namely, that he could draw on Baudelaire, whose characteristic language on these matters—not unrelated, to be sure, to that nascent psychology contemporaneous with him—is certainly far more elegant; for him, the man in the
crowd was "a kaleidoscope equipped with consciousness."[6] Yet the ideological content is much the same; we generally here confront the picture of a relatively placid
organism now increasingly bombarded by the multiple stimuli of the big city, from
street crossings to clock time and harried appointments, from "the passing glance"
(here in Simmel not eroticized, but rather the bearer of repulsion and loathing) to the
classic and henceforth Benjaminian or Baudelairean crowd, or *foule*. It is philosophically prescient of Simmel to have made this side of his pendant or diptych the place of
sheer difference and ever more minute differentiation as such, something that should
not distract us from the recognition of everything stereotypical about the characterization of its opposite number, the countryside, as a place of identities and the identification of everything with everything else.

   Yet this initial hypothesis—multiple stimuli—is little more than the "foundation" on which a series of other characterizations will be based. The identification of
the city with Reason is only the most incidental and functional of these, for what he
really has in mind is *Verstand*, instrumental or sheerly calculating reason, and behind
that, as an even more fundamental form, what he calls "intellectualism." This concept
is related not only by causality, as we shall see in a moment, but also by connotation to
the whole notion of the nervous system, nerves playing a fundamental role in the
ideology of this whole period from the "American nervousness" of the 1880s to
Proust's "neurasthenia." For a big-city nervousness will be developed in two direc-
tions, both of which are significantly characterized as blasé or indifferent. On the one
hand, indifference results from exhaustion of the nervous centers:

> Just as an immoderately sensuous life makes one blasé because it stimulates the
> nerves to their utmost reactivity until they finally can no longer produce any
> reaction at all, so, less harmful stimuli, through the rapidity and the contradic-
> toriness of their shifts, force the nerves to make such violent responses, tear
> them about so brutally that they exhaust their last reserves of strength and,
> remaining in the same milieu, do not have time for new reserves to form.
> ("MM" 329; "GG" 193)

A passage of this kind might, to be sure, serve as an exhibit for the medical ideologies
of the period (which in any case themselves are profoundly complicitous with all the
other social ones). What interests us here primarily is its inconsistency with the other
account Simmel gives us of the blasé mentality, namely its function as a defense
mechanism *against* stimuli. Now, on the other hand, "indifference" is said to be
somehow "unnatural" ("MM" 331; "GG" 195–96), and it comes to be explained as
"a protective organ" that guards "against the profound disruption with which the
fluctuations and discontinuities of the external milieu threaten" the city dweller

("MM" 326; "GG" 189). We thus move from homology (the blasé as the exhaustion of multiple stimuli) to an attempted negation (in which the blasé attitude holds the stimuli at bay or neutralizes them). The variation still lies in what I will call a vertical model, a relationship of synchronic levels to one another, but it foreshadows a very different structural solution, which I will come to in a moment and which may illustrate Simmel's creative ability to break out of these initial ideological positions and stereotypes.

At any rate, it is clear that this is what Benjamin appreciated in Simmel's essay, for he himself abandoned the medical stereotypes of exhausted nerves and only retained the concept of a defense mechanism, which, reinforced by the authority of Sigmund Freud and Bergson, he then wheeled around in a different direction, to turn it on the question of experience and its expression in narrative form. Simmel was, however, to pursue his own urban diagnosis in a development unique to him, which did not, as far as I know, greatly interest Benjamin, and that is in the area of money as such. For the twin areas of indifference opened up by city life—a protective indifference to other people and a kind of numbing of perception to the qualitative distinctions among things—are insensibly combined, and under the dominance of the second of these forms, come to be identified as the indifference of the monetary form, of sheer equivalence as such. So in a final identification big-city "intellectualism" (with its precisions and calculations, its clock time, its measurabilities) finds its ultimate form in the money economy as such (and only much later, at the very end of the society, in the division of labor). At this point, and into this breach, all the intricacies of Simmel's *The Philosophy of Money* may be expected to flow, but we have not yet reached the climax of this first section of the essay, which emerges when the metropolis and its multiple stimuli, the intellectualistic and the blasé, equivalence and the money form, are finally *interpreted,* and the word *freedom* is at length pronounced.

Now suddenly the whole structure of the essayistic discourse changes, and we witness a move from an essentially vertical or analytic thinking to a horizontal or oscillating one, which I will characterize as a transformation from the elaboration of an ideological position to the exercise of a kind of dialectical thinking (with all the qualifications we will want to make on the use of this term, particularly when we come to describe the arrested dialectic of *The Philosophy of Money*). However one wishes to characterize it, the change in thought mode is striking and inescapable indeed, for the first section of the essay seemed to offer, however reluctantly, a catalogue of alienations, without expressing any particular nostalgia for the opposite term—the simplicity of rural life. (On this score Benjamin is far more ambiguous, or perhaps industrialization in his period had come to seem far more inevitable and inescapable. The wholeness of experience realized in the storytelling of the peasant village or sailors' and travelers' narratives can thus be affirmed without fear of any regression to the pastoral or to older modes of production.)

But where these characterizations of big-city life and its *mentalité* have mildly negative and unpleasant connotations—the loss of qualitative distinctions, the antipathy to other people aroused by their sheer multiplicity, if not by economic competition itself—the sudden introduction of the motif of freedom modulates to the major key and transforms the tonality of the previous negative descriptions into a philosophical problem in its own right. Now, the specificity of the metropolis and its mental life having been secured, the deeper interest and attention of the reader is shifted in the somewhat different direction of the way in which such negative features can be reconciled with the evidently positive connotations of the concept of freedom.

In short, at this point, the properly dialectical problem of the unity of negativity and positivity arises, and the strategy of the essay must be modified to oscillate from the negative to the positive aspects of urban freedom as such. At this point, even the critique of urban equivalence and intellectualism is drawn into the argument in a new way: no longer outside the description, in the alternate social space of the countryside and the peasantry, but now within it and identified with the names of critics such as John Ruskin and Nietzsche, whose popularity and readership become a big-city event, the critique of the city being consumed most avidly by the city itself.

This dialectical oscillation is pursued on into "historiosophy" itself, with a brief allusion to the opposition between left-wing ideals of social equality and right-wing glorifications of uniqueness, genius, and the individual personality, only to reach a peculiar moment of neutralization in which both political positions may seem to have been canceled out in favor of a third or contemplative one, which, as he puts it, "transcend[s] the sphere in which a judge-like attitude on our part is appropriate" such that "it is our task not to complain or to condone but only to understand" ("MM" 339; "GG" 206). It would be abusive to try to make Simmel over into a political figure (and the *The Philosophy of Money* will make it clearer why this would be a misplaced effort), but I believe that this conclusion of the metropolis essay does not amount to "a plague on both your houses." Rather, it should be read as an effort to fulfill and complete the dialectic's first function, namely the suspension of the moralizing judgment, the transcendence of good and evil, which is to say, the neutralization of some choice between the negative and the positive judgment. But perhaps this suspension of judgment in the face of the unity of the positive and the negative may be contrasted with that empty place of judgment Adorno thought he found to have been reserved for the absent reader of Benjamin's great Arcades montages.

I would thus be less inclined to see Simmel's contemplative position here as a political symptom than as a hesitation to theorize, to produce the concept. If so, we need to seek the explanation elsewhere, in *The Philosophy of Money* itself (whose first publication in 1900, to be sure, preceded that of "The Metropolis and Mental Life" by some three years). The search will not be lightened by Simmel's methodological decision, in this his *Hauptwerk,* to organize his materials as it were vertically rather than horizontally, or, in other words, following what might be called the Thomas Mann principles ("only the exhaustive is truly interesting"), to say everything all at once, and on the occasion of each separate topic, in such a way that the text itself sometimes strikes one as a carefully lined up series of digressions, linked by the frailest of thematic threads. I think that in fact this is not so, but the method runs several significant risks: first, in the explanatory stance itself, which can quickly arouse the reader's subconscious resentment at being thus condescended to whenever the brilliance of the explanation flags in the slightest; and second, in the tension thus aroused between what we may call the spatial and the temporal dimensions of this book. We have often heard it said of "modernist" long projects that they cannot be read but only reread; something the sort surely holds for *The Philosophy of Money*, where so much initial energy must be expended on the parts themselves—the explanations and digressions—that their sequence and temporal form can only be grasped on some secondary review, at fast-forwarding speed. One has to learn the parts, so to speak, before the whole can be "performed" as some immense Mahlerian continuity.

Add to this a certain perverseness in the adjustment of the subject matter itself. This "philosophy" will deal with everything about money save precisely its economic function as such, which can be left to the economists. It is a decision that will frustrate readers who had hoped this "metaphysical" approach might make economics more meaningful for them, and it will also mislead those like ourselves who are interested in the place of theory as such, which they may be tempted (wrongly, I think) to identify with this immense hold at the very center of the work. In any case, it is surely always a strategic mistake to exclude parts of a topic at the outset for disciplinary reasons; the disciplines and their territorial demarcations are always part of the problem, indeed, part of the content, and ought never to benefit from some blanket amnesty before the fact. It is clear that Simmel would have been perfectly capable of performing the same kind of logical dissection of economic pseudo-concepts that his contemporary Bergson so thoroughly enacted for the experimental psychology of his time. On the other hand, such misleadings may themselves turn out to have been misled, and we should be willing to entertain the possibility that Simmel's omission of economics as such is less a mark of respect than of contempt, and that the empty place assigned it here will also turn out to be a kind of interpretation in its own right.

At any rate the arrangement of the material in two sections (of three chapters each, each of those equally subdivided into three sections, whether out of some numerological impulse I cannot say, although the pursuit of such patterns down into the smallest details would certainly also tell us much about Simmel's thought pro-cesses) is a perfectly plausible one. It separates our topic into preconditions and consequences, and opens a phenomenological space *avant la lettre* for what, socially, historically, and psychologically, needs to be in place for the money mechanism to come into full play, just as it reserves a dimension of cultural speculation for the aftereffects of money on social life and *mentalité* (some of which we have already encountered in very abbreviated form in "The Metropolis and Mental Life"). The first section, then, on money's conditions of possibility, the so-called analytical part, aims "to construct a new story beneath historical materialism" (*PM* 56; *PG* viii). Unsurprisingly, it begins with the question of value as such, whose internal concep-tual problems must first be laid in place before the two concluding chapters can take up the problems—more immediately related to money as such—of the "substance" of coinage (must its material intrinsically have value independent of the money function?) and then of the again more philosophical issue of money as a means (and its subsequent effect on the very existence of ends as such).

Yet the style of these investigations is already set in the first chapter, which goes to great lengths not merely to stress the effect of the concept of value as an objectifica-tion of our desires but also to underscore its temporal variability, that is to say, its very nature as a distance from the desired object, from desire itself, and from my own subjective desire, a distance that will clearly enough vary with the possibility of consumption. To keep faith, then, with this temporal irregularity in the phenomena of value requires us to respect a certain oscillation in its concept, which must not be allowed to become overly objective, nor overly subjective, but rather variably open and released to this very fluctuation. This is to say that our mode of concept-formation must be adjusted accordingly.

Nor does the logical next step—the discussion of exchange—modify this conceptual state of things. Simmel's treatment of exchange is very different from Marcel Mauss's more famous and influential one, which projects a visionary typology of distinct social relationships, as well as from Karl Marx's, which extrapolates the paradoxes and peculiarities of this form onto the structure of capitalism as a whole. Simmel wants to problematize exchange only in the sense of using its temporality, its nature as a process, to undermine our reified habits of grasping its elements as so many givens or things (in much the same way that the very notion of objectification is supposed to problematize our notion of objects as entities). Thus, "exchange is the representative of the distance between subject and object which transforms subjective feelings into objective valuation"; but if this is what exchange is, then any independent assessment of the subjective or the objective becomes difficult indeed, and even more so if the phenomenon of exchange is a separate one that is the mere "representative" of that process (PM 90; PG 45). "Exchange," Simmel adds, "is not the mere addition of two processes of giving and receiving, but a new third phenomenon, in which each of the two processes is simultaneously cause and effect" (PM 90; PG 45–46). But this formula is also frustrating: For the welcome anticipation of the transformation of exchange into a phenomenon in its own right (a "representative," a "third phenomenon"), about which we could finally form some thinglike or substantive concept is then at once dispelled again by the final clause, which returns us to its internal alternation.

At this point, Simmel seems to show his hand; he introduces a topic and a philosophical entity—relativism—which, far from being a precondition of the money economy, would seem to belong rather to its cultural consequences and to offer something like its social meaning. This is not so, I think, but the misinterpretation can only enhance the reading of the work as a whole by adding a question about what the possible meaning might ultimately be, if it is not this one. Let's keep it in mind; the eventual answer is an astonishing one indeed, as we shall see.

But it is true enough that Simmel never solves the problem of priority here, if indeed he raises it at all; the problem of whether the achievement of a money economy demands the development of a relativistic world view, or the other way round. Presumably they happen simultaneously; furthermore, the search for phenomenological preconditions is not that kind of historical inquiry, even though the historical development of money does get outlined later on, for philosophical purposes ("the historical development of money from *substance* to *function*") (PM 168; PG 151; my emphasis).

The topic of relativism serves a rather different purpose, which is to train us in the kind of thinking and conceptualization we will need to understand money itself. In other words, we do not only need to link the topic of relativism to that of money in order to understand each of them more fully; we also need to understand how to think relativistically in order to learn how to think money, and the way to do so lies not in some relativistic reduction of the truth content of each of the moments in a relativistic sequence but rather in maintaining the absolute truth content of each moment until we abandon it for the next one. Simmel's relativism, in other words, does not mean a reduction in "truths" but a multiplication and intensification of them. But perhaps its spirit can be more accessibly conveyed by the now rather stereotypical distinction between a substance-oriented and a process-oriented kind of thinking. It would be fatuous to suggest that Simmel somehow "prefers" the latter; rather, the whole drama of *The Philosophy of Money* lies in the visible demonstration of the imposition of process-oriented thought on the author by virtue of the very nature of his subject matter itself.

In a revealing phrase, indeed, he evokes the way in which, here, "relativity, i.e., the reciprocal character of the significance of criteria of knowledge, appears in the form of succession or alternation" (*PM* 113; *PG* 77–78). It is precisely this momentum or temporality that forestalls concept formation, postponing it indefinitely at the same time that it yields the elements and constituent parts of the concept that cannot be fully elaborated. Before quoting at greater length Simmel's most elaborate theorization of this internal and structural hesitation before theory as such, we probably need to draw on the illustrative material that follows, not least in order to show how this technical problem is intimately related to the conceptual problems posed by money in itself, which might under other circumstances be characterized as antinomies.

For one thing, money is both multiple and infinitely various and, on the other hand, stable and unified as an expression of value; indeed, this philosophical tension between multiplicity and unity will be a central category problem throughout Simmel's immense inventory of monetary phenomena. Thus, at the most abstract level,

> money derives its content from its value; it is value turned into a substance, the value of things without the things themselves. By sublimating the relativity of things, money seems to avoid relativity. . . . Money as abstract value expresses nothing but the relativity of things that constitute value; and, at the same time . . . money, as the stable pole, contrasts with the eternal movements, fluctuations and equations of the objects. (*PM* 121; *PG* 88–89)

This "dual role"—outside and within the series of concrete values—gives us one way of understanding why the conceptualization of money must always remain somehow incomplete, since its other dimension of existence lies outside the plane to which the theory in question belongs: "money is therefore one of those normative ideas that obey the norms that they themselves represent" (*PM* 122; *PG* 90).

Yet the dilemma can be formulated in more concrete or empirical terms than this, as with the notion of scarcity, for example, which can be meaningful only as a moment and not as an absolute ("scarcity can only become significant above a considerable volume"); or, above all, in the well-known tension between money's two functions as a measure of value and as a means of exchange (*PM* 72; *PG* 20). These functions do not necessarily entail each other; thus for example, "the function of money in measuring values does not impose upon it the character of being itself a valuable object" (*PM* 142; *PG* 115).

> In ancient Egypt prices were determined by the *uten*, a piece of coiled copper wire, but payments were made in all kinds of goods. In the Middle Ages price was often determined in money terms, but the buyer was free to pay in whatever manner was convenient. In many places in Africa at the present day the exchange of goods is carried out according to a monetary standard which is sometimes quite complicated, while money itself for the most part does not even exist. The business of the very important Genoese exchange market in the sixteenth century was based upon the standard of the *scudo de'marchi*. This standard was almost entirely imaginary and did not exist in any actual coinage. (*PM* 192; *PG* 181–82)

It is as though here a fourth-dimensional reality intersected the world of three dimensions to leave its incomprehensible traces—impalpable mental categories and antinomies marking the real world in symptomatic ways that cannot be accounted for by commonsense physical or realistic laws. A similar inventory of empirically derivable paradoxes is to be found in the incommensurability of large and small coinage, which turns on the paradoxes involved in thinking quantity as such:

> The largest coins even of precious metals are found almost exclusively among less developed peoples where barter still prevails. . . . The same sentiment about the importance of quantity reserved the privilege of minting the largest coins to the highest authorities, while the smaller coins, though of the same metal, were coined by lower authorities. . . . Under primitive barter conditions, money transactions took place not for the small needs of everyday life, but only for the acquisition of larger and more valuable objects. (*PM* 145; *PG* 119–20)

These phenomena are then philosophically related to the matter of divisibility and the requirement that a monetary standard have the capability of expressing the smallest fractions of value and the multiplicity of valuable objects. They document Simmel's insistence on the gradual and historical extension and conquest of a universal monetary form as such: "actually, a general money value did not formerly exist at all" (*PM* 267; *PG* 279).[7] Analogous to Marx's insistence on the universality of wage labor as a condition for understanding capitalism, the historical universalization of money has perhaps an opposite epistemological effect in Simmel, where it may be said that everything that has come to seem natural to us in a money economy blocks our ability to grasp its conceptual peculiarities. Yet the paradigm case of all these antinomies and incommensurabilities remains, of course, the problem of precious metals and the question about the "real value" of the monetary vehicle (a problem related to those of prices and their fluctuations, and finally to the whole concept of the wealth of nations as such).

After all that has been said, we will not be surprised to find that Simmel's solution, if it can be called that, is a temporal one, in the spirit of the doctrine of "succession or alternation." He sets in place the more obvious contemporary solution to the dilemma, namely, the appeal to state power (along with the accompanying requirement of the unification of the national terrain within which the currency is to be respected), without being fully satisfied with this explanation, which of course obliterates the peculiarities of the money phenomenon and transfers the causality to a wholly different, political level. For what Simmel wants to stage here is the contradictory appeal of the two absolute alternatives, neither of which can be satisfactory in itself, but also not completely wrong, namely, the idea that money is wholly conventional (the henceforth standard appeal to "trust" in effect returns us to an explanation in terms of the state) along with the conviction that money must be intrinsically valuable and in practice take the form of this or that precious metal (see *PM* 99; *PG* 58). The temporality of the concept will allow both these explanations to be thought within a new kind of conceptualization, which I will wish to relate to the dialectic while distinguishing it from the latter in certain crucial ways.

For money must obviously be somehow valuable, yet the very conception of the value of its "substance" tends to project the whole phenomenon of value onto a quite different, nonmonetary plane (something which modern theory has described, following Freudian and Lacanian psychoanalysis, as the exclusion of the material of value from the realm of exchange):

> If it is claimed that the value of money consists in the value of its material, this means that its value is embodied in the qualities or powers of the substance which are not those of money. The apparent paradox indicates that money does not necessarily have to be based upon substances that are intrinsically valuable, i.e., valuable in some other respect. It is sufficient if the ability to function as money is transferred to any substance, the other qualities of which are quite irrelevant. (*PM* 153; *PG* 130)

In other words, as Simmel will here try to demonstrate by way of ethical and aesthetic examples, what counts is the memory of the preceding stage, and the fact that the monetary value was *once* based on precious metal, "the attraction" as he puts it quaintly, that springs simply from the passing of a preceding form of life" (*PM* 153; *PG* 131). Value lies in the sequence of moments, not in the thing itself; and Simmel reaches his most dialectical register when he characterizes this phenomenon as the "influence of not-being on being" (*PM* 153; *PG* 131), as also when he later tells us, "Money performs its services best when it is not simply money" (*PM* 165; *PG* 146). Meanwhile, in the next chapter, which seeks to localize the structural peculiarity of money in its initial mode of use as a tool, but as a means that can at any moment become a new end in its own right, the appreciation begins to modulate into the language of mediation, which vanishes when we seek to contemplate money in its own right:

> Money is the purest reification of means, a concrete instrument which is absolutely identical with its abstract concept. . . . The tremendous importance

of money for understanding the basic motives of life lies in the fact that money embodies and sublimates the practical relation of man to the objects of his will, his power and his impotence; one might say, paradoxically, that man is an indirect being [das indirekte Wesen]. (PM 211; PG 206)

All of which perhaps now puts us in a better position to grasp the implications of the lengthy meditation on theory, which I have postponed quoting until now but which can be said to offer Simmel's own description, not so much of his method, as rather of the conceptual dynamics into which this particular object has forced him:

It is necessary to consider our mental existence under two categories that complement each other: in terms of its content and in terms of the process that, as an event of consciousness, carries or realizes this content. The structure of these categories is extremely different. We must conceive the mental process as a continuous flux, in which there are no distinct breaks, so that one mental state passes into the next uninterruptedly, in the manner of organic growth. The contents, abstracted from this process and existing in an ideal independence, appear under a totally different aspect: as an aggregate, a graduate scheme, a system of single concepts or propositions clearly distinguished from one another. The logical connection between any two concepts reduces the distance between them but not the discontinuity, like the steps of a ladder that are sharply separated from each other but yet provide the means for a continuous movement of the body. The relation among the contents of thought is characterized by the fact that the foundations of thought, considered as a whole, seem to move in circles, because thought has to support itself "by being suspended" and has no που στω [Archimedean point] which supports it from outside. The contents of thought provide a background to each other so that each gets its meaning and colour from the other; they are pairs of mutually exclusive opposites and yet postulate each other for the creation of a possible worldview. Every particular content becomes the ground of proof for the other through the whole chain of what is knowable. The process of thinking, however, by which this relation is psychologically accomplished, follows a direct and continuous chronological course; it continues according to its own inner meaning, although the death of the individual brings it to an end. The two categories of our reflection are divided into these two forms, which make knowledge illusory in particular cases but possible in general. Knowledge follows a course of infinite regress, of infinite continuity, of boundlessness, which yet is limited at any particular moment—whereas the contents exhibit the other form of infinity, that of the circle, in which every point is a beginning and an end, and all the parts condition each other mutually (PM 115; PG 80–81)

The statement is no doubt in itself a kind of ontologization of the thought process and its dilemma, couched, however, in the language of content rather than process. It thereby illustrates the dilemma in question by virtue of its own inability to theorize it on its own terms; the revenge of this particular dualism is to force its own theory to adopt one or the other of its alternatives, both of which are unsatisfactory. If, as in this version, the content is emphasized at the expense of process, the opposition takes on the form of a kind of immense world structure, a sort of cosmic yin and yang; if, on the other hand, processes are emphasized then, as with relativism in the earlier discussion, the truth content of the various terms is lost and a frivolous temporal movement results, in which none of the moments of the process is taken seriously. This is, in effect, the practice of the dialectic without its theory, which is not to say that some stereotypical Hegelian "synthesis" ought to have been evoked at this point. Indeed, the spirit of the latter is perhaps better captured by C. S. Peirce's doctrine of "thirdness," or sheer relationality ("firstness" being immediacy, "second-ness" being the resistance of an outside),[8] but we have already noted the way in which "thirdness" has been elided in all of Simmel's formulations, most dramatically in the omission of the officially economic itself in the overall plan of the work. But "third-ness" would be the very place of dialectical theory as such, and this evasion or elision is what suggests that Simmel's eminently dialectical thinking finally stops short of its own theory (or, as Hegel might say, does not manage to be equal to its concept). There are, however, other reasons for this, which we need to sketch out briefly in conclusion.

For one thing, the implications of the peculiar conceptual dilemmas that Simmel finds himself confronting again and again are redirected and even recon-tained by a discursive pathos we have already found at work in the conclusion to "The Metropolis and Mental Life," a pathos which seals and certifies the impossibility of any resolution to these dilemmas by appealing to the tragic mode as such. In this case it is not, as elsewhere, the impossibility of choosing between life and form that is at stake but rather a somewhat different dialectic, one that anticipates the developments in the second part of Simmel's work, which explores the consequences of a money economy: "What one might term the tragedy of human concept formation lies in the fact that the higher concept, which through its breadth embraces a growing number of details, must count upon increasing loss of content" (*PM* 221; *PG* 219). This view clearly enough spells the end of the historical optimism projected by the Hegelian attempt at a system; perhaps it also augurs, in a very different way, the culture pessimism of Freud's *Civilization and Its Discontents*. What Simmel has immediately in mind here, however, is our old friend "abstraction" or "intellectualization," which played so central a role in the shorter essay on the city and the money economy; in fact, this remark comes as a gloss on a first premonition of the blasé relationship to life that will be one of the central themes of the second half of *The Philosophy of Money*.

In that second part, which we will not deal with in great detail, this register of tragic pathos is also extended to the discussion of freedom as such and its paradoxes, which are analogous. But where the motif of freedom opened up the themes of the essay on the metropolis to some properly dialectical exercise of its negative and positive aspects, here the same logic is enlisted in a litany of the unresolvable (and thereby "tragic") paradoxes of modern freedom, at one and the same time more individualistic and more dependent on the complex networks of an interdependent social fabric. The rhetoric of this entire second section, which may considered to be Simmel's contribution to a theory of modernity that takes its cue from the centrality of money in modern society, is suffused with the inescapable pathos of the double bind. Money's other juridical and social consequence in the emergence of property is grasped as an enrichment of the self at the same time that its static and object-oriented tendencies are denounced (one of the most interesting features of this discussion lies in Simmel's suggestion, which anticipates Sartrean existentialism, that we should think of ownership as an activity and a process rather than a state; this is, of course, very consistent with the methodological remarks previously quoted) (see *PM* 332, 304; *PG* 346, 323). Freedom itself is not only linked to the social division of labor but as a consequence becomes characterized as an "internal division of labour," in which the multiplicity of the older group becomes ascribed to the formerly individual entity who was once nothing but a constituent part of that group (*PM* 313; *PG* 333). But this formulation then immediately rehearses yet again the deeper tension between multiplicity and unity that was the drama of the money form itself. Thus the contradiction between individualism and group cohesion "has its origin in the fact that the individual is only one element and member of the social unity, while at the same time being himself a whole entity, whose elements form a relatively closed unity" (*PM* 350; *PG* 381). As for abstraction in modern life, Simmel summarizes his position as follows:

> We have pointed out in the preceding chapters how much money, on the basis of its general availability and objectivity, none the less facilitates the growth of individuality and subjectivity, how much its unchanging uniformity, its qualitatively communistic character, leads to each quantitative difference becoming a qualitative one. This extension of the power of money that is incomparable with that of any other cultural factor, and which gives equal rights to the most contradictory tendencies in life, is manifested here as the condensation of the purely formal cultural energy that can be applied to any content in order to strengthen it and to bring about its increasingly purer representation. (*PM* 440; *PG* 494)

This exceedingly dense and enigmatic passage foreshadows the most interesting subsection of this second part of Simmel's work, which deals with the whole question of styles in modernity, and which deserves a discussion and an appreciation in its own right.

What I must now observe, in conclusion, is that the organization of Simmel's dialectic around the irreducibly empirical form of money, which has enabled the extraordinary richness of his social *Darstellung*, now finally exacts its price, so to speak, in the form of some ultimate limitation and paradoxical constriction. What he was able to project as a pure form out of the phenomenon of money—an absolute unity that is at one and the same time a ceaseless multiplicity of contents and differences of all kinds—now returns to seal his conceptualization of modernity as being inseparable from money and from the money economy as such.

Already he had formally noted the conceptual or categorical kinship of the money form with theological speculations:

It may appear as an irony that, as the moment when the satisfying and ultimate purposes of life become atrophied, precisely that value that is exclusively a means and nothing else takes the place of such purposes and clothes itself in their form. In reality, money in its psychological form, as the absolute means and thus as the unifying point of innumerable sequences of purposes, possesses a significant relationship to the notion of God—a relationship that only psychology, which has the privilege of being unable to commit blasphemy, may disclose. The essence of the notion of God is that all diversities and contradictions in the world achieve a unity in him, that he is—according to a beautiful formulation of Nicolas de Cusa—the *coincidentia oppositorum*. Out of this idea, that in him all estrangements and all irreconcilables of existence find their unity and equalization, there arises the peace, the security, the all-embracing wealth of feeling that reverberate with the notion of God which we hold. (*PM* 236; *PG* 240)

Now this theological property of the money form seizes on Simmel's thinking itself and determines an ultimate ontological outburst:

Money is the symbol in the empirical world of the inconceivable unity of being, out of which the world, in all its breadth, diversity, energy and reality, flows. (*PM* 497; *PG* 567)

It is an astonishing climax, accompanied on the level of empirical decoration by a no less revealing remark in passing to the effect that "the roundness of coins which make them 'roll' symbolizes the rhythm of the movement that money imparts to transactions" and by implication the rhythm of Being itself, in its unified yet infinite differentiation (*PM* 506; *PG* 578). The greatness of Simmel's work lies in its ceaseless and varied use of the money form to unearth and conceptually reveal incommensurabilities of all kinds, in social reality fully as much as in thought itself. Money was thus a ladder that he was unwilling to push away after use, and it was well that Benjamin, who learned so much from Simmel, was unwilling to follow him in this immensely productive fascination, which, however, like the coin itself, became a vicious circle in which the sociologist was ultimately trapped.

Notes

1.   Walter Benjamin (1994), letter to Theodor W. Adorno, 23 February 1939, *The Correspondence of Walter Benjamin, 1910–1940,* trans. Manfred R. Jacobson and Evelyn M. Jacobson, ed. Gershom Scholem and Theodor W. Adorno (Chicago: University of Chicago Press), 599; see also ibid. letter to Scholem, 23 December 1917, 106.

2.   Quoted in Donald N. Levine (1971), introduction to Georg Simmel, *On Individuality and Social Forms: Selected Writings,* ed. Donald N. Levine (Chicago: University of Chicago Press), xiii.

3.   Ibid., "The Metropolis and Mental Life," trans. Edward A. Shils, *On Individuality,* 324; hereafter abbreviated "MM". Ibid., "Die Großstädte und das Geistesleben," *Jahrbuch der Gehe-Stiftung zu Dresden* 9 (Winter): 187; hereafter abbreviated "GG."

4.   Georg Lukács (1971), *History and Class Consciousness: Studies in Marxist Dialectics,* trans. Rodney Livingstone (Cambridge, Mass.: MIT), 186. But juxtapose Simmel's equally significant position: "Money as such is the most terrible destroyer of form," Georg Simmel (1978), *The Philosophy of Money,* trans. Tom Bottomore and David Frisby (London), 272, hereafter abbreviated *PM.* Georg Simmel (1958), *Philosophie des Geldes* (Berlin), 285, hereafter abbreviated *PG*).

5.   Simmel, "The Conflict in Modern Culture," trans. K. Peter Etzkorn, *On Individuality,* 377.

6.   "Un kaleidoscope doué de conscience." Charles Baudelaire, "Le Peintre de la vie modern," *Oeuvres complètes* (1976), 2 vols. ed. Claude Pichois and Jean Ziegler, (Paris: Gallimard), 2: 692; quoted in Walter Benjamin (1968), "On Some Motifs in Baudelaire," *Illuminations,* trans. Harry Zohn, ed. Hannah Arendt (New York), 175.

7.   This is the moment to note Simmel's interesting thoughts on Greece, in particular his account of the cultural and philosophical results of an incompletely monetary economy in ancient Greece, which produced an emphasis on consumption rather than, as in modernity, on production (uncertainty of time and the future, compensatory over-emphasis on the concept of substance); see *PM,* 323–24; *PG,* 235–37.

8.   See, for example, Charles Sanders Peirce (1960), *Principles of Philosophy,* in *Collected Papers of Charles Sanders Peirce* 1960, 8 vols. In 5, ed. Charles Hartshorne and Paul Weiss (Cambridge, Mass.: Harvard University Press), vol. 1: 182–95.

2

The Frankfurt School and British Cultural Studies: The Missed Articulation

Douglas Kellner

For some decades now, British cultural studies has tended either to disregard or caricature in a hostile manner the critique of mass culture developed by the Frankfurt School.[1] The Frankfurt School has been repeatedly stigmatized as elitist and reductionist, or simply ignored in discussion of the methods and enterprise of cultural studies. This is an unfortunate oversight, as I will argue, since despite some significant differences in method and approach, there are also many shared positions that make dialogue between the traditions productive. Likewise, articulation of the differences and divergences of the two traditions could be fruitful since, as I will argue, both traditions to some extent overcome the weaknesses and limitations of the other. Consequently, articulation of their positions could produce new perspectives that might contribute to developing a more robust cultural studies. Thus, I will argue that rather than being antithetical, the Frankfurt School and British cultural studies approaches complement each other and can be articulated in new configurations.

As we enter a new millenium and a new cultural environment being dramatically transformed by global media and computer technologies, we need a cultural studies that analyzes the political economy of the now global culture industries, the proliferation of new media technologies and artifacts, and their multifarious appropriations by audiences. In this article, I will discuss some of the theoretical resources needed for these tasks. My argument is that the Frankfurt School is extremely useful for analyzing the current forms of culture and society because of its focus on the intersections between technology, the culture industries, and the economic situation in contemporary capitalist societies. Since the present age is being dramatically shaped by new media and computer technologies, we need perspectives that articulate the intersection of technology, culture, and everyday life. In my view, both the Frankfurt School and British cultural studies offer us resources to analyze and transform our current social situation and thus to develop a critical social theory and cultural studies with a practical intent.

The Frankfurt School, Cultural Studies, and Regimes of Capital

To a large extent, the Frankfurt School inaugurated critical studies of mass communication and culture, and thus produced an early model of cultural studies (see Kellner 1982, 1989a and 1995a). During the 1930s, the Frankfurt School developed a critical and transdisciplinary approach to cultural and communications studies, combining critique of political economy of the media, analysis of texts, and audience reception studies of the social and ideological effects of mass culture and communications.[2] They coined the term "culture industries" to signify the process of the industrialization of mass-produced culture and the commercial imperatives which drove the system. The critical theorists analyzed all mass-mediated cultural artifacts within the context of industrial production, in which the commodities of the culture industries exhibited the same features as other products of mass production: commodification, standardization, and massification. The culture industries had the specific function, however, of providing ideological legitimation of the existing capitalist societies and of integrating individuals into the framework of its system.

Adorno's analyses of popular music (1978 [1932], 1941, 1982, and 1989), Lowenthal's studies of popular literature and magazines (1984), Herzog's studies of radio soap operas (1941), and the perspectives and critiques of mass culture developed in Horkheimer and Adorno's famous study of the culture industries (1972 and Adorno 1991) provide many examples of the value of the Frankfurt School approach. Moreover, in their theories of the culture industries and critiques of mass culture, they were the first to systematically analyze and criticize mass-mediated culture and communications within critical social theory. They were the first social theorists to see the importance of what they called the "culture industries" in the reproduction of contemporary societies, in which so-called mass culture and communications stand in the center of leisure activity, are important agents of socialization, mediators of political reality, and should thus be seen as major institutions of contemporary societies with a variety of economic, political, cultural, and social effects.[3]

Furthermore, they investigated the cultural industries in a political context as a form of the integration of the working class into capitalist societies. The Frankfurt School was one of the first neo-Marxian groups to examine the effects of mass culture and the rise of the consumer society on the working classes, which were to be the instrument of revolution in the classical Marxian scenario. They also analyzed the ways that the culture industries and consumer society were stabilizing contemporary capitalism and accordingly sought new strategies for political change, agencies of political transformation, and models for political emancipation that could serve as norms of social critique and goals for political struggle. This project required rethinking Marxian theory and produced many important contributions—as well as some problematical positions.

The Frankfurt School focused intently on technology and culture, indicating how technology was becoming both a major force of production and formative mode of social organization and control. In a 1941 article, "Some Social Implications of Modern Technology," Herbert Marcuse argued that technology in the contemporary era constitutes an entire "mode of organizing and perpetuating (or changing) social relationships, a manifestation of prevalent thought and behavior patterns, an instrument for control and domination" (414). In the realm of culture, technology produced mass culture that habituated individuals to conform to the dominant patterns of thought and behavior, and thus provided powerful instruments of social control and domination.

Victims of European fascism, the Frankfurt School experienced firsthand the ways that the Nazis used the instruments of mass culture to produce submission to fascist culture and society. While in exile in the United States, the members of the Frankfurt School came to believe that American "popular culture" was also highly ideological and worked to promote the interests of American capitalism. Controlled by giant corporations, the culture industries were organized according to the strictures of mass production, churning out mass-produced products that generated a highly commercial system of culture, which in turn sold the values, lifestyles, and institutions of American capitalism.

In retrospect, one can see the Frankfurt School work as articulation of a theory of the stage of state and monopoly capitalism that became dominant during the 1930s.[4] This was an era of large organizations, theorized earlier by Hilferding as "organized capitalism" (1980 [1910]), in which the state and giant corporations managed the economy and in which individuals submitted to state and corporate control. This period is often described as "Fordism" to designate the system of mass production and the homogenizing regime of capital that wanted to produce mass desires, tastes, and behavior. It was thus an era of mass production and consumption characterized by uniformity and homogeneity of needs, thought, and behavior producing a "mass society" and what the Frankfurt School described as "the end of the individual." No longer was individual thought and action the motor of social and cultural progress; instead giant organizations and institutions overpowered individuals. The era corresponds to the staid, ascetic, conformist, and conservative world of corporate capitalism that was dominant in the 1950s with its organization men and women, its mass consumption, and its mass culture.

During this period, mass culture and communication were instrumental in generating the modes of thought and behavior appropriate to a highly organized and massified social order. Thus, the Frankfurt School theory of "the culture industries" articulates a major historical shift to an era in which mass consumption and culture was indispensable to producing a consumer society based on homogeneous needs and desires for mass-produced products and a mass society based on social organization and homogeneity. It is culturally the era of highly controlled network radio and television, insipid top forty pop music, glossy Hollywood films, national magazines, and other mass-produced cultural artifacts.

Of course, media culture was never as massified and homogeneous as in the Frankfurt School model and one could argue that the model was flawed even during its time of origin and influence and that other models were preferable (such as those of Walter Benjamin, Sigfried Krakauer, Ernst Bloch, and others of the Weimar generation and, later, British cultural studies, as I argue below). Yet the original Frankfurt School model of the culture industry did articulate the important social roles of media culture during a specific regime of capital and provided a model, still of use, of a highly commercial and technologically advanced culture that serves the needs of dominant corporate interests, plays a major role in ideological reproduction, and in enculturating individuals into the dominant system of needs, thought, and behavior.

British cultural studies, then, from historical perspective emerges in a later era of capital, on the cusp of what became known as "post-Fordism" and a more varie-gated and conflicted cultural formation. The forms of culture described by the earliest phase of British cultural studies in the 1950s and early 1960s articulated conditions in an era in which there were still significant tensions in England and much of Europe between an older working-class-based culture and the newer mass-produced culture whose models and exemplars were the products of American culture industries. The initial project of cultural studies developed by Richard Hoggart, Raymond Williams, and E. P. Thompson attempted to preserve working-class culture against onslaughts of mass culture produced by the culture industries. Thompson's inquiries into the history of British working-class institutions and struggles, the defenses of working-class culture by Hoggart and Williams, and their attacks on mass culture were part of a socialist and working class–oriented project that assumed that the industrial work-ing class was a force of progressive social change and that it could be mobilized and organized to struggle against the inequalities of the existing capitalist societies and for a more egalitarian socialist one. Williams and Hoggart were deeply involved in projects of working-class education and oriented toward socialist working-class poli-tics, seeing their form of cultural studies as an instrument of progressive social change.

The early critiques in the first wave of British cultural studies of Americanism and mass culture, in Hoggart, Williams, and others, thus paralleled to some extent the earlier critique of the Frankfurt School, yet valorized a working class that the Frankfurt school saw as defeated in Germany and much of Europe during the era of fascism and which they never saw as a strong resource for emancipatory social change. The early work of the Birmingham school, as I will now argue, was continuous with the radicalism of the first wave of British cultural studies (the Hoggart-Thompson-Williams "culture and society" tradition) as well, in important ways, with the Frank-furt School. Yet the Birmingham project also paved the way, as I suggest below, for a postmodern populist turn in cultural studies, which responds to a later stage of capitalism.

The Trajectories of Cultural Studies

It has not yet been recognized (as far as I know) that the second stage of the development of British cultural studies—starting with the founding of the University of Birmingham Centre for Contemporary Cultural Studies in 1963–1964 by Hog-gart and Stuart Hall—shared many key perspectives with the Frankfurt School. During this period, the Centre developed a variety of critical approaches for the analysis, interpretation, and criticism of cultural artifacts.[5] Through a set of internal debates, and responding to social struggles and movements of the 1960s and the 1970s, the Birmingham group came to focus on the interplay of representations and ideologies of class, gender, race, ethnicity, and nationality in cultural texts, including media culture. They were among the first to study the effects of newspapers, radio, television, film, and other popular cultural forms on audiences. They also focused on how various audiences interpreted and used media culture in varied and different ways and contexts, analyzing the factors that made audiences respond in contrasting ways to media texts.

The now classical period of British cultural studies from the early 1960s to the early 1980s continued to adopt a Marxian approach to the study of culture, one especially influenced by Althusser and Gramsci (see, especially Hall 1980a). Yet although Hall usually omits the Frankfurt School from his narrative, some of the work done by the Birmingham group replicated certain classical positions of the Frankfurt School, in their social theory and methodological models for doing cultural studies, as well as in their political perspectives and strategies. Like the Frankfurt School, British cultural studies observed the integration of the working class and its decline of revolutionary consciousness, and studied the conditions of this catastrophe for the Marxian project of revolution. Like the Frankfurt School, British cultural studies concluded that mass culture was playing an important role in integrating the working class into existing capitalist societies and that a new consumer and media culture was forming a new mode of capitalist hegemony.

Both traditions focused on the intersections of culture and ideology and saw ideology critique as central to a critical cultural studies (CCCS 1980a and 1980b). Both saw culture as a mode of ideological reproduction and hegemony, in which cultural forms help to shape the modes of thought and behavior that induce individuals to adapt to the social conditions of capitalist societies. Both also see culture as a form of resistance to capitalist society and both the earlier forerunners of British cultural studies, especially Raymond Williams, and the theorists of the Frankfurt School see high culture as forces of resistance to capitalist modernity. Later, British cultural studies would valorize resistant moments in media culture and audience interpretations, and use of media artifacts—while the Frankfurt School tended, with some exceptions, to see mass culture as a homogeneous and potent form of ideological domination, a difference that would seriously divide the two traditions.

From the beginning, British cultural studies was highly political in nature and focused on the potentials for resistance in oppositional subcultures, first valorizing the potential of working class cultures, then youth subcultures, to resist the hegemonic forms of capitalist domination. Unlike the classical Frankfurt School (but similar to Herbert Marcuse), British cultural studies turned to youth cultures as providing potentially new forms of opposition and social change. Through studies of youth subcultures, British cultural studies demonstrated how culture came to constitute distinct forms of identity and group membership and appraised the oppositional potential of various youth subcultures (see Jefferson 1976 and Hebdige 1979). Cultural studies came to focus on how subcultural groups resist dominant forms of culture and identity, creating their own style and identities. Individuals who conform to dominant dress and fashion codes, behavior, and political ideologies thus produce their identities within mainstream groups, as members of specific social groupings (such as white, middle-class, conservative Americans). Individuals who identify with subcultures, like punk culture, or black nationalist subcultures, look and act differently from those in the mainstream, and thus create oppositional identities, defining themselves against standard models.

But British cultural studies, unlike the Frankfurt School, has not adequately engaged modernist and avant-garde aesthetic movements, limiting its focus by and large to products of media culture and "the popular" which has become an immense focus of its efforts. However, the Frankfurt School engagement with modernism and avant-garde art in many of its protean forms strikes me as more productive than ignoring modernism and to some extent high culture as a whole, by much of British cultural studies. It appears that in its anxiety to legitimate study of the popular and to engage the artifacts of media culture, British cultural studies has turned away from so-called "high" culture in favor of the popular. But such a turn sacrifices the possible insights into all forms of culture and replicates the bifurcation of the field of culture into a "popular" and "elite" (which merely inverts the positive/negative valorizations of the older high/low distinction). More important, it disconnects cultural studies from attempts to develop oppositional forms of culture of the sort associated with the "historical avant-garde" (Burger 1984). Avant-garde movements like Expressionism, Surrealism, and Dada wanted to develop art that would revolutionize society, that would provide alternatives to hegemonic forms of culture.

The oppositional and emancipatory potential of avant-garde art movements was a primary focus of the Frankfurt School, especially Adorno, and it is unfortunate that British and North American cultural studies have largely neglected engaging avant-garde art forms and movements. Indeed, it is interesting that such a focus was central to the project of *Screen*, which was in some ways the hegemonic avant-garde of cultural theory in Britain in the 1970s, with powerful influence throughout the world. In the early 1970s, *Screen* developed a founding distinction between "realism" and "modernism" and carried out a series of critiques of both bourgeois realist art and the sorts of media culture that reproduced the ideological codes of realism. In addition, they positively valorized avant-garde modernist aesthetic practices, which were championed for their political and emancipatory effects. This project put *Screen* theory in profound kinship with the Frankfurt School, especially Adorno, though there were also serious differences.

British cultural studies developed systematic critiques of the theoretical positions developed by *Screen* in the 1970s and early 1980s that, as far as I know, were never really answered.[6] Indeed, what became known as "*Screen* theory" itself fragmented and dissolved as a coherent theoretical discourse and practical program by the 1980s. While many of the critiques of *Screen* theory developed by British cultural studies were convincing, I would argue that the emphasis on avant-garde practices championed by *Screen* and the Frankfurt School constitute a productive alternative to the neglect of such practices by current British and North American cultural studies.

British cultural studies—like the Frankfurt School—insists that culture must be studied within the social relations and system through which culture is produced and consumed, and that thus study of culture is intimately bound up with the study of society, politics, and economics. The key Gramscian concept of hegemony led British cultural studies to investigate how media culture articulates a set of dominant values, political ideologies, and cultural forms into a hegemonic project that incorporates individuals into a shared consensus, as individuals became integrated into the consumer society and political projects like Reaganism or Thatcherism (see Hall

1998). This project is similar in many ways to that of the Frankfurt School, as are their metatheoretical perspectives that combine political economy, textual analysis, and study of audience reception within the framework of critical social theory.

British cultural studies and the Frankfurt School were both founded as fundamentally transdisciplinary enterprises that resisted established academic divisions of labor. Indeed, their boundary crossing and critiques of the detrimental effects of abstracting culture from its sociopolitical context elicited hostility among those who are more disciplinary-oriented and who, for example, believe in the autonomy of culture and renounce sociological or political readings. Against such academic formalism and separatism, cultural studies insists that culture must be investigated within the social relations and system through which culture is produced and consumed, and that thus analysis of culture is intimately bound up with the study of society, politics, and economics. Employing Gramsci's model of hegemony and counterhegemony, it sought to analyze "hegemonic," or ruling, social and cultural forces of domination and to seek "counterhegemonic" forces of resistance and struggle. The project was aimed at social transformation and attempted to specify forces of domination and resistance in order to aid the process of political struggle and emancipation from oppression and domination.

Some earlier authoritative presentations of British cultural studies stressed the importance of a transdisciplinary approach to the study of culture that analyzed its political economy, process of production and distribution, textual products, and reception by the audience—positions remarkably similar to the Frankfurt School. For instance, in his classical programmatic article, "Encoding/Decoding," Stuart Hall began his analysis by using Marx's *Grundrisse* as a model to trace the articulations of "a continuous circuit," encompassing "production-distribution-consumption-production" (1980b, 128ff). Hall concretizes this model with focus on how media institutions produce meanings, how they circulate, and how audiences use or decode the texts to produce meaning. Moreover, in a 1983 lecture published in 1985/1986, Richard Johnson provided a model of cultural studies, similar to Hall's earlier model, based on a diagram of the circuits of production, textuality, and reception, parallel to the circuits of capital stressed by Marx, illustrated by a diagram that stressed the importance of production and distribution. Although Johnson emphasized the importance of analysis of production in cultural studies and criticized *Screen* for abandoning this perspective in favor of more idealist and textualist approaches (63ff.), much work in British and North American cultural studies has replicated this neglect.

In more recent cultural studies, however, there has been a turn—throughout the English-speaking world—to what might be called a postmodern problematic that emphasizes pleasure, consumption, and the individual construction of identities in terms of what Jim McGuigan (1992) has called a "cultural populism." Media culture from this perspective produces material for identities, pleasures, and empowerment, and thus audiences constitute the "popular" through their consumption of cultural products. During this phase—roughly from the mid-1980s to the present—cultural studies in Britain and North America turned from the socialist and revolutionary politics of the previous stages to postmodern forms of identity politics and less critical perspectives on media and consumer culture. Emphasis was placed more and more on the audience, consumption, and reception, and displaced focus on production and distribution of texts and how texts were produced in media industries.

A Postmodern Cultural Studies?

In this section, I wish to argue that the forms of cultural studies developed from the late 1970s to the present, in contrast to the earlier stages, theorize a shift from the stage of state monopoly capitalism, or Fordism, rooted in mass production and consumption, to a new regime of capital and social order, sometimes described as "post-Fordism" (Harvey 1989), or "postmodernism" (Jameson 1991), and characterizing a transnational and global capital that valorizes difference, multiplicity, eclecticism, populism, and intensified consumerism in a new information/entertainment society. From this perspective, the proliferating media culture, postmodern architecture, shopping malls, and the culture of the postmodern spectacle became the promoters and palaces of a new stage of technocapitalism, the latest stage of capital, encompassing a postmodern image and consumer culture.[7]

Consequently, I would argue that the turn to a postmodern cultural studies is a response to a new era of global capitalism. What is described as the "new revisionism" (McGuigan 1992, 61ff.) severs cultural studies from political economy and critical social theory. During the current stage of cultural studies there is a widespread tendency to decenter, or even ignore completely, economics, history, and politics in favor of emphasis on local pleasures, consumption, and the construction of hybrid identities from the material of the popular. This cultural populism replicates the turn in postmodern theory away from Marxism and its alleged reductionism, master narratives of liberation and domination, and historical teleology.[8]

In fact, as McGuigan (1992, 45ff.) has documented, British cultural studies have had an unstable relationship with political economy from the beginning. Although Stuart Hall and Richard Johnson grounded cultural studies in a Marxian model of the circuits of capital (production-distribution-consumption-production), Hall and other key figures in British cultural studies have not consistently pursued economic analysis, and most practioners of British and North American cultural studies from the 1980s to the present have pulled away from political economy altogether. Hall's swervings toward and away from political economy are somewhat curious. Whereas in the article cited above Hall begins cultural studies with production and recommends traversing through the circuits of capital (1980b) and while in "Two Paradigms" (1980a), Hall proposes synthesizing on a higher level, à la the Frankfurt School "culturalism" and "structuralism," he has been rather inconsistent in articulating the relationship between political economy and cultural studies, and rarely deployed political economy in his work.

In the "Two Paradigms" article, for example, Hall dismisses the political economy of culture paradigm because it falls prey to economic reductionism. Hall might be right in rejecting some forms of the political economy of culture then circulating in England and elsewhere, but, as I will argue below, it is possible to do a political economy of culture à la the Frankfurt School without falling prey to reductionism yet using the same sort of model of reciprocal interaction of culture and economy. In particular, the Frankfurt model posits a relative autonomy to culture, which is often defended by Hall, and does not entail economic reductionism or determinism.

Generally speaking, however, Hall and other practioners of British cultural studies (i.e., Tony Bennett, John Fiske, Angela McRobbie, et al.) either simply dismiss the Frankfurt School as a form of economic reductionism or simply ignore it.[9] The blanket charge of economic reductionism is in part a way of avoiding political economy altogether. Yet while many practioners of British cultural studies ignore political economy totally, Hall, to be sure, has occasionally made remarks that might suggest the need to articulate cultural studies with political economy. In a 1983 article, Hall suggests that it is preferable to conceive of the economic as determinate in "the first instance" rather than in "the last instance," but this play with Althusser's argument for the primacy of the economic is rarely pursued in actual concrete studies (see the critique in Murdock 1989 and McGuigan 1992, 34).

Hall's analysis of Thatcherism as "authoritarian populism" (1988) related the move toward the hegemony of the right to shifts in global capitalism from Fordism to post-Fordism, but for his critics (Jessop et al. 1984) he did not adequately take account of the role of the economy and economic factors in the shift toward Thatcherism. Hall responded that with Gramsci he would never deny "the decisive nucleus of economic activity" (1988, 156), but it is not certain that Hall himself adequately incorporates economic analysis into his work in cultural studies and political critique. For example, Hall's writing on the "global postmodern" suggests the need for more critical conceptualizations of contemporary global capitalism and theorizing of relations between the economic and the cultural of the sort associated with the Frankfurt School. Hall states (1991):

> the global postmodern signifies an ambiguous opening to difference and to the margins and makes a certain kind of decentering of the Western narrative a likely possibility; it is matched, from the very heartland of cultural politics, by the backlash: the aggressive resistance to difference; the attempt to restore the canon of Western civilization; the assault, direct and indirect, on multicultural; the return to grand narratives of history, language, and literature (the three great supporting pillars of national identity and national culture); the defense of ethnic absolutism, of a cultural racism that has marked the Thatcher and the Reagan eras; and the new xenophobias that are about to overwhelm fortress Europe.

For Hall, therefore, the global postmodern involves a pluralizing of culture, openings to the margins, to difference, to voices excluded from the narratives of Western culture. But one could argue in opposition to this interpretation in the spirit of the Frankfurt School that the global postmodern simply represents an expansion of global capitalism on the terrain of new media and technologies, and that the explosion of information and entertainment in media culture represents powerful new sources of capital realization and social control. To be sure, the new world order of technology, culture, and politics in contemporary global capitalism is marked by more multiplicity, pluralism, and openness to difference and voices from the margins, but it is controlled and limited by transnational corporations, which are becoming powerful new cultural arbitrators who threaten to constrict the range of cultural expression rather than to expand it.

The dramatic developments in the culture industries in recent years toward merger and consolidation represent the possibilities of increased control of information and entertainment by ever fewer superconglomerates. One could argue already that the globalization of media culture is an imposition of the lowest denominator homogeneity of global culture on a national and local culture, in which CNN, NBC, BBC, the Murdock channels, and so on impose the most banal uniformity and homogeneity on media culture throughout the world. To be sure, the European cable and satellite television systems have state television from Germany, France, Italy, Spain, Sweden, and Russia, and so on, but these state television systems are not really open to that much otherness, difference, or marginality. Indeed, the more open channels, like public access television in the United States and Europe, or the SBS service, which provides multicultural television in Australia, are not really part of the global postmodern, and are funded or mandated for the most part by the largess of the state and are usually limited and local in scope and reach.

Certainly, there are some openings in Hall's global postmodern, but they are rather circumscribed and counteracted by increasing homogenization. Indeed, the defining characteristics of global media culture are the contradictory forces of identity and difference—homogeneity and heterogeneity, the global and the local—impinging on each other, clashing, simply peacefully coexisting, or producing new symbioses as in the motto of MTV Latino, which combines English and Spanish: *Chequenos!*—meaning "Check us out!" Globalization by and large means the hegemony of transnational cultural industries, largely American. In Canada, for instance, about 95 percent of films in movie theaters are American; U.S. television dominates Canadian television; seven American firms control distribution of sound recordings in Canada; and 80 percent of the magazines on newsstands are non-Canadian (*Washington Post Weekly,* 11–17 September 1995: 18). In Latin America and Europe the situation is similar with American media culture, commodities, fast food, and malls creating a new global culture that is remarkably similar on all continents.[10]

Evocations of the global postmodern diversity and difference should thus take into account countervailing tendencies toward global homogenization and sameness—themes constantly stressed by the Frankfurt School.

For Hall (1991), the interesting question is what happens when a progressive politics of representation imposes itself on the global postmodern field, as if the global field was really open to marginality and otherness. But in fact the global field itself is structured and controlled by dominant corporate and state powers and it remains a struggle to get oppositional voices in play and is probably impossible where there is not something like public access channels or state-financed open channels as in Holland. Of course, things look different when one goes outside of the dominant media culture—there *is* more pluralism, multiplicity, openness to new voices, on the margins—but such alternative cultures are hardly part of the global postmodern that Hall elicits. Hall's global postmodern is thus too positive and his optimism should be tempered by the sort of critical perspectives on global capitalism developed by the Frankfurt School and the earlier stages of cultural studies.

The emphasis in postmodernist cultural studies, in my view, articulates experiences and phenomena within a new mode of social organization. The emphasis on active audiences, resistant readings, oppositional texts, utopian moments, and the like describes an era in which individuals are trained to be more active media consumers, and in which they are given a much wider choice of cultural materials, corresponding to a new global and transnational capitalism with a much broader array of consumer choices, products, and services. In this regime, difference sells, and the differences, multiplicities, and heterogeneity valorized in postmodern theory describes the proliferation of differences and multiplicity in a new social order predicated on proliferation of consumer desires and needs.

The forms of hybrid culture and identities described by postmodern cultural studies correspond to a globalized capitalism with an intense flow of products, culture, people, and identities with new configurations of the global and local and new forms of struggles and resistance (see Appadurai 1990 and Cvetkovich and Kellner 1997). Corresponding to the structure of a globalized and hybridized global culture, are new forms of cultural studies that combine traditions from throughout the world. Cultural studies has indeed has become globalized during the past decade with the proliferation of articles, books, conferences, and internet sites and discussions throughout the world.

The question arises as to the continued use-value of the older traditions of Frankfurt School theory and British cultural studies in this new and original condition. To begin, these traditions continue to be relevant because there are continuities between our present stage and the earlier ones. Indeed, I would argue that we are in an interregnum period, between the modern and the postmodern, and that the current regime of capital has strong continuities with the mode of production and social organization of the earlier stages described by the Frankfurt School and British cultural studies. Contemporary culture is more commodified and commercialized than ever and so the Frankfurt School perspectives on commodification are obviously still of fundamental importance in theorizing our current situation. The hegemony of capital continues to be the dominant force of social organization, perhaps even more so than before. Likewise, class differences are intensifying, media culture continues to be highly ideological and to legitimate existing inequalities of class, gender, and race, so that the earlier critical perspectives on these aspects of contemporary culture and society continue to be of importance.

My argument will be that the new global constellation of technocapitalism is based on configurations of capital and technology, producing new forms of culture, society, and everyday life. I have been arguing that the Frankfurt School furnishes resources to analyze this conjuncture because their model of the culture industries focuses on the articulations of capital, technology, culture, and everyday life that constitute the current sociocultural environment. Although there is a tendency of Frankfurt School thinkers to occasionally offer an overly one-sided and negative vision of technology as an instrument of domination—building on Weber's theory of instrumental rationality—there are also aspects that make possible a critical theory of technology that articulates both its emancipatory and oppressive aspects (see Marcuse 1941; Kellner 1984 and 1989a). The Frankfurt School thus complements British cultural studies in providing a more intense focus on the articulations of capital and technology, and thus theorizing contemporary culture and society in the context of the current constellation of global capitalism.

In the next section, accordingly, I will examine what theoretical resources the Frankfurt School and tradition of British cultural studies contain to critically analyze and transform contemporary societies and culture. I will be concerned to articulate some overlapping similarities in perspective between the two traditions, but also differences in which the traditions complement each other and force us to produce new perspectives in order to do cultural studies in the present conjuncture. My argument is that cultural studies today should return to the earlier models of British cultural studies and put in question the current rejection of political economy, class, ideology, and other concepts central characteristic of the postmodern turn in cultural studies. I believe that the turn away from the problematic shared to some extent with the Frankfurt School has vitiated contemporary British and North American cultural studies and that a return to critical social theory and political economy is a necessary move for a revitalized cultural studies. This project requires a new cultural studies that articulates the sort of analysis of political economy developed by the Frankfurt School with the emphasis on subversive moments of media culture, oppositional subcultures, and an active audience developed by British cultural studies. I believe that the neglect of political economy truncates cultural studies and would argue for its importance, not only for generally understanding media culture, but also for analyzing texts and audience use of texts that are deeply influenced by the system of production and distribution within which media products circulate and are received (see Kellner 1995a).[11]

Border Crossing, Transdisciplinarity, and Cultural Studies

I have been arguing that there are many important anticipations of key positions of British cultural studies in the Frankfurt School, that they share many positions and dilemmas, and that a dialogue between these traditions is long overdue. I would also propose seeing the project of cultural studies as broader than that taught in the contemporary curricula and as encompassing a wide range of figures from various social locations and traditions. There are indeed many traditions and models of cultural studies, ranging from neo-Marxist models developed by Lukàcs, Gramsci, Bloch, and the Frankfurt School in the 1930s to feminist and psychoanalytic cultural studies to semiotic and poststructuralist perspectives. In Britain and the United States, there is a long tradition of cultural studies that preceded the Birmingham school.[12] And France, Germany, and other European countries have also produced rich traditions that provide resources for cultural studies throughout the world.

The major traditions of cultural studies combine—at their best—social theory, cultural critique, history, philosophical analysis, and specific political interventions, thus overcoming the standard academic division of labor by surmounting specialization arbitrarily produced by an artificial academic division of labor. Cultural studies thus operates with a transdisciplinary conception that draws on social theory, economics, politics, history, communication studies, literary and cultural theory, philosophy, and other theoretical discourses—an approach shared by the Frankfurt School, British cultural studies, and French postmodern theory. Transdisciplinary approaches to culture and society transgress borders between various academic disciplines.[13] In regard to cultural studies, such approaches suggest that one should not stop at the border of a text, but should see how it fits into systems of textual production, and how various texts are thus part of systems of genres or types of production, and have an intertextual construction—as well as articulating discourses in a given sociohistorical conjuncture.

Rambo is a film, for instance, that fits into the genre of war films and a specific cycle of return to Vietnam films, but it also articulates anticommunist political discourses dominant in the Reagan era (see Kellner 1995a). It replicates the right-wing discourses concerning POWs left in Vietnam and the need to overcome the Vietnam syndrome (i.e., shame concerning the loss of the war and overcoming the reluctance to again use U.S. military power). But it also fits into a cycle of masculinist hero films, antistatist right-wing discourses, and the use of violence to resolve conflicts. The figure of Rambo itself became "global popular," which had a wide range of effects throughout the world. Interpreting the cinematic text of *Rambo* thus involves the use of film theory, textual analysis, social history, political analysis and ideology critique, effects analysis, and other modes of cultural criticism.

One should not, therefore, stop at the borders of the text or even its intertextuality, but should move from text to context, to the culture and society that constitutes the text and in which it should be read and interpreted. Transdisciplinary approaches thus involve border crossings across disciplines from text to context, and thus from texts to culture and society. Raymond Williams was especially important for cultural studies because of his stress on borders and border crossings (1961, 1962, and 1964). Like the Frankfurt School, he always saw the interconnection between culture and communication, and their connections with the society in which they are produced, distributed, and consumed. Williams also saw how texts embodied the political conflicts and discourses within which they were embedded and reproduced.

Crossing borders inevitably pushes one to the boundaries and borders of class, gender, race, sexuality, and the other constituents that differentiate individuals from each other and through which people construct their identities. Thus, most forms of cultural studies, and most critical social theories, have engaged feminism and the various multicultural theories that focus on representations of gender, race, ethnicity, and sexuality, enriching their projects with theoretical and political substance derived from the new critical discourses that have emerged since the 1960s. Transdisciplinary cultural studies thus draw on a disparate range of discourses and fields to theorize the complexity and contradictions of the multiple effects of a vast range of cultural forms in our lives and differentially demonstrate how these forces serve as instruments of domination, but also offer resources for resistance and change. The Frankfurt School, I would argue, inaugurated such transdisciplinary approaches to cultural studies, combining analysis of the production and political economy of culture with textual analysis that contextualize cultural artifacts in their sociohistorical milieu, with studies of audience reception and use of cultural texts.[14]

Yet there are serious flaws in the original program of critical theory that require a radical reconstruction of the classical model of the culture industries (Kellner 1989a and 1995a). Overcoming the limitations of the classical model would include: more concrete and empirical analysis of the political economy of the media and the processes of the production of culture; more empirical and historical research into the construction of media industries and their interaction with other social institutions; more empirical studies of audience reception and media effects; more emphasis on the use of media culture as providing forces of resistance; and the incorporation of new cultural theories and methods into a reconstructed critical theory of culture and society. Cumulatively, such a reconstruction of the classical Frankfurt School project would update the critical theory of society and its activity of cultural criticism by incorporating contemporary developments in social and cultural theory into the enterprise of critical theory.

In addition, the Frankfurt School dichotomy between high culture and low culture is problematical and should be superseded for a more unified model that takes culture as a spectrum and applies similar critical methods to all cultural artifacts ranging from opera to popular music, from modernist literature to soap operas. In particular, the Frankfurt School model of a monolithic mass culture contrasted with an ideal of "authentic art," which limits critical, subversive, and emancipatory moments to certain privileged artifacts of high culture, is highly problematic. The Frankfurt School position that all mass culture is ideological and homogenizing, having the effects of duping a passive mass of consumers, is also objectionable. Instead, one should see critical and ideological moments in the full range of culture, and not limit critical moments to high culture and identify all of low culture as ideological. One should also allow for the possibility that critical and subversive moments could be found in the artifacts of the cultural industries, as well as the canonized classics of high modernist culture that the Frankfurt School seemed to privilege as the site of artistic opposition and emancipation.[15] One should also distinguish between the encoding and decoding of media artifacts, and recognize that an active audience often produces its own meanings and use for products of the cultural industries.

British cultural studies overcomes some of these limitations of the Frankfurt School by systematically rejecting high/low culture distinctions and taking seriously the artifacts of media culture. Likewise, they overcome the limitations of the Frankfurt School notion of a passive audience in their conceptions of an active audience that creates meanings and the popular. Yet it should be pointed out that Walter Benjamin—loosely affiliated with the Frankfurt School but not part of their inner circle—also took seriously media culture, saw its emancipatory potential, and posited the possibility of an active audience. For Benjamin (1969), the spectators of sports events were discriminating judges of athletic activity, able to criticize and analyze sports events. Benjamin postulated that the film audience can also become experts of criticism and dissect the meanings and ideologies of film. Yet I believe that we need to synthesize the concepts of the active and manipulated audience to grasp the full range of media effects, thus avoiding both cultural elitism and populism.

Indeed, it is precisely the critical focus on media culture from the perspectives of commodification, reification, technification, ideology, and domination developed by the Frankfurt School that provides a perspective useful as a corrective to more populist and uncritical approaches to media culture that surrender critical perspectives—as is evident in some current forms of British and North American cultural studies. In fact, the field of communications study was initially bifurcated into a division, described by Paul Lazarsfeld (1941) in an issue edited by the Frankfurt School on mass communications, between the critical school associated with the Institute for Social Research contrasted to administrative research, which Lazarsfeld defined as research carried out within the parameters of established media and social institutions and that would provide material that was of use to these institutions—research with which Lazarsfeld himself would be identified. Hence, it was the Frankfurt School that inaugurated critical communications research, and I am suggesting that a return to a reconstructed version of the original model would be useful for media and cultural studies today.

Although the Frankfurt School approach itself is partial and one-sided, it does provide tools to criticize ideological forms of media culture and how it provides ideologies that legitimate forms of oppression. Ideology critique is a fundamental constituent of cultural studies and the Frankfurt School is valuable for inaugurating systematic and sustained critiques of ideology within the cultural industries. The Frankfurt School is especially useful in providing contextualizations of their cultural criticism. Members of the group carried out their analysis within the framework of critical social theory, thus integrating cultural studies within the study of capitalist society and the ways that communications and culture were produced within this order and the roles and functions that they assumed. Thus, the study of communication and culture became an important part of a theory of contemporary society, in which culture and communication were playing ever more significant roles.[16]

In the next section, I will argue that the neglect in current versions of British cultural studies of the sort of political economy and critical social theory found in the Frankfurt School work has vitiated contemporary cultural studies that can be enriched by incorporation of the version of political economy—closely connected with critical social theory—found in the Frankfurt School. I develop this argument with engagement of some key texts within British cultural studies, and criticize some current versions that are shown to be problematical precisely through their abandoning of the earlier, more Marxist-oriented perspectives that defined earlier versions of British cultural studies and the work of the Frankfurt School.

Political Economy and Cultural Studies

Thus, against the turn away from political economy in cultural studies, I believe it is important to situate analysis of cultural texts within their system of production and distribution, often referred to as the "political economy" of culture.[17] But this requires some reflection on what sort of political economy might be useful for cultural studies. The references to the terms "political" and "economy" call attention to the fact that the production and distribution of culture takes place within a specific economic system, constituted by relations between the state, the economy, the media, social institutions and practices, culture, and everyday life. Political economy thus encompasses economics and politics and the relations between them and the other central dimensions of society and culture.

In regard to media institutions, for instance, in Western democracies, a capitalist economy dictates that cultural production is governed by laws of the market, but the democratic imperatives mean that there is some regulation of culture by the state. There are often tensions within a given society concerning which activities should be governed by the imperatives of the market alone and how much state regulation or intervention is desirable, to assure a wider diversity of broadcast programming, or the prohibition of phenomena agreed to be harmful, such as cigarette advertising or pornography (see Kellner 1990).

Political economy highlights that capitalist societies are organized according to a dominant mode of production that structures institutions and practices according to the logic of commodification and capital accumulation so that cultural production is profit- and market-oriented. Forces of production (such as media technologies and creative practice) are deployed according to dominant relations of production that are important in determining what sort of cultural artifacts are produced and how they are consumed. However, "political economy" does not merely refer solely to economics, but to the relations among the economic, political, and other dimensions of social reality. The term thus links culture to its political and economic context and opens up cultural studies to history and politics. It refers to a field of struggle and antagonism and not an inert structure as caricatured by some of its opponents.

Political economy also calls attention to the fact that culture is produced within relationships of domination and subordination and thus reproduces or resists existing structures of power. Such a perspective provides a normative standard for cultural studies whereby the critic can attack aspects of cultural texts that reproduce class, gender, racial, and other hierarchal forms of domination and positively valorize aspects that resist or subvert existing domination, or depict forms of resistance and struggle against them. In addition, inserting texts into the system of culture within which they are produced and distributed can help elucidate features and effects of the texts that textual analysis alone might miss or downplay. Rather than being antithetical approaches to culture, political economy can contribute to textual analysis and critique, as well as audience reception and uses of media texts—as I attempt to demonstrate below. The system of production often determines what sort of artifacts will be produced, what structural limits there will be about what can and cannot be said and shown, and what sort of audience expectations and usage the text may generate.

Consideration of Stuart Hall's famous distinction between encoding and decoding (1980b) suggests some of the ways that political economy structures both the encoding and decoding of media artifacts. As the Frankfurt School pointed out, media culture is produced within an industrial organization of production in which products are generated according to codes and models within culture industries that are organized according to industrial models of production (Horkheimer and Adorno 1972). What codes are operative and how they are encoded into artifacts is thus a function of the system of production. In a commercial system of media culture, production is organized according to well-defined genres with their own codes and modes of production.

Film, television, popular music, and other genres of media culture are highly codified into systems of commercial enterprise, organized in accordance with highly conventional codes and formulas. In the system of commercial broadcasting in the United States, for instance, network television is organized into a few dominant genres such as talk shows, soap operas, action-adventure series, and situation comedies. Each genre has its own codes and format, with situation comedies invariably using a structure of conflict and resolution, with the solving of the problem suggesting a moral message or upholding dominant values or institutions. Within the genre, each series has its own codes and formats that are followed according to the dictates of the production company; each series, for instance, uses a manual (or "story bible") that tells writers and production teams what to do and not to do, defines characters and plot lines, and the conventions of the series; continuity experts enforce the following of these codes rigorously (as do network censors that do not allow content that transgresses dominant moral codes).

Sometimes, of course, the codes of media culture change, often dramatically and usually in accordance with social changes that lead media producers to conclude that audiences will be receptive to new forms more relevant to their social experience. So for some years during the 1950s and 1960s happy, middle-class nuclear families ruled the U.S. situation comedy during an era of unparalleled post–World War II affluence that came to an end in the early 1970s. Precisely then new working class comedies appeared, such as Norman Lear's *All in the Family,* which focused on social conflict and economic problems, and that did not offer easy solutions to all of the standard conflicts. Lear's subsequent series on the working class, *Mary Hartman,* combined situation comedy codes with soap opera codes, which endlessly multiplied problems rather than providing solutions. During the protracted economic recession of the 1980s and 1990s, triggered by a global restructuring of capitalism, new "loser television" situation comedy series appeared featuring the victims of the economic downswing and restructuring (i.e., *Roseanne, Married . . . with Children,* and *The Simpsons*). *Beavis and Butt-Head* takes loser television even further, combining situation comedy formats with music video clips and the commentary of two mid-teenage animated cartoon characters without apparent families, education, or job prospects (see the discussion in Kellner 1995a).

Other popular 1990s sitcoms feature singles, reflecting the decline of the family and proliferation of alternative life styles in the present moment (e.g., *Murphy Brown, Seinfeld, Friends,* etc.). The most popular U.S. sitcoms of the 1990s thus break the codes of happy affluent families easily solving all problems within the nuclear family ("It's all in the family."). The codes of the texts are produced by changes in production codes with media corporations deciding that audiences want a new sort of program that better reflects their own situation and in turn creates new audience codes and expectations. The concept of "code" therefore intersects articulations of media industries and production, texts, and audience reception in a circuit of production-consumption-production in which political economy is crucial.

Increased competition from ever-proliferating cable channels and new technologies led network television in the 1980s and 1990s to break many of the conventions rigorously followed in series TV in order to attract declining audiences. Programs like *Hill Street Blues, L.A. Law, Law and Order,* and *N.Y.P.D. Blue,* for instance, subverted previous conventions and taboos of the television crime drama. *Hill Street Blues* employed handheld cameras to create a new look and feel, multiplied its plot lines with some stories lasting for weeks, and did not always provide a positive resolution to the conflicts and problems depicted. Previous TV police dramas rigorously followed a conflict/resolution model with a crime, its detection, and an inevitable happy ending, projecting the message that crime did not pay and providing idealizations of the police and the criminal justice system. But the later police shows mentioned above depicted corrupt members within the law enforcement and judicial system, police committing crimes, and criminals getting away with their misdeeds.

Yet even the code-breaking series have their own codes and formulas that cultural analysis should delineate. The relatively young and liberal production team of *Hill Street Blues,* for instance, conveyed socially critical attitudes toward dominant institutions and sympathy for the oppressed marked by the experiences of sixties radicalism (see Gitlin 1983's study of Steven Bochco and his production team). The team's later series *L.A. Law* negotiates the emphasis on professionalism and rising mobility of the Reaganite 80s with concern for social problems and the oppressed. Bochco's series *N.Y.P.D. Blue* reflects growing cynicism toward police, law enforcement, and the society as a whole. The success of these series obviously points to an audience that shares these attitudes and is tiring of idealized depictions of police, lawyers, and the criminal justice system.

Thus, situating the artifacts of media culture within the system of production and the society that generate them can help illuminate their structures and meanings. The encoding of media artifacts is deeply influenced by systems of production so that study of the texts of television, film, or popular music, for instance, is enhanced by studying the ways that media artifacts are actually produced within the structure and organization of the culture industries. Since the forms of media culture are structured by well-defined rules and conventions, the study of the production of culture can help elucidate the codes actually in play and thus illuminate what sorts of texts are produced. Because of the demands of the format of radio or music television, for instance, most popular songs are three to four minutes, fitting into the format of the distribution system. Because of its control by giant corporations oriented primarily toward profit, film production in the United States is dominated by specific genres and since the 1970s by the search for blockbuster hits, thus leading to proliferation of the most popular sorts of comedies, action-adventure films, fantasies, and seemingly never-ending sequels and cycles of the most popular films. This economic factor explains why Hollywood film is dominated by major genres and subgenres, explains sequelmania in the film industry, crossovers of popular films into television series,[18] and a certain homogeneity in products constituted within systems of production with rigid generic codes, formulaic conventions, and well-defined ideological boundaries.

Likewise, study of political economy can help determine the limits and range of political and ideological discourses and effects, and can help indicate which discourses are dominant at a specific conjuncture. The rigid production code implemented for Hollywood films in 1934, for instance, strictly forbade scenes showing explicit sexuality, use of drugs, critical references to religion, or stories in which crime did indeed pay. By the 1960s, the production code was thoroughly subverted and eventually abandoned during an era of falling audiences where the film industries broke previous taboos in order to attract audiences to the movie theaters. In addition, the wave of youth and counterculture films of the 1960s responded to what film studios saw as a new film generation that made up a significant chunk of the audience (Kellner and Ryan 1988). Low-budget films like *Easy Rider* made high profits and Hollywood spun off genre cycles of such films. Likewise, when low-budget blaxploitation films made high profits a cycle of films featuring black heroes, often outlaws, against the white power structure proliferated. After consolidation of the film industry in the 1970s, however, and megablockbuster hits like *Jaws* and *Star Wars*, Hollywood aimed at more mainstream genre blockbuster films, driving more subcultural fare to the margins.

Thus, economic trends in the film industry help explain what sorts of films were made over the past decades. Television news and entertainment and its biases and limitations can also be illuminated by study of political economy. My study of television in the United States, for instance, disclosed that the takeover of the television networks by major transnational corporations and communications conglomerates was part of a "right turn" within U.S. society in the 1980s whereby powerful corporate groups won control of the state and the mainstream media (Kellner 1990). For example, during the 1980s all three U.S. networks were taken over by major corporate conglomerates: ABC was taken over in 1985 by Capital Cities, NBC was taken over by General Electric, and CBS was taken over by the Tisch Financial Group. Both ABC and NBC sought corporate mergers and this motivation, along with other benefits derived from Reaganism, might well have influenced them to downplay criticisms of Reagan and to generally support his conservative programs, military adventures, and simulated presidency—and then to support George Bush in the 1988 election (see the documentation in Kellner 1990).

Reaganism and Thatcherism constituted a new political hegemony, a new form of political common sense, and the trend in the 1990s has been for deregulation and the allowing of "market forces" to determine the direction of cultural and communications industries. Hence, in 1995–1996 megamergers between Disney and ABC, Time Warner and Turner Communications, CBS and Westinghouse, and NBC and Microsoft, and mergers among other major media conglomerates were negotiated and more recently Time Warner and AOL. Merger mania was both a function of the general atmosphere of deregulation and a FCC ruling under the Clinton administration that allowed television networks to own and produce their own programming (whereas previously independent Hollywood production companies created programs and the networks distributed them). Relaxing of these rules and visions of "synergy" between production and distribution units has led to even greater concentration of media conglomerates and will thus probably lead to a narrower range of programming and voices in the future.

Thus, analysis of political economy allows illumination of the major trends in the information and entertainment industries. Furthermore, one cannot really discuss the role of the media in specific events like the Gulf War without analyzing the production and political economy of news and information, as well as the actual text of the war against Iraq and its reception by its audience (see Kellner 1992 and 1995a). Likewise, in appraising the full social impact of pornography, one needs to be aware of the sex industry and the production process of, say, pornographic films, and not just limit analysis to the texts themselves and their effects on audiences. Nor can one fully grasp the success of Michael Jackson or Madonna without analyzing their marketing strategies, their use of the technologies of music video, advertising, publicity, and image management.

Toward a Multiperspectival Cultural Studies

To conclude, I am proposing that cultural studies develop a multiperspectival approach that includes investigation of a wide range of artifacts interrogating relationships within the three dimensions of (1) the production and political economy of culture; (2) textual analysis and critique of its artifacts; and (3) study of audience reception and the uses of media/cultural products.[19] This proposal involves suggesting, first, that cultural studies itself be multiperspectival, getting at culture from the perspectives of political economy and production, text analysis and audience reception.[20] I would also propose that textual analysis and audience reception studies utilize a multiplicity of perspectives, or critical methods, when engaging in textual analysis, and in delineating the multiplicity of subject positions, or perspectives, through which audiences appropriate culture. Moreover, I would argue that the results of such studies need to be interpreted and contextualized within critical social theory to adequately delineate their meanings and effects.

Which perspectives will be deployed in specific studies depends on the subject matter under investigation, the goals of the study, and its range. Obviously, one cannot deploy all the perspectives circulating in every single study, but I would argue if one is doing a study of a complex phenomena like the Gulf War, Madonna, the *Rambo* phenomena, rap music, or the "war on terrorism," one needs to deploy the perspectives of political economy, textual analysis, and audience reception studies to illuminate the full dimensions of these spectacles of media culture. In this paper, I have limited myself to some arguments concerning how Frankfurt School perspectives on the cultural industries can enrich cultural studies, and for a final example of the fruitfulness of this approach let us reflect on the Madonna and Michael Jackson phenomena. There have been a large number of readings of their texts and a vast literature on Madonna's effects on her audiences, but less study of how their mode of production and marketing strategies have helped create their popularity.

My argument would be that Madonna and Michael Jackson have deployed some of the most proficient production and marketing teams in the history of media culture and this dimension should therefore be considered in analyses of their meanings, effects, and uses by their audiences. Just as Madonna's popularity was in large part a function of her marketing strategies and her production of music videos and images that appealed to diverse audiences (see Kellner 1995a), so too has Michael Jackson's media machine employed topflight production, marketing, and public relations personnel. Both Madonna and Michael Jackson reached superstardom during the era when MTV and music videos became central in determining fame within the field of popular music and arguably became popular because of their look and spectacular presentations in expensive music videos with exceptionally high production values. In both cases, it is arguably the marketing of their image and the spectacle of their music videos or concerts—rather than, say, their voices or any specific musical talent—that account for their popularity. Both deployed top musical arrangers, choreographers, and cinematographers in the production of music videos and performed in highly spectacular and well-publicized concerts that were as much spectacle as performance. Both employed powerhouse publicity machines and constantly kept themselves in the public eye. In particular, both were celebrated constantly by MTV, which had entire weekends, and even weeks, devoted to publicizing their work and fame.

Both therefore succeeded because of their understanding and use of the machinery of musical production and promotion by the culture industries. Interestingly, Michael Jackson targeted mainstream audiences from the beginning, attempting to appeal equally to black and white, preteen and teenage, audiences. Indeed, his look erased racial markers as he became whiter and whiter after recurrent plastic surgery; likewise, he cultivated an androgenous look and image that collapsed distinctions between male and female, child and adult, appearing both childlike and sexy, as a naïve innocent and canny businessperson, thus appealing to multiple audiences. Madonna, by contrast, targeted first teenage girl audiences, then various ethnic audiences with performers of color and distinct ethnic markers appearing in her music videos and concerts.

Both also appealed to gay audiences with Madonna in particular pushing the boundaries of the acceptable in music videos, leading MTV to ban a 1990 video "Justify My Love" with what was deemed excessively extreme sexuality. Both became highly controversial, Madonna because of her exploitation of sexuality and Michael Jackson because of accusations of child molestation. Indeed, the latter created a serious public relations problem for Jackson who had presented himself as a lover of children. But when this image became too literal he needed to refurbish his public persona. After settling financially with the family of the boy who had claimed that Jackson had sexually abused him, Jackson undertook a series of desperate attempts to refurbish his image in the mid-1990s. He married Lisa Marie Presley, Elvis's daughter in 1994, thus positioning him as a husband, a father (of Lisa Marie's children by a previous marriage), and as in the lineage of the King of Rock, the successor to the throne. With the 1995 release of *HisStory*, a multirecord collection of his greatest hits and current work, Jackson undertook a massive publicity campaign with Sony records supported with a $30 million budget. The record did not match his earlier sales, but at least brought Jackson back into the limelight as it was accompanied by an un-paralleled media blitz in summer 1995 with ABC Television dedicating entire special programs to Jackson and his wife, and to Jackson on-line with his fans in a live Internet interaction. Not to be outdone, MTV devoted an entire week's prime time programming to Jackson.

Yet Jackson and Lisa Marie Presley split up in 1996 and once again rumors circulated that he was continuing to engage in pedophilia, and these rumors and the breakup of his marriage created bad press and retarnished his image. In the midst of this crisis, Jackson declared that a long time friend was pregnant with his child and he married her in Fall 1996, once again trying to produce a positive image as husband and father. But, again, negative media reports circulated and Jackson's image was again in crisis. Ironically, in a Fall 2001 concert broadcast on CBS, Jackson allegedly spent thousands of dollars on a digital darkening of his visual image so that he would appear more black! He who lives by the media can also die by the media, though like old soldiers, media celebrities sometimes just fade away rather than merely disappearing.

In any case, analyzing the marketing and production of stardom and popularity can help to demystify the arguably false idols of media culture and to produce more critical audience perception. Analyzing the business dimension of media culture can help produce critical consciousness as well as better understanding of its production and distribution. Such a dimension enhances cultural studies and contributes to developing a critical media pedagogy that supplements analysis of how to read media texts and how to study audience use of them.

Consequently, a cultural studies that is critical and multiperspectival provides comprehensive approaches to culture that can be applied to a wide variety of artifacts from pornography to Michael Jackson and Madonna, from the Gulf War to Beavis and Butt-Head, from modernist painting to postmodern architecture. Its comprehensive perspectives encompass political economy, textual analysis, and audience research and provide critical and political perspectives that enable individuals to dissect the meanings, messages, and effects of dominant cultural forms. Cultural studies is thus part of a critical media pedagogy that enables individuals to resist media manipulation and to increase their freedom and individuality. It can empower people to gain sovereignty over their culture and to be able to struggle for alternative cultures and political change. Cultural studies is thus not just another academic fad, but can be part of a struggle for a better society and a better life.

Notes

1. As I argue in this text, the classical texts of British cultural studies ignore or denigrate the Frankfurt School and most succeeding texts on cultural studies continue to either superficially caricature or hostilely attack the tradition of critical theory. For my own earlier appreciations and criticisms of the Frankfurt School tradition that I draw upon here, see Kellner 1989a and Kellner 1995a.

2. On the Frankfurt School theory of the cultural industries, see Horkheimer and Adorno 1972; Adorno 1991; the anthology edited by Rosenberg and White 1957; the readers edited by Arato and Gebhardt 1982 and Bronner and Kellner 1989; the discussions of the history of the Frankfurt School in Jay 1971 and Wiggershaus 1994; and the discussion of the Frankfurt School combination of social theory and cultural criticism in Kellner 1989a.

3. I've analyzed some of these effects from a reconstructed critical theory perspective in analyses of Hollywood film with Michael Ryan (1988), two books on American television (Kellner 1990 and 1992), and a series of media cultural studies (in Kellner 1995a and Best and Kellner, forthcoming).

4. See Kellner 1989a and the texts in Bronner and Kellner 1989.

5. For standard accounts of this phase of British cultural studies, see Hall 1980b; Johnson 1986–1987; Fiske 1986; O'Conner 1989; Turner 1990; Grossberg 1989; Agger 1992; and McGuigan 1992. For readers who document the positions of British cultural studies, see the articles collected in Grossberg, Nelson, Triechler 1992, and During 1992.

6. See the critique of "*Screen* theory" in Hall et al. 1980.

7. For detailed description of this new form of culture and society, see Best and Kellner 1997 and forthcoming; for critical analysis of the postmodern theories that emerged during the 1970s and 1980s, see Best and Kellner 1991.

8. The most extreme version of "the end of political economy" is found in Jean Baudrillard (1993) and French postmodern theory, but is present in some versions of British and North American cultural studies. See Kellner 1989b and 1995a.

9. Among the few engagements with the Frankfurt School in the vast literature explaining the origins and trajectory of British cultural studies, or on the positions the Birmingham school critically engaged, are an article by Tony Bennett (1982: 30ff), who tended to read the Frankfurt School as a left variant of the mass society model that cultural studies was rejecting in an anthology containing Open University texts used for cultural studies. Earlier, there was an article by Phil Slater in the Birmingham Centre journal on "The Aesthetic Theory of the Frankfurt School," which was highly dismissive, and "A Bibliography of the Frankfurt School" by Chris Pawling in the journal published by the Centre for Contemporary Cultural Studies, *Cultural Studies* 6 (Autumn 1974): 172–215. In one of his genealogies of the Centre, Hall (1990: 16) notes how the British New Left encountered major works of European Marxism—including "the Frankfurt School, then of Benjamin, and then of Gramsci"—through the translations of *New Left Review*, but Hall never describes his wrestling with the devilish angels of the Frankfurt School—as he frequently does vis-à-vis Althusser and Gramsci. Thus, there has been no real critical engagement with the Frankfurt School that I could find and certainly no recognition of the shared positions.

10. In Europe, American films constitute 75 to 80 percent of the market; *Time,* 27 February 1995: 36. It is predicted that new digital technologies will create even greater penetration of world markets by American media products.

11. Here I agree with McGuigan who writes, "the separation of contemporary cultural studies from the political economy of culture has been one of the most disabling features of the field of study. The core problematic was virtually premised on a terror of

economic reductionism. In consequence, the economic aspects of media institutions and the broader economic dynamics of consumer culture were rarely investigated, simply bracketed off, thereby severely undermining the explanatory and in effect, critical capacities of cultural studies" (1992, 40–41).

12. On earlier traditions of cultural studies in the United States, see Aronowitz 1993 and for Britain, see Davies 1995.

13. Articles in the 1983 *Journal of Communications* issue on *Ferment in the Field* (33, 3 [Summer]) noted a bifurcation of the field between a culturalist approach and more empirical approaches in the study of mass-mediated communications. The culturalist approach was largely textual, centered on the analysis and criticism of texts as cultural artifacts, using methods primarily derived from the humanities. The methods of communications research, by contrast, employed more empirical methodologies, ranging from straight quantitative research, empirical studies of specific cases or domains, or historical research. Topics in this area included analysis of the political economy of the media, audience reception and study of media effects, media history, the interaction of media institutions with other domains of society and the like. See Kellner 1995b for analyses of how the Frankfurt School, British cultural studies, and French postmodern theory all overcome the bifurcation of the field of culture and communications into text- and humanities-based approaches opposed to empirical and social science–based enterprises. As I am arguing here, a transdisciplinary approach overcomes such bifurcation and delineates a richer and broader perspective for the study of culture and communications.

14. The contributions of the Frankfurt School to audience reception theory is often overlooked completely, but Walter Benjamin constantly undertakes studies of how audiences use the materials of popular media and inaugurated a form of reception studies; see Benjamin (1969, 217ff.). Leo Lowenthal also carried out reception studies of literature, popular magazines, political demagogues, and other phenomena (with Norbert Gutterman 1949; and 1957; 1961). On Frankfurt experiments with studies of media effects see Wiggershaus (1994, 441ff.).

15. There were, to be sure, some exceptions and qualifications to this "classical" model: Adorno would occasionally note a critical or utopian moment within mass culture and the possibility of audience reception against the grain; see the examples in Kellner 1989a. But although one can find moments that put in question the more bifurcated division between high and low culture and the model of mass culture as consisting of nothing except ideology and modes of manipulation that incorporate individuals into the existing society and culture, generally the Frankfurt School model is overly reductive and monolithic and thus needs radical reconstruction—which I have attempted to do in my work over the past two decades.

16. In the 1930s model of critical theory, theory was supposed to be an instrument of political practice. Yet the formulation of the theory of the culture industries by Horkheimer and Adorno (1972 [1947]) in the 1940s was part of their turn toward a more pessimistic phase in which they eschewed concrete politics and generally located resistance within critical individuals, like themselves, rather than within social groups, movements, or oppositional practices. Thus, the Frankfurt School ultimately is weak on

the formulation of oppositional practices and counterhegemonic cultural strategies with the exception, as noted, of Walter Benjamin.

17.   For a survey of recent literature on the political economy of the media and efforts at "rethinking and renewal," see Mosco 1995.

18.   Curiously, whereas during the 1970s and the 1980s, there were frequent spin-offs of television series from popular movies, in more recent years the trend has reversed with popular classical television series spun-off into films like *The Fugitive, The Beverly Hillbillies, The Flintstones, The Addams Family* series, *The Brady Bunch, The Mod Squad, Charlie's Angels,* and many others. Yet the synergy continues with a 1995 TV series based on a film derived from John Grisham's *The Client* and 1996 series based on the films *Dangerous Minds* and *Clueless.*

19.   I set out this multiperspectival approach in an earlier article and book on the Gulf War as a cultural and media event (Kellner 1992a and 1992b), and illustrate the approach in studies of the Vietnam war and its cultural texts, Hollywood film in the age of Reagan, MTV, TV entertainment like *Miami Vice,* advertising, Madonna, cyberpunk fiction, and other topics in Kellner 1995a. Thus, I am here merely signaling the metatheory that I have worked out and illustrated elsewhere.

20.   Curiously, Raymond Williams (1981) equates precisely this multiperspectival approach in his textbook on the sociology of culture to a mainstream "observational sociology" perspective, though I am suggesting more critical approaches to production, textual analysis, and audience reception. Yet, interestingly, Williams privileges an institution and production approach in his sociology of culture, whereas British and North American cultural studies have neglected these dimensions for increasing focus on audiences and reception.

References

Adorno, Theodor W. 1941. "On Popular Music," (with G. Simpson), *Studies in Philosophy and Social Science* 9, 1: 17–48.

———. 1978 (1932). "On the Social Situation of Music," *Telos* 35 (Spring): 129–65.

———. (1982) "On the Fetish Character of Music and the Regression of Hearing," in *The Essential Frankfurt School Reader.* Edited by Andrew Arato and Eike Gebhardt. New York: Continuum. 270–299.

———. 1989. "On Jazz," in *Critical Theory and Society: A Reader.* Edited by Stephen Bronner and Douglas Kellner. New York: Routledge. 199–209.

———. 1991. *The Culture Industry.* London: Routledge.

Agger, Ben. 1992. *Cultural Studies.* London: Falmer Press.

Appadurai, Arjun. 1990. "Disjuncture and Difference in the Global Cultural Economy" in *Global Culture: Nationalism, Globalization and Modernity.* Edited by Mike Featherstone. 295–310.

Arato, Andrew, and Eike Gebhardt. 1982. *The Essential Frankfurt School Reader.* New York: Continuum.

Aronowitz, Stanley. 1993. *Roll Over Beethoven.* Hanover, N.H.: University Press of New England.

Baudrillard, Jean. 1993. *Symbolic Exchange and Death.* London: Sage Books.

Benjamin, Walter. 1969. *Illuminations.* New York: Shocken.

Bennett, Tony. 1982. "Theories of the Media, Theories of Society," in *Culture, Society, and the Media.* Edited by Michael Gurevitch, et al. London: Macmillan.

Best, Steven, and Douglas Kellner 1991. *Postmodern Theory: Critical Interrogations.* London and New York: Macmillan and Guilford Press.

———. 1997. *The Postmodern Turn.* New York: Guilford Press.

———. Forthcoming. *The Postmodern Adventure.* New York: Guilford Press.

Bloch, Ernst. 1986. *The Principle of Hope.* Cambridge, Mass.: MIT Press.

Blundell, et al. 1993. *Relocating Cultural Studies.* New York: Routledge.

Bronner, Stephen, and Douglas Kellner. 1989. *Critical Theory and Society: A Reader.* New York: Routledge.

Bürger, Peter. 1984 (1974). *Theory of the Avant-Garde.* Minneapolis, Minn.: University of Minnesota Press.

Centre for Contemporary Cultural Studies. 1980a. *On Ideology.* London: Hutchinson.

———. 1980b. *Culture, Media, Language.* London: Hutchinson.

Cvetkovich, Ann, and Douglas Kellner. 1997. *Articulating the Global and the Local: Globalization and Cultural Studies.* Boulder, Colo.: Westview Press.

Davies, Ioan. 1995. *Cultural Studies, and After.* London and New York: Routledge.

Dieterle, William. 1941. "Hollywood and the European Crisis." *Studies in Philosophy and Social Science* 9: 96–103.

During, Simon, ed. 1993. *The Cultural Studies Reader.* London and New York: Routledge.

Featherstone, Mike, ed. 1990. *Global Culture: Nationalism, Globalization and Modernity.* London: Sage.

Fiske, John. 1986. "British Cultural Studies and Television," in *Channels of Discourse.* Edited by R. C. Allen. Chapel Hill, N.C.: University of North Carolina Press. 254–89.

Gitlin, Todd. 1983. *Inside Prime Time.* New York: Pantheon.

Grossberg, Lawrence. 1989. "The Formations of Cultural Studies: An American in Birmingham." *Strategies* 22: 114–49.

Grossberg, Lawrence; Nelson, Cary; and Paula Treichler. 1992. *Cultural Studies.* New York: Routledge.

Hall, Stuart, et al. 1980. *Culture, Media, Language.* London: Hutchinson.

———. 1980a. "Cultural Studies and the Centre: Some Problematics and Problems," in ibid. 15–47.

———. 1980b. "Encoding/Decoding," in ibid. 128–38.

———. 1983. "The Problem of Ideology—Marxism Without Guarantees," in *Marx 100 Years On.* Edited by B. Matthews. London: Lawrence & Wishart.

———. 1988. *The Hard Road to Renewal.* London: Verso.

———. 1991. Lecture on Globalization and Ethnicity, University of Minnesota, Videotape.

Harvey, David. 1989. *The Condition of Postmodernity.* Cambridge: Blackwell.

Hebdige, Dick. *Subculture. The Meaning of Style.* London: Methuen.

Herzog, Herta. 1941. "On Borrowed Experience. An Analysis of Listening to Daytime Sketches," *Studies in Philosophy and Social Science,* Vol. IX, No. 1: 65-95.

Hilferding, Rudolf. 1981 (1910). *Finance Capital.* London: Routledge and Kegan Paul.

Horkheimer, Max, and T.W. Adorno. 1972. *Dialectic of Enlightenment.* New York: Herder and Herder.

Jameson, Fredric. 1991. *Postmodernism, or the Cultural Logic of Late Capitalism.* Durham, N.C.: Duke University Press.

Jay, Martin. 1973. *The Dialectical Imagination.* Boston: Little, Brown.

Jefferson, Tony, ed. 1976. *Reistance through Rituals.* London: Hutchinson.

Jessop, Bob, et al. 1984. "Authoritarian Populism, Two Nations, and Thatcherism," *New Left Review* 147.

Johnson, Richard. 1986–1987. "What is Cultural Studies Anyway?" *Social Text* 16: 38–80.

Kellner, Douglas. 1982. "Kulturindustrie und Massenkommunikation. Die Kritische Theorie und ihre Folgen," in *Sozialforschung als Kritik.* Edited by Wolfgang Bonss and Axel Honneth. Frankfurt: Suhrkamp, 482–514.

———. 1984. *Herbert Marcuse and the Crisis of Marxism.* London and Berkeley: Macmillan and University of California Press.

———. 1989a. *Critical Theory, Marxism, and Modernity.* Cambridge and Baltimore: Polity and John Hopkins University Press.

———. 1989b. *Jean Baudrillard: From Marxism to Postmodernism and Beyond.* Cambridge and Palo Alto, Polity and Stanford University Press.

———. 1990. *Television and the Crisis of Democracy.* Boulder, Colo.: Westview Press.

———. 1992a. *The Persian Gulf TV War.* Boulder, Colo.: Westview Press.

———. 1992b. "Toward a Multiperspectival Cultural Studies." *Centennial Review* 26, 1 (Winter): 5–42.

———. 1995a. *Media Culture. Cultural Studies, Identity, and Politics Between the Modern and the Postmodern.* London and New York: Routledge.

———. 1995b. "Media Communications vs. Cultural Studies: Overcoming the Divide." *Communication Theory* 5, 2 (May): 162–77.

———, and Michael Ryan. 1988. *Camera Politica: The Politics and Ideology of Contemporary Hollywood Film.* Bloomington, Ind.: Indiana University Press.

Lazarsfeld, Paul. 1941. "Administrative and Critical Comunications Research." *Studies in Philosophy and Social Science* 9, 1: 2–16.

Lowenthal, Leo, with Norbert Guttermann. 1949. *Prophets of Deceit.* New York: Harper & Row.

———. 1957. *Literature and the Image of Man.* Boston: Beacon Press.

———. 1961. *Literature, Popular Culture and Society.* Englewood Cliffs, N.J.: Prentice-Hall.

Marcuse, Herbert. 1941. *Studies in Philosophy and Social Science* 9, 1: 414–39.

McGuigan, Jim. 1992. *Cultural Populism.* London and New York: Routledge.

Mosco, Vincent. 1996. *The Political Economy of Communication. Rethinking and Renewal.* London: Sage.

Murdock, Graham. 1989. "Cultural Studies at the Crossroads," *Australian Journal of Communication* 16.

O'Connor, Alan. 1989. "The Problem of American Cultural Studies." *Critical Studies in Mass Communication* (December): 405–13.

Rosenberg, Bernard, and David Manning White, eds. 1957. *Mass Culture.* Glencoe, Ill.: The Free Press.

Turner, Graeme. 1990. *British Cultural Studies: An Introduction.* New York: Unwin Hyman.
Wiggershaus, Rolf. 1994. *The Frankfurt School.* Cambridge, Eng.: Polity Press.
Williams, Raymond. 1961. *The Long Revolution.* London: Chatto and Windus.
———. 1962. *Communications.* London: Penguin.
———. 1974. *Television, Technology, and Cultural Form.* London: Fontana.
———. 1981. *Communications.* London: Penguin.

3

The Limits of Culture:
The Frankfurt School and/for
Cultural Studies

Imre Szeman

We had compulsions that made us confuse shopping with
creativity . . .

—Douglas Coupland, *Generation X*

Cultural Studies and Populism

For better or for worse, cultural studies has come to be identified as a practice whose highest ambition is to salvage meaning and significance out of what most others in the academy would still see as the junk of popular culture. Invoke the phrase "cultural studies" today and chances are that associations are made not only to studies of visual culture (television, film, etc.) and working-class cultural practices (as in the early projects of the Birmingham Centre), but to books about alien abductions, body piercing, theme parks, pornography, and the revolutionary potential of cyberspace, i.e., quasi-sociological, impressionistic studies of those trends that just happen to be cresting the wave of the cultural *Zeitgeist*. The antipopulist tone of much recent work in cultural studies—a tone that it shares with a growing number of its critics[1]— seems intended to correct the impression that it has thus become nothing more than a kind of "slacker" discipline, one that is more interested in reading resistance in *South Park* and Japanese *anime* than in (say) defining cultural policy or in understanding precisely the complicated relationship of culture to politics. The various calls that have been made recently to fundamentally rethink cultural studies (e.g., to think it transnationally),[2] to explore its largely unexplored philosophical underpinnings (which has become Larry Grossberg's primary project),[3] or to "return" it to its initial (i.e., "better") trajectory,[4] all seem to originate out of a widely shared sense that cultural studies needs to recover the critical and democratizing impulses that an uncritical populism has confused or obscured. What is perhaps less clear is whether in an effort to clear it of the kind of bad reputation that has allowed Pierre Bourdieu to dismiss cultural studies out-of-hand as "one of the most perverse forms of academic pedantry" (1998, 9), the antipopulism within cultural studies constitutes a rejection of populism altogether, or whether the intent is to recover a "true" populism from its degeneration into the cruder varieties embraced by some versions of cultural studies and manufactured as a component of mass culture itself.[5]

Even though it has seemed to be on the increase as of late, this disavowal of populism within cultural studies is not an entirely new phenomenon. More than a decade ago—a long time in the relatively short history of cultural studies—Meaghan Morris had already issued warnings about the effects of a naive or crude populism on cultural studies. In her influential essay, "Banality in Cultural Studies," Morris notes with alarm that the guiding thesis of some versions of cultural studies had already become

> perilously close to this kind of formulation: people in modern mediatized societies are complex and contradictory, mass cultural texts and complex and contradictory, therefore people using them produce complex are contradictory culture. To add that this popular culture has critical and resistant elements is tautological—unless one has a concept of culture so rudimentary that it excludes criticism and resistance from the practice of everyday life. (1998, 19)[6]

Yet, as necessary as it has become for cultural studies to distance itself from such a simplistic understanding of culture that would locate resistance everywhere, it nevertheless seems that such disavowals—especially when through repetition they become a defining element of cultural studies itself—can only produce an identity crisis for cultural studies. For if cultural studies is not to be identified with *some* kind of populism, it might be asked in what way it can still be understood *as* cultural studies: an attention to the popular seems to be one of it defining characteristics, so much so that without it, it is no longer clear what remains of this practice.[7] Nevertheless, it seems that cultural studies has decided, even at the risk of its own identity, that there is more to be gained than lost by treating the objects and subjects of contemporary mass culture with a good deal more suspicion than it has in the past, especially in terms of what it means to locate resistance in and to what now passes for "culture."

Turning: From Cultural Studies to the Frankfurt School

In the context of the accelerated commodification and corporatization of culture over this past decade (a process whose most visible sign has been the formation of vertically *and* horizontally integrated global media giants, a situation that harkens back to the 1940s and 1950s), it might be possible to read the disavowal of populism as a sign of a belated *turn* to the Frankfurt School's equally suspicious view of the "culture industry." It has been common practice to view the characteristics of successive moments in the development of cultural studies in relationship to immediate political circumstances. For example, more than one commentator has taken the consolidation of cultural studies as an academic practice in the 1980s as a symptom of the troubled (apolitical) state of the left in the era of Reagan, Thatcher, and Mulroney. The past decade has seen a further intensification and deepening of this neoconservative revolution, so much so that it has become clear that whatever it was that cultural studies had hoped to accomplish politically, it hasn't. As cultural studies begins to reach the limits of its effectivity as a critical practice,[8] and correspondingly, as it tries to seek out a new way forward, could we be witnessing what would amount to a rethinking of the Frankfurt School by cultural studies—not a rethinking of the Frankfurt School as such, but of its potential contribution to the practice and development of cultural studies?

This is an important question to consider given its repercussions for the analysis of contemporary culture. But before it is even possible to begin to address this question, it is necessary to examine the relationship between the Frankfurt School and cultural studies more generally. I believe that the work of the Frankfurt School, particularly its work on culture, has a great deal to contribute to cultural studies, especially now, at a time when cultural studies has become more concerned with self-definition than with the practice of cultural analysis. However, it is not by accident that I described the antipopulism within cultural studies as a sign of a potential turn to the Frankfurt School—a *turn*, and not a *return*. Even if one has the sense that whatever their differences, cultural studies and the Frankfurt School share at least a family resemblance as practices that attempt to understand (among other things, in the case of the Frankfurt School) the culture of commodity culture, there are numerous barriers that separate these two critical practices. While it *seems* almost natural to assume that cultural studies has not only drawn inspiration from the Frankfurt School and its work on mass culture, but that its theoretical roots lie in the fertile ground first cultivated by the Frankfurt School, the truth of the matter is that the connection between the work of the Frankfurt School and the development of contemporary cultural studies has been less clearly articulated than one might expect. There is a surprising silence on the question of the importance and influence of work such as Herbert Marcuse's "The Affirmative Character of Culture" or Max Horkheimer and Theodor Adorno's "The Culture Industry" on the practice of cultural studies.[9] But perhaps this silence is less surprising once the role that the Frankfurt School has played in defining cultural studies becomes clear. Whenever the work of the Frankfurt School is addressed in works of cultural studies, its importance derives almost entirely from the *negative* lesson that is to taken from it. In the various histories that have been offered of cultural studies, the Frankfurt School represents nothing but its "bad" other, the polar opposite of the kind of cultural analysis that cultural studies proposes to undertake. References to the work of the Frankfurt School are thus made only to produce a negative maxim: whatever else cultural studies may be or might become, it should take the practice of the Frankfurt School as an example of something to be avoided at all costs.[10]

This is perhaps nowhere so clear as in Simon During's *The Cultural Studies Reader*, which begins with an abridged version of "The Culture Industry" from the *Dialectic of Enlightenment*. Its position at the beginning of the collection suggests that it is an originary text for cultural studies, even if During makes little reference to it in the general historical overview of cultural studies that forms the introduction to the book. However, the brief comments with which During introduces "The Culture Industry" itself suggests a different reason for starting off the book with Horkheimer and Adorno: it is through its explicit *contrast* to the Frankfurt School's approach to culture that cultural studies assumes its raison d'être, the animating logic that links together the rest of the essays in the collection. In his editorial comments, During finds it important to explain, or even to explain away, the well-known pessimism of Horkheimer and Adorno's essay. He does this by suggesting that the positions that they take have to be seen as a function of the historical moment during which "The Culture Industry" was produced. During writes,

> it is worth emphasizing that when this essay was written the culture industry was less variegated that it was to become, during the 1960s in particular. Hollywood, for instance, was still "vertically integrated" [in the mid-1940s] so that the five major studios owned the production, distribution, and exhibition arms of the film business between them; television was still in its infancy; the LP and the single were unknown; the cultural market had not been broken into various demographic sectors—of which, in the 1950s, the youth segment was to become the most energetic. (1993, 29–30)

"This explains," During concludes, "how Adorno and Horkheimer neglect what was to become central to cultural studies: the ways in which the cultural industry, while in the service of organized capital, also provides the opportunities for all kinds of individual and collective creativity and decoding" (30).

In addition to providing what amounts to a working definition of cultural studies, this short paragraph manages to reveal a whole history of the relationship—or better yet, the lack of one—between cultural studies and the Frankfurt School. I will point to just two elements of this relationship here. First, and perhaps most notably, a temporal identification is made between cultural studies and the recent past and present of capitalism. Strictly speaking, During does not want to suggest that the analysis of contemporary culture offered by Horkheimer and Adorno is wrong. Rather, it seems that what he wishes to emphasize is that further developments in capitalist cultural production—developments that have made the cultural field more variegated—have somehow opened up space for "collective creativity and decoding." For During, the fracturing of the social field into a multitude of demographic categories, something that has only happened since the 1950s, necessitates a less restrictive and less pessimistic view of culture industry. To put this into concrete terms, the claim is that we should take the abundance of video titles now available in even smaller towns, neatly categorized into genres and forms appealing to different audiences, or the numerous available forms of recorded music (rap, country, alternative, alternative country,[11] etc.), as examples of the way in which new spaces have been opened up for agency and identity-construction within commodity culture.[12] This is a troubling claim, and one that I will return to by way of conclusion, but what I want to stress here is the periodizing effect of this claim: the temporal field that cultural studies claims is *necessarily* late modernity/postmodernity, the period in which cultural production becomes central to capitalism, and a period for which the (supposedly) anachronistic analysis offered by Horkheimer and Adorno is found wanting. In this respect, it would amount to something like a category mistake to presume to be able to perform cultural studies of nineteenth-century culture or even of "third-world" culture prior to the wholesale development of commodity culture in these regions.[13] The second point is that while there is an admission of the limits imposed by contemporary cultural production, which During concedes is "in the service of organized capital," this is nevertheless accompanied by the suggestion that there is still room for the subject to maneuver in the culture of late capitalism, a fact that cultural studies has wanted to emphasize as much as Horkheimer and Adorno seem to have wanted to deny. Together, these two points form the basic logic of cultural studies: if the field of analysis of cultural studies is the immediate past and the present, it is only by being able to see the culture that it studies as porous, ambivalent, and incompletely "colonized" by capitalist rationality that cultural studies can undertake its imagined political function, locating multiple spaces of resistance within a hegemony that is much less stable and threatening than the gloom-and-doom rhetoric of the Frankfurt School might suggest.

It is important to emphasize that this is not an idiosyncratic rendering of the relationship between cultural studies and the Frankfurt School. The same contrast between the Frankfurt School and cultural studies, a contrast that makes them out to be nothing less than polar opposites, is made in numerous other places. For example, in his summation of the work of critical theory in comparison to other modes of cultural analysis, Larry Grossberg reduces the work of the Frankfurt School to the following formula: "For critical theory, the cultural object is pure exchange value, with no use value whatsoever, except perhaps as an ideological mystification in the service of the already existing structures of power" (109). In a related fashion, in *An Introduction to Theories of Popular Culture*, Dominic Strinati points out that in contrast to the Frankfurt School, cultural studies "stresses the democratic and participatory rather than the authoritarian and repressive potential of contemporary popular culture" (1995, 85). Finally, in *Doing Cultural Studies*, the "production as consumption" view of the Frankfurt School is dismissed out of hand because it doesn't allow for "agency"—a concept that is presumed to be a precondition for social analysis instead of one that requires careful theoretical articulation (87–88). It seems then that cultural studies and the Frankfurt School can only live each other's death. One affirms what the other denies, and if a choice must be made between the two, it is the relentless contemporaneity of cultural studies that stands a better chance of making sense of the contemporary politics of culture—even if present conditions of popular cultural production have once again begun to resemble the conditions of monopoly and vertical integration encountered by Horkheimer and Adorno in the 1940s.[14] If this is indeed the nature of the relationship between the Frankfurt School and cultural studies, the question of how cultural studies might rethink the Frankfurt School—rethink it, that is, while retaining its own theoretical and critical imperatives—requires careful elaboration before it can be even tentatively answered.

Bad Connections

It is perhaps evident that what I have just identified as two essential elements of cultural studies—elements, furthermore, that are produced through a contrast with the work of the Frankfurt School—are also what I take to mark the very real limitations of this approach to culture. If there is anything that the work of the

Frankfurt School could "add" to cultural studies, it would therefore first have to
destabilize the latter's fundamental logic as a practice. The surprising ahistorical
character of cultural studies—a practice that often treats culture as something spon-
taneously generated after the invention of television, or that views contemporary
culture as having somehow obliterated previous forms of culture in the nuclear blast
of its contemporary reinvention in the era of technological transmission—has been a
source of a great deal of the criticism that has been directed toward cultural studies
from within the left. For instance, Michael Sprinker has pointed out that cultural
studies' "preoccupation with the products of late capitalist culture . . . effectively
blocks a more comprehensive, historically differentiated theorization of culture"
(1997, 390). What the emphasis on the present means is that within cultural studies,
"the possibility that culture might occupy different positions in the hierarchy of social
practices in distinct social formations tends to be lost in the irreducible presentism of
these discourses. The 'popularity' of, say, Elizabethan historical drama cannot be
directly equated with the 'popularity' of Dickens's novels or Chaplin's films; the
appeal of each was to a fundamentally different social group with distinctive tastes
and for whom the products of art performed a historically specific social function"
(390).[15] And while cultural studies might (as During himself does) pay lip service to
the idea that contemporary culture is commodity culture, Sprinker also rightly makes
the claim that "cultural studies for the most part has lost sight of the fact that mass
culture is a historical phenomenon of comparatively recent origin, that it is a distinctive feature only in late capitalist society, and that this fact entails serious consequences for the analysis of its possible ideological effects" (391).[16] Yet having said
this, it seems to me, finally, unhelpful to simply propose (as Sprinker more or less
does) to do away with cultural studies, or to abandon it in favor of the work of the
Frankfurt School and Marxism—that is, to simply choose the approach of the
Frankfurt School over that of cultural studies. It is unhelpful both because such
wholesale criticisms are possible only by reducing everything called "cultural studies"
to its most stereotypical characteristics, negating the very sophisticated work carried
out by (for example) Stuart Hall, Meaghan Morris, Larry Grossberg, and others, and
also because it is equally reductive not to pay attention to the historical and social
circumstances that have produced what Fredric Jameson has described as "the desire
called Cultural Studies" (Jameson 1993, 17). In other words, in order to rethink the
Frankfurt School for cultural studies (and thus for contemporary cultural analysis
as well), one has to take the imperatives of cultural studies seriously, rather than
dismissing them as premised from the outset on a set of enormous theoretical
miscalculations.

　　Just as it will not help to understand contemporary culture or the practice of
cultural studies by drawing attention to the massive theoretical errors that (supposedly) provide the very foundations of cultural studies, it seems to me that arguing
for some kind of rapprochement between the Frankfurt School and cultural studies is
not without its own problems. While Michael Sprinker might argue that the missed
articulation between these two traditions is an outcome of the theoretical limits of
cultural studies, Douglas Kellner has taken roughly the opposite approach. For
Kellner, the production of a discourse of cultural theory that is a hybrid of cultural

studies and the Frankfurt School is eminently desirable, since "both traditions overcome the weaknesses and limitations of the other" (Kellner 1997, 12).[17] Kellner frames the opposition between these two traditions in the usual stereotypical terms: cultural studies needs the Frankfurt School's emphasis on political economy and on its analysis of the political possibilities inherent in modernist and avant-garde aesthetic movements, while the Frankfurt School could benefit from the more empirical approach that cultural studies takes toward contemporary culture, its critique of the distinctions between high and low culture, and its insistence that mass culture can be seen to provide moments of resistance to the dominant ideology that produces it. The problems with this approach are similar to the ones that I identified above: the merger of the Frankfurt School and cultural studies can take place only through a significant reduction of each practice's history and theoretical operations. In order to produce what amounts to a superdiscourse of cultural theory, Kellner places the work of the Frankfurt School and cultural studies on the same level, characterizing each as working on essentially the same problems with the same set of concepts; the differences between them thus occur only because they pay attention to different aspects of culture. It is for this reason that Kellner believes that a "total" theory of culture can be produced by the addition of these two different practices—even if this means that one has to suppress (for instance) Adorno's repeated jeremiads against positivism and empiricism of any kind. If Sprinker's criticisms represent an argument against cultural studies from the side of the Frankfurt School, Kellner's argument produces an engagement of the two discourses, but only by transforming the Frankfurt School into something akin to cultural studies. For while Kellner would want to identify himself with the critical theory of the Frankfurt School (he has self-consciously described his work as a continuation of the legacy of critical theory), it is striking that the almost infinitely flexible hybrid theoretical practice that Kellner characterizes as a "multiperspectival cultural studies" (Kellner 1994, 34–36) sounds almost exactly like the way in which Grossberg has repeatedly characterized cultural studies. The cultural studies that Grossberg describes in "The Circulation of Cultural Studies," for example, hardly needs to be supplemented by the specific emphases of the Frankfurt School on mass culture. Like the hybrid Frankfurt School–cultural studies approach that Kellner describes, which is "multiperspectival, getting at culture from the perspectives of political economy and production, text analysis and audience reception" (Kellner 1997, 34), Grossberg's cultural studies encompasses "multiple positions" in order to examine "how specific practices are placed—and their productivity determined—between the social structures of power and the lived realities of everyday life" (Grossberg 1997, 238).

Instead of imagining the possible points of connection between the Frankfurt School and cultural studies as a choice between these practices, or in terms of the ideal supplementary that Kellner suggests, I want to propose a different way of thinking about the connections between Frankfurt School and cultural studies. For cultural studies to rethink the work of the Frankfurt School, the first thing that it needs to do is to take it up in the same spirit as it has investigated popular culture: to see the work of the Frankfurt School on culture as containing both productive *and* problematic insights into contemporary cultural production. In other words, it needs to take up the Frankfurt School *dialectically*, an approach that has the advantage of also affirming the Frankfurt School's own critical process. For cultural studies to rethink the Frankfurt School by simply embracing the latter's pessimism about popular culture signals nothing more than a failure to really consider what the Frankfurt School might be able to contribute to cultural studies; adopting an antipopulist pose only reinforces the absolute difference through which cultural studies has defined itself in relation to the Frankfurt School. To rethink dialectically the potential contribution of the work of the Frankfurt School to cultural studies is a far more dangerous process, since it cannot help but initiate the end of what is now known as cultural studies. And yet it seems to be the only way to shake cultural studies out of its present critical lethargy, the only way to get it beyond seeing contemporary culture through the reductive either/or of pessimism/optimism that has prevented cultural studies from fully mapping out the space of contemporary culture.

Given what I have identified as both the defining logic of cultural studies *and* the site of its theoretical limitations, the most productive place for such a dialectical engagement between the Frankfurt School and cultural studies concerns the question of "culture" itself. To understand what I take this site of engagement to be, let me return once again to the conclusion that During makes in his introductory comments to "The Culture Industry." During writes that what Horkheimer and Adorno fail to grasp is "the ways in which the cultural industry, while in the service of organized capital, also provides the opportunities for all kinds of individual and collective creativity and decoding." If there is one element here that seems to be undertheorized in the practice of cultural studies as a whole it is this: that the culture industry *is* inescapably in the service of capital. As Fredric Jameson reminds us, " 'the 'Culture Industry' is not a theory of culture but the theory of an *industry*" (*Late* 1993, 144). The field of cultural studies—the study of contemporary popular culture, from television to film to pop music, as well as all of the iconic and symbolic apparati that go along with it—is the field of the production of culture in the framework of capitalism. Our sense of what constitutes culture has in fact become so restricted by this framework that it has become difficult to imagine "culture" (except in the terms of some anthropological fantasy or bad faith gesture to a more authentic past) as anything other than the consumption of the cultural objects produced in and by capitalism: watching films, listening to CDs, shopping for clothing, adopting styles, and so on. Even the distinctions made by Raymond Williams between culture as "whole ways of life" and culture as that which is embodied in various cultural forms, has collapsed in many contemporary accounts of culture: our "ways of life" have been reduced to the ways that we live in/with/through cultural commodities. As has so often been pointed out, the production of culture is no longer some kind of epiphenomenal aspect of capitalist production, but has long since become its main motive force. That we can deal creatively with the cultural products churned out by the culture industry (to whatever degree we can) is therefore not a politically insignificant fact. But the significance of this creative decoding has to be considered against the larger background of a consumer capitalism in which culture has been reduced to the status of something that is consumed. Not reduced without remainder, purely to exchange value, of course; but then it must be remembered that this remainder, too, lives out a life in a social setting heavily overdetermined by consumer capitalism, and that simply by being "more than" exchange value it does not thereby automatically congregate with concepts that are all too easy to abstract from the sites at which they are socially produced, i.e., pleasure, identity, imagination, and even "decoding" and "creativity" as well.

Affirming Culture

It is by reestablishing this larger framework within which the contemporary limits of "culture" can be actively considered that an encounter with the Frankfurt School is most productive for cultural studies. In one of his many formulations, Grossberg describes cultural studies as "concerned with describing and intervening in the ways in 'texts' and 'discourses' (i.e., cultural practices) are produced within, inserted into, and operate in the everyday life of human beings and social formations, so as to reproduce, struggle against, and perhaps transform the existing structures of power" (*Bringing* 1997, 237). It is this sense of "culture" as the primary site of mediation between subjects and historical and social formations that needs to be more carefully considered. What the Frankfurt School can contribute to the project of cultural studies is a permanent suspicion about dealing with contemporary culture only as a reified set of objects—from popular to high cultural objects, forms, and genres— rather than as a set of processes on which the particular forms of "culture" that we identify *as* culture are dependent. Furthermore, it can help to break through the sacred character that cultural studies lends to this reified culture, revealing the ideo- logical function of what is one of the most insidious elements of cultural studies. For while proclaiming to study the "everyday," the life of the popular, and the mass, cultural studies nevertheless imbues the cultural commodities that it studies with a more traditional "cultural" character. By this I mean the sense of "culture" that Herbert Marcuse characterized as "affirmative,"

> in which the spiritual world is lifted out of its social context, making culture a (false) collective noun and attributing (false) universality to it. This . . . con- cept of culture, clearly seen in expressions such as "national culture," "Ger- manic culture" or "Roman culture," plays off the spiritual world against the material world by holding up culture as the realm of authentic values and self- contained ends in opposition to the world of social utility and means. Through the use of this concept, culture is distinguished from civilization and so- ciologically and valuationally removed from the social process. (Marcuse 1988, 94–95)

Though Marcuse seems to refer almost exclusively to bourgeois culture in his elaboration of the freedom and unfreedom that affirmative culture simultaneously embodies, his formulation of the function of culture under capitalism seems equally applicable to mass culture. At the very least, the way in which cultural studies has imbued mass culture with social significance and meaning has had the effect of affirming culture—of rendering it spiritual—however much it might imagine that it is doing just the opposite: reconnecting the "torn halves of an integral freedom" (Adorno in Bloch et al. 1994, 123) in a manner that gets one beyond the arrested dialectic within which Marcuse circles endlessly. What animates this belief, of course, is cultural studies' emphasis on popular/mass culture rather than bourgeois culture, an emphasis that is taken in and of itself as a negation of Marcuse's problematic. Every time, however, individual cultural commodities are probed like works of art for their cultural resonance and social significance, they are (unintentionally, unavoidably) endowed with the false spiritually of affirmative culture in a way that simultaneously connects the present of culture to the cultural forms of the past. Far from sidestepping affirmative culture, cultural studies reaffirms it, and does so in a more dangerous way by linking this unacknowledged reaffirmation to the eclipse of the spiritual in culture. The solution to affirmative culture lies elsewhere: remember, for Adorno, "the torn halves of an integral freedom" could never add up to something whole.

It is in fact this suspicion about the affirmative character of contemporary culture—the way it both mirrors bourgeois culture's spirituality and denies this spirituality in the guise of "the popular"—that lends to Horkheimer and Adorno's "The Culture Industry" its infamous antipopulist tone. It is sometimes difficult to read "The Culture Industry" as anything but one long rant against the horrors of the mass cultural environment that Horkheimer and Adorno encountered during their period of exile in America. Nevertheless, if we understand the essay as participating in a dialogue with Marcuse's characterization of affirmative culture, the approach that Horkheimer and Adorno take in their examination of contemporary culture can prove to be an instructive one for cultural studies. First of all, the essay on the culture industry is far more heterogeneous and complex than its reputation suggests; indeed, even though it might be one of the poorest examples of the real subtlety with which members of the Frankfurt School dealt with mass and popular culture,[18] there is nevertheless more going on here than most critics have suggested. Although the numerous theoretical positions, gestures, and statements that Horkheimer and Adorno make in the essay originate from a core philosophical position that extends throughout *Dialectic of Enlightenment,* it is nevertheless difficult to link these rapid-fire statements of discontent into anything approaching a rigid theoretical position. Among the many things that Horkheimer and Adorno address in the essay are the control of the individual consciousness by the culture industry, the use of distinction to mask the essential sameness of contemporary life, the degradation of art, the obliteration of form and detail, the cultural modes of social reproduction, the appropriation and manufacture of newness and the corresponding generation of permissible deviance from the system, the significance of style, the reality of individual conformity under the sign of the unique qualities of the bourgeois individual, the myth of success and the ideology of chance, sublimation in art versus repression in popular culture, and the culturally induced modes of pleasure and helplessness. These represent an enormously varied set of themes, each of which contributes to an understanding of the culture industry, but that are irreducible to a simple, general position. And yet a consideration of the detailed way in which Horkheimer and Adorno consider twentieth-century culture has been consistently sacrificed in favor of the dominant impression that the essay leaves behind as all of these themes are rushed together, heaped on top of one another and interjected in a scattershot way throughout the text: the culture industry has rendered all resistance futile; "fun is a medicinal bath. The pleasure industry never fails to prescribe it" (Horkheimer and Adorno 1988, 140).

It is by failing to consider the "minianalyses" that together produced this dominant pessimistic impression that the larger horizon against which these details are positioned becomes lost. For far less important than the "conclusions" that Horkheimer and Adorno offer about the culture industry is the mode of analysis that is exemplified in both the form and content of the essay. "The Culture Industry" is a critique of the present that is firmly rooted in a *historical* consideration of the changing significance of culture for the subject and for society. What is ultimately for Horkheimer and Adorno the most troubling aspect of contemporary culture is not its lack of depth, or the degree to which culture has approached becoming purely exchange value, but that it closes off any consideration of its own history and thus of the logic of its conditions of possibility. "The Culture Industry" shows that the problem of cultural studies with respect to history is not that it begins only at the historical point where the Frankfurt School leaves off, which confines it to examining a relatively small sliver of time. The problem is, rather, that by accepting commodity culture *as* culture, and by consequently affirming the spiritual dimension of this culture, cultural studies circulates in a perpetual present in which the reality of present-day culture amounts to no more and no less than *all* that culture is and can be. The cultural past, dominated by what cultural studies considers to be the lumbering dinosaurs of bourgeois high culture, is closed off from it—but so is the future, since the present of culture is taken as fate. For Horkheimer and Adorno, it is precisely this that they wish to attack: the present of the culture industry is *not* to accepted as is, nor is it to be taken as the limits within which various forms of cultural resistance must necessarily work. "The Culture Industry" *is* a lament about the impoverished actualization of potentialities that existed beforehand. But it is important to emphasize that the easy charge that has been made about the politics of culture in "The Culture Industry," that of an elitist commitment to the supposed authenticity of high, bourgeois art and culture, is a false one. Even as they suggest the possibilities inherent in bourgeois art, they clearly point to its limits. "The promise held out by the work of art that it will create truth by lending new shape to the conventional social forms is as necessary as it is hypocritical. It unconditionally posits the real forms of life as it is by suggesting that fulfillment lies in their aesthetic derivatives. To this extent the claim of art is always ideology too" (130). The longstanding interest of various members of the Frankfurt School in political and avantgarde artistic practices does not simply reflect their unquestioned bourgeois acceptance of certain cultural forms and derision of others. It is just that such practices might be able to do what no Disney film can: attempt to broach the limits of the culture that has been produced by commodity culture in order to generate a historical response to the dead objects of contemporary cultural experience.[19] At one point in "The Culture Industry," Horkheimer and Adorno ask what would happen "if most of the radio stations and movie theaters were closed down?" (Horkheimer and Adorno

1988, 139). We may not agree with his answer: "consumers would probably not lose so very much . . . as soon as the very existence of these institutions no longer made it obligatory to use them there would be no great urge to do so" (Horkheimer and Adorno 1988, 139). But it is the structural ability to pose the question that is important, an ability that exists (perhaps paradoxically) more within the supposedly closed system of Horkheimer and Adorno's reflections on the culture industry, than in the *amor fati* of contemporary cultural studies, which has learned to love the fate the culture industry has made for it.

The Limits of Culture

What I am then suggesting is that if read in the right way, it is in the very object of its derision—the pessimistic analysis of mass culture in "The Culture Industry"—that cultural studies can find a model for a renewed cultural studies that is invigorated by a historical dimension that it all too frequently lacks. I want to end by pointing out how a recognition of the limits of culture in cultural studies, limits that an engagement with the work of the Frankfurt School would help to define *as* limits, has practical as well as theoretical implications. One area of growing interest in cultural studies over the past several years has been to consider the utility of cultural studies in examinations of cultural policy.[20] In a chapter in which he also examines Horkheimer and Adorno's essay on the culture industry, Jim McGuigan describes a situation in which the insights of cultural studies were in effect "put into action" in the realm of policy making. In an attempt to radically democratize its funding of arts and culture, the Labor Party–controlled Greater London Council (GLC) of 1981–1986 initiated a "cultural industries strategy," as outlined in position papers developed in 1983 by the cultural and media theorist, Nicholas Garnham. The initial attempt by the GLC to move beyond funding mainly elite institutions with relatively small, privileged audiences, such as the National Theatre and the English National Opera, was to make funds available to various grass-roots and community-based arts projects. However, a report on these activities found that "community arts facilities were used very largely by highly educated middle-class people who were not wholly dissimilar in social origin from the core audiences for the 'traditional arts' " (McGuigan 1996, 82). In an effort to expand the reach of government funding of culture, Garnham proposed a much more substantial reorientation of arts funding, one that embraced the market rather than rejecting it. As McGuigan writes, "Garnham argued that the community arts critique of 'elitism' in public arts patronage was inadequate because it remained within the dominant cultural policy paradigm, in effect acquiescing with the marginal role ascribed to public agencies in the cultural field. It failed to address the real power structures of culture, which are 'private' rather than 'public', capitalist controlled and not dependent on the interventionist policies of the national and local states" (McGuigan 1996, 83).

In order to shatter "the idealist tradition of arts patronage" (83) on which government cultural funding was based, the decision was made by the GLC on the basis of Garnham's proposals to intervene in the production and distribution of cultural goods in the private sector, a policy that represented a decided shift away from support for the production of nonmarket art and culture. In a context in which, in Garnham's words, "most people's cultural needs and aspirations are being, for better or worse, supplied by the market as goods and services" (Garnham in McGuigan 1996, 83–84), it was decided that monies would be best directed toward the establishment (through investment and loan programs) of small and medium-sized cultural industries that would emphasize the *distribution* of those cultural forms that had a limited market. Under the terms of the "culture industries strategy," the GLC helped to create community recording studies, a Black publishing house, and a radical book distribution network. Though this strategy represents a wholesale shift in the funding of arts and culture, it is clear that the initial aims, at least, were not all that dissimilar from the grassroots or community-based model. The emphasis was still placed on the support of marginal cultural forms, with the ultimate goal being, perhaps, to make these marginal forms "popular" through their enhanced distribution.

While this might seem to be an innovative way for governments to democratize their funding of arts and culture, the final outcome of this project shows the limits of the "culture" of cultural studies that is at work here. Garnham's acceptance of the "dominant cultural process," (McGuigan 1998, 84) in which markets make the culture that defines the entire space of culture, led to his proposal that governments wishing to support cultural production should do so with the model of market in mind. Yet, as McGuigan points out, "while the initial aims [of such projects] tend to emphasize representation . . . (a)s time passes, however, economic goals and job training are increasingly stressed. The logic of a cultural industries strategy, then, becomes rather more industrial than culture, often unrealistically so" (McGuigan 1998, 87). Once governments establish these cultural industries as a way of supporting the production of marginal cultural forms, the need for them to succeed *as* industries quickly displaces their cultural (and critical) function. In other words, as soon as the calculus of the market enters the equation, these government-sponsored culture industries begin to function like all other culture industries, producing culture in order to produce profit. After a few years, industries developed to publish radical books and record controversial Black British hip-hop acts were transformed into producers of mass-market (if still "alternative") best sellers and top-twenty recording artists.

In the overview of the "culture industry" argument that he provides as a prelude to his discussion of the policies of the GLC, McGuigan is highly critical of Horkheimer and Adorno's view of the culture industry. While he describes the work of Benjamin and Horkheimer and Adorno as equally "romantic," he takes Benjamin's hopeful depiction of democratizing potential of mass culture as "closer to cultural actualities . . . (t)he unqualified pessimism of Horkheimer and Adorno has little resonance now outside the shrinking coteries of artistic refusal of mass-popular culture" (McGuigan 1998, 80). What I want to draw attention to in looking at the policy implications of cultural studies is how the understanding of culture that it operates with gives it very little room for maneuver, even, or perhaps especially, as it imagines itself to be changing the overall orientation of cultural policy. As arts funding shifts from support for the production of marginal cultural forms to their distribution, there is a corresponding ideological shift from left to right insofar as this policy unapologetically and unproblematically embraces the capitalist system of cultural production. And as it does so, it does so disingenuously. For even as critics of Horkheimer and Adorno speak of limits of the "artistic refusal of mass-popular culture," in terms of the culture industries strategy this ideological shift is disguised in part by the support of cultural producers that exist outside of the mainstream, very often *because* of their refusal to accommodate the logic of the commodity culture. In its acceptance of the present-day space of culture *as* culture, the impact of cultural studies on cultural policy seems to be (perhaps unintentionally) the elimination of every space outside of the market in the name of democratizing the way in which governments spend their monies; a cultural studies that had engaged with the work of the Frankfurt School would be less inclined to make this error—not simply because of its pessimism toward the culture industry, but because of the critical horizon that it would perpetually hold open concerning the struggle that is being constantly waged over the definition of what constitutes "culture."

Coda: The End of Mass Culture, 2002

Though I came upon it belatedly, much of what I have been trying to say here is articulated in a different form in Michael Denning's exceptional essay "The End of Mass Culture." Written in 1989, Denning's essay reflects on two attempts a decade earlier to overcome the opposition between Frankfurt School critiques of culture and a populism associated with cultural studies: Fredric Jameson's "Reification and Utopia in Mass Culture" and Stuart Hall's "Notes on Deconstructing 'the Popular'." In these formative essays for contemporary cultural critique, Jameson and Hall express in slightly different ways a view that has now become a critical commonplace: mass culture is ideological and utopian at the same time. What Denning tries to understand is just what it means for this view of mass culture to have become dominant, and especially, what kind of questions this view of mass culture tends to rule out.

Denning's conclusions in "The End of Mass Culture" seem to me to be simultaneously appealing and problematic. On the one hand, he makes an absolutely essential claim that should constitute the ground zero of all work on contemporary culture: "All culture is mass culture under capitalism. There is no working-class culture that is not saturated with mass culture" (Denning 1991, 258). On the other, he offers ways of conceptualizing and mobilizing a distinctive working-class culture that he has, in a sense, just ruled out. He argues, for instance, for a way (the correct way) of thinking about Gramsci's notion of hegemony that doesn't reduce it to "domination through managed consumption and manipulated desire" (262), and that in turn refocuses attention on the long-term struggle to build, tear down, and rebuild hegemonic formations through institutions and "long-term historic projects" (264). It is probably unhelpful to see these as contradictory; rather, together they lay out the framework that cultural studies should work within but doesn't. Denning distinguishes contemporary investigations of mass culture—which are underwritten in general by an ethos derived from Jameson and Hall—from at least three previous "waves" of cultural criticism: worries about the new, powerful, and potentially manipulative powers of broadcast media; postwar critiques of Popular Front culture; and hostility to the counterculture and the New Left (257–58). He argues that "the work of these intellectual tendencies was not a clever game of finding subversive moments in each piece of pop culture, not a ritual invocation of a dialectic between the ideological and the utopian . . . Rather [they] attempted to change the way we thought about culture generally" (258). This is just what is lacking in contemporary cultural studies—a way of thinking culture *differently*. Denning's argument—which has been mine as well—is in this respect of a piece with Raymond Williams' distinction between mass culture and working-class culture in *Culture and Society*. For Williams (and for Denning), it was important not to reduce working-class culture to mass culture, in part because working-class culture offered a different vision of culture than bourgeois culture—a way of life centered on the community rather than the individual. Whatever qualms one might have about asserting too easily the necessity of a renewed focus on working-class culture—as if it was just out there waiting to be discovered, separate or at least separable from mass culture—one can at least take it as the name for what I have here called history. Without such a concept or structure, cultural studies is unable to resolve the dialectic between ideology and utopia in a satisfactory way, or even to see the need for such a resolution.

What interests me here is not just the content of Denning's analysis, but that so little has changed in the decade between the writing of his essay and the composition of my own. Denning concludes his essay by claiming that "We have come to the end of 'mass culture'; the debates and positions which named 'mass culture' as an other have been superseded" (267). This seems right to me—and yet my own argument about the absence of the Frankfurt School from cultural studies retraces not only Denning's own, but also in part those of Jameson and Hall. It is as if there has been no movement forward over more than twenty years of sustained critical reflection and argumentation. This suggests to me that there is something fundamentally lacking in our conceptualization of the present and of the role of mass culture within it, something that should push us to think the present differently. The desire for working-class culture present in Denning still seems to represent a desire for an outside (like the Third World in some of Jameson's writings) that seems to me to no longer exists in any way—a claim that should not be taken as an assertion of the bad idea of hegemony that Denning warns us against.

I was tempted to end by pointing to more concrete sites from which one could develop a Frankfurt School cultural studies. The recent English translations of Adorno's *The Stars Come Down to Earth and Other Essays on the Irrational in Culture*, *The Psychological Technique of Martin Luther Thomas' Radio Addresses*, and *Introduction to Sociology*, seems to offer such a site or sites. But while Routledge might hope to generate sales by categorizing Adorno's work on the *Los Angeles Times* astrology column as "cultural studies," this label is appropriate only because Adorno's object of analysis mirrors the kind of objects that might be taken up in cultural studies analyses today. In truth, Adorno had very different ends in mind in his analyses of the irrational in contemporary culture; and as the late lectures collected in *Introduction to*

Sociology make clear, his suspicions about empirical sociology never deviated from the view he expressed toward certain kinds of cultural analysis in "Why Philosophy?":

> Neither is philosophy turning to advantage the approach of that professor who, in the pre-Fascist era, experienced an urge to rectify the ills of the times, and examined Marlene Dietrich's film, *The Blue Angel,* in order to obtain, at first hand, an idea of how bad things really were. Excursions of that kind into tangible realities turn philosophy into the refuse of history, with the subject-matter of which it is confused, in the manner of a fetishistic belief in culture per se." (2000, 53)

Once more, what the Frankfurt School might be able to offer cultural studies can be summarized by a negative maxim: don't fetishize culture.

Ultimately, however, this can't help but seem unsatisfying. Purely pragmatically and somewhat crudely, it certainly doesn't offer much of a hint concerning how one might continue in good faith to produce journal-length essays analyzing specific cultural objects or practices. Tentatively, I'd like to suggest that the real historical originality of contemporary mass culture (and by this I mean mass culture since the mid-1970s) is that it *has* in fact superseded the dialectic of affirmative culture, a dialectic, however, within which cultural criticism continues to belatedly circulate. Cultural criticism seems tied to the concept of *mediation,* a concept which itself implies an understanding of society and politics as organized according to the logic of transcendence. In *Empire,* Michael Hardt and Antonio Negri argue that what is unique about the present moment is that capitalism no longer requires the guise of transcendence: it has become immanent in a way that has created problems for our attempts to explain and theorize the circulation of contemporary power. It would be a difficult task to summarize Hardt and Negri's massive book and its implications for cultural studies in the short space available to me here.[21] What I would like to claim, however, is that it is possible to see cultural studies as symptomatic of this shift of capital (or more properly, a shift of its sovereignty) from transcendence to immanence in the much the same way as Hardt and Negri see postcolonial and postmodern studies as symptoms of the end of modern sovereignty—as kinds of critique that can only emerge once modern sovereignty is no longer the framework for control and domination. If those theorists "who advocate a politics of difference, fluidity, and hybridity in order to challenge the binaries and essentialism of modern sovereignty have been outflanked by strategies of power" (Hardt and Negri 2000, 138), it is because the modern form of sovereignty, which can be encapsulated as a form of binary (or even dialectical) logic that operates on an ultimately unsustainable separation of inside and outside, transcendent and immanent, has been eclipsed in the transformation of imperialist capitalism into Empire. What is needed then is a mode of critique that can directly address the contemporary form of power that now exists. The work of the Frankfurt School might not, on its own, provide us with this form of critique; it does, however, allow us to see how and why we have become stuck and how we might move forward.

Notes

1. The main focus of recent criticisms of cultural studies has been to contrast its exclusively "cultural" politics with the need for the left to renew its attention to matters of "real" politics. Writers representing a broad range of positions have taken cultural studies to task for its claim to articulate a politics at all. See, for example, Thomas Frank, 2000, *One Market Under God: Extreme Capitalism, Market Populism and the End of Economic Democracy* (New York: Doubleday); Todd Gitlin, 1995, *Twilight of Our Common Dreams* (New York: Metropolitan Books) and, 1997, "The Anti-Populism of Cultural Studies" in *Cultural Studies in Question,* ed. Marjorie Ferguson and Peter Golding (London: Sage): 102–20; Richard Rorty, 1999, *Achieving Our Country: Leftist Thought in 20th Century America* (Cambridge, Mass.: Harvard University Press); Michael Tomasky, 1996, *Left for Dead: The Life, Death and Possible Resurrection of Progressive Politics in America* (New York: The Free Press); and even Michael Bérubé's "Cultural Criticism and the Politics of Selling Out" (Available on-line at: http://www.altx.com/ ebr/ebr2/2berube.htm). For a defense of cultural studies against these kind of charges, see Judith Butler, 1998, "Merely Cultural," *New Left Review* 227: 33–44; and recent work by Henry Giroux, 2000, *Stealing Innocence: Youth, Corporate Power and the Politics of Culture* (New York: St. Martin's Press) and, 2000, *Impure Acts: The Practical Politics of Cultural Studies* (New York: Routledge).

2. See Henry Schwarz and Richard Dienst, ed., 1996, *Reading the Shape of the World: Toward an International Cultural Studies* (Boulder, Colo.: Westview Press).

3. See 1996, "The Space of Culture, The Power of Space," in *The Postcolonial Question: Common Skies, Divided Horizons,* ed. Iain Chambers and Lidia Curti (New York: Routledge): 169–88; and 1998, "The Victory of Culture, Part 1 (Against the Logic of Mediation)" *Angelaki* 3.3: 3–29.

4. See Andrew Goodwin and Janet Wolff, 1997, "Conserving Cultural Studies" and Richard Johnson, "Reinventing Cultural Studies: Remembering for the Best Version," both in *From Sociology to Cultural Studies,* ed. Elizabeth Long (Malden, Mass.: Blackwell): 123–49 and 452–88, respectively. The need to "conserve" cultural studies first becomes an issue in the worries expressed by Stuart Hall over the transformation of cultural studies into an academic discipline in the United States. See Hall, 1992, "Cultural Studies and its Theoretical Legacies," in *Cultural Studies,* ed. Cary Nelson, Paula Treichler, and Lawrence Grossberg (New York: Routledge).

5. In one sense, after all, the popular is coincident with market demand, which is itself the subject of a vast *techne* (advertising, demographic research, test marketing, etc.) whose sole intention is to create and generate popularity. The coincidence between the study of "popular" culture and the marketing of commodities in order to generate their popularity leads Michael Sprinker to ask:

    > What, one cannot help asking, do the current doyens of cultural studies envision as the outcome of their work, both in the classroom and in the community of professionals for whom they principally write? Teaching their students to decipher the racial and gender codings in film, television, and popular music? The entertain-

ment industry would like nothing better, since this pedagogy advertises their products—and for free!—and helps them to sustain a taste for their products among the educated who might, other things being equal, just stop consuming them. The one conclusion never reached in cultural studies is that analyzing contemporary mass culture might not be worth the effort expended on it (1997, 392).

While it is important to consider the possible complicity of cultural studies with the culture industry (and there has certainly been extensive hand-wringing over this), Sprinker's statement is not without its own problems. Sprinker makes presumptions about the ways in which ideas are transmitted and tastes formed that are simplistic and unsustainable. (If you analyze Jerry Springer, you can't help but like him!) There is not only a rush to aesthetic judgment about the objects that cultural studies examines, but a grounding of this judgment in barely disguised class terms: after Bourdieu's *Distinction* and the work of Simon Frith (for instance) one might think that it would not be quite so easy to concede legitimate taste to the "educated." And there is also a failure to consider the pedagogic function that popular culture plays in the lives of most students who will take a university course on cultural studies: decoding popular cultural forms is to simultaneously decode the ways in which one's subjectivity has been formed. The infinity of traces that any future Gramsci might want to explore will of necessity have to pass through the televisual screen and the earphones of the Sony Walkman, as much as through the logics of class and capital.

6.   There are numerous other essays that critically explore the position of the popular in cultural studies. A representative selection of these are collected in John Storey, ed., *Cultural Theory and Popular Culture: A Reader*. Second Edition. (Athens: University of Georgia Press, 1998). See also Scott Cutler Shershow's "New Life: Cultural Studies and the Problem of the 'Popular'." *Textual Practice* 12.1 (1998): 23–47.

7.   Stuart Hall famously declared that popular culture "matters" because "it is one of the sites where [the] struggle for and against a culture of the powerful is engaged . . . it is one of the places where socialism might be constituted . . . Otherwise, to tell you the truth, I don't give a damn about it." Hall, 1981, "Notes on Deconstructing 'the Popular'," in *People's History and Socialist Theory*, ed. Raphael Samuel (London: Routledge & Kegan Paul), 239. Nevertheless, I think that it is fair to suggest that a study of popular culture remains constituitive of cultural studies as a practice, though it may well be the case that the politics it names doesn't necessitate a focus on mass/popular culture.

8.   In "The Victory of Culture," Grossberg outlines a set of contemporary conditions that "makes the available formations of cultural studies relatively ineffective" (1997, 5). These include: "the growing power of and investment in a politics organized around modern (cultural) difference" (3); a lack of attention to the body and affect; the contemporary displacement of economics and politics by culture; and an increasingly cynical inflection to ideology (in Zizek's formulation: "they know what they are doing but they are doing it anyway").

9.   For example, in what many still consider to be the central document of cultural studies—the collection entitled *Cultural Studies*—there is one lone reference to Horkheimer and Adorno in over seven hundred pages of text. See Cary Nelson, Paula Treichler, and Lawrence Grossberg, eds., 1992, *Cultural Studies* (New York: Routledge).

10. The exception to the rule has been the generally positive reception of Walter Benjamin's "The Work of Art in the Age of Mechanical Reproduction." But then this is perhaps the one essay related to the Frankfurt School that can be seen to confirm the more positive view that cultural studies takes toward the democratizing potential of the mechanical reproduction of art.

11. With the invention of the term "alternative," which continually oscillates between being an adjective and a noun, the record industry has managed to effectively deal with one of central contradictions of cultural commodity production—the need to continually produce new products to replace other cultural commodities that are never entirely used up in the process of being consumed. "Alternative" names both a body of work with its own historical antecedents (Hüsker Dü, the Replacements, the Ramones, etc.) *and* designates a category of infinite flexibility that captures the latest styles and trends in music geared toward white youth. The current generation of neo-Swing bands are most commonly categorized as alternative rather than jazz.

12. Though see Franco Moretti's discussion of video stores in New York City. Moretti and his students found an enormous difference in the kinds of videos available in different parts of the city. "It may be summarized thus: in the Bronx and in Harlem, the presence of the genres 'Action/Adventure' and (to a lesser extent) 'Horror/Sci-Fi' is roughly three times higher than elsewhere, and adds up to 50 percent of the total". 2000, *New Left Review* 5: 111–15.

13. In order to capitalize on the imagined saleability of cultural studies to undergraduate students, there *have* been attempts to generalize the practice of cultural studies. Members of my own department have argued about the need to include medieval or Renaissance cultural studies in the cultural studies program that we have been (belatedly) developing.

14. To cite just one well-known example, the Disney Corporation now owns theme parks, motion picture studios (Touchstone, Hollywood, Buena Vista, and the "indie" distributor Miramax), record companies (including the "indie" label Mammoth), radio and television stations that each reach 25 percent of the U.S. population, sport teams, broadcast and cable channels (including ABC, ESPN, Lifetime, A&E, the History Channel), over 600 Disney stores, a planned community (Celebration), and an island in the Bahamas. Indeed, in the wake of recent consolidations in the cultural field, it is hard to envision how much more vertically integrated contemporary capitalist enterprises can become. For a discussion of these issues, see Janine Jaquet, 8 June 1998, "The Media Nation: TV: Who Controls Television?" *The Nation* 266, 21: 23–24; and the "Special Hollywood Issue" 5/12 April 1999, of *The Nation* 268, 13.

15. For a related critique, see Donald K. Hendrick, 1997, "Dumb and Dumber History: The Transhistorical Popular," in *Class Issues: Pedagogy, Cultural Studies, and the Public Sphere,* ed. Amitava Kumar (New York: New York University Press): 65–75.

16. I remain partial to Richard Ohmann's claim that mass culture originates in the United States with the birth of the mass circulation magazines of the late nineteenth century. See Ohmann, 1996, *Selling Culture: Magazines, Markets, and Class at the Turn of the Century* (New York: Verso.). Even so, the characteristics and social effectivity of mass culture have to be seen as changing significantly over the course of the twentieth century: its identity isn't fixed at birth.

17. Kellner has tried to effect similar rapproachments between cultural studies and other practices. See 1995, "Media Communications vs. Cultural Studies: Overcoming the Divide," *Communication Studies* 5.2: 162–77; and "Overcoming the Divide: Cultural Studies and Political Economy," in 1997, *Cultural Studies in Question,* ed. Marjorie Ferguson and Peter Golding (London: Sage): 102–20.

18. Adorno's "empirical" work beginning with Paul Lazarfeld's Princeton Radio Project is one example, but I am also thinking here of the underestimated work of Leo Lowenthal.

19. In "The Culture Industry Reconsidered," Adorno makes a case for the "seriousness" of *both* high and low art. The problem with the culture industry is that it attacks high *and* low, forcing them together in a way that strips both of their potential to resist total social control. What Adorno identifies as an element of certain forms of avant-garde literature and art he thus sees as residing in the "rebellious resistance" of the low as well. In other words, it is simply *not* the case that Adorno sees only "high" art as having a political potentialities. The problem with contemporary culture is not that it is "low," but that its political and social effectivity has declined. See "The Culture Industry Reconsidered," in *The Adorno Reader,* ed. 2000, Brian O'Connor (Oxford: Blackwell): 230–38 and "Why Philosophy?" 40–53.

20. I am thinking here not only of work that directly addresses cultural policy, but also studies of tourism, the "heritage" industry, and examinations of various forms of cultural imperialism from a cultural studies perspective. See, for example, G. J. Ashworth and D. J. Larkham, eds., 1994, *Building a New Heritage: Tourism, Culture and Identity in the New Europe* (New York: Routledge); Eric Michaels, 1994, *Bad Aboriginal Art* (Minneapolis: University of Minnesota Press, 1994); and Barbara Kirshenblatt-Gimblett, 1998, *Destination Culture* (Berkeley: University of California Press). On the implications of cultural studies for cultural policy, see Tony Bennett, 1992, "Putting Policy into Cultural Studies," in *Cultural Studies,* ed. Cary Nelson, Paula Treichler, and Lawrence Grossberg (New York: Routledge): 23–33; and Ellen Messer-Davidow, 1997, "Whither Cultural Studies?" in *From Sociology to Cultural Studies,* ed. Elizabeth Long (Malden, Mass.: Blackwell): 489–522.

21. I take this issue up explicitly in 2001, "Plundering the Empire: Globalization, Cultural Studies and Utopia," *Rethinking Marxism* 13.3, 13.3/4: 173–189.

Works Cited

Adorno, Theodor. 1994. *The Stars Come Down to Earth and Other Essays on the Irrational in Culture.* Stanford, Calif.: Stanford University Press.

———. "Letter to Walter Benjamin, 18 March 1936." In Ernst Bloch, et al. *Aesthetics and Politics.* New York: Verso, 1994: 123.

———. 2000. *Introduction to Sociology.* Ed. Christoph Godde. Trans. Edmund Jephcott. Stanford, Calif.: Stanford University Press, 2000.

———. 2000. *The Psychological Technique of Martin Luther Thomas' Radio Addresses.* Stanford, Calif.: Stanford University Press, 2000.

———. 2000. "Why Philosophy?" In *The Adorno Reader.* Ed. Brian O'Connor. Oxford, Eng.: Blackwell: 40–53.

Bourdieu, Pierre. 1998. *On Television.* Trans. Priscilla Parkhurst Ferguson. New York: New Press.

Coupland, Douglas. 1991. *Generation X.* New York: St. Martin's Press.

Denning, Michael. 1991. "The End of Mass Culture." In *Modernity and Mass Culture.* Ed. James Naremore and Patrick Bratlinger. Bloomington: Indiana University Press, 1991: 253–68.

Du Gay, Paul, et al., 1996. *Doing Cultural Studies: The Story of the Sony Walkman.* London: Sage.

During, Simon, ed. 1993. *The Cultural Studies Reader.* New York: Routledge.

Grossberg, Larry. 1997. *Bringing It All Back Home: Essays on Cultural Studies.* Durham, N.C.: Duke University Press.

Hardt, Michael, and Antonio Negri. 2000. *Empire.* Cambridge, Mass.: Harvard University Press.

Horkheimer, Max, and Theodor Adorno. 1988. *Dialectic of the Enlightenment.* Trans. John Cumming. New York: Continuum.

Jameson, Fredric. 1990. *Late Marxism—Adorno, or, The Persistence of the Dialectic.* New York: Verso.

———. 1993. "On 'Cultural Studies'." *Social Text* 34: 17–52.

Kellner, Douglas. 1997. "Critical Theory and Cultural Studies: The Missed Articulation." *Cultural Methodologies.* Ed. Jim McGuigan. Thousand Oaks, Calif.: Sage: 12–41.

Marcuse, Herbert. 1988. *Negations: Essays in Critical Theory.* Trans. Jeremy J. Shapiro. London: Free Association Books.

McGuigan, Jim. 1996. *Culture and the Public Sphere.* New York: Routledge.

Morris, Meaghan. "Banality in Cultural Studies." *Discourse* 10, 2: 3–29.

Sprinker, Michael. 1997. "We Lost It at the Movies." *MLN* 112, 3: 385–99.

Strinati, Dominic. 1995. *An Introduction to Theories of Popular Culture.* New York: Routledge.

Williams, Raymond. 1983. *Culture and Society 1780–1950.* New York: Columbia University Press.

4

The Frankfurt School and the Political Economy of Communications

Ronald V. Bettig

The purpose of this chapter is threefold. First, I will review the Frankfurt School's historical influence on the field of mass communications theory and research.[1] From roughly the late 1930s up through the 1970s, the Frankfurt School provided a critical alternative to the empirically oriented, administrative research produced within the dominant paradigm. Second, I will explore the links between the work of the Frankfurt School and the contemporary study of the political economy of communications.

The Frankfurt theorists made us think about how the logic of capital shapes the structure and output of the culture industry, particularly in Max Horkheimer and Theodor Adorno's second section of *Dialectic of Enlightenment,* "The Culture Industry: Enlightenment as Mass Deception."[2] This essay was one of the first attempts to understand the effects of the commodification of culture and the way in which exchange value rather than use value drives cultural production. Finally, I will suggest ways in which we might rethink the Frankfurt School on the question of social change and the role of communications in this process. Like the studies of the Frankfurt School, studies of the political economy of communications generally conclude that the media play a prominent role in preventing social change and that our capitalist media system is inherently undemocratic. The critique leaves us with the difficult and inevitable question posed by Lenin: "What is to be done?"[3]

The Frankfurt School: On Mass Communications "Science"

Within the received history of mass communications theory and research, the Frankfurt School is credited with producing the most developed critique of the dominant paradigm in the "science of communications" that prevailed from the early 1930s to the early 1960s.[4] Scholars working within the dominant paradigm sought to demonstrate media effects using empirically-oriented, social-behavioral approaches—usually laboratory or survey research. This quantitative orientation served two purposes: first, within the academy, it helped to legitimize the study of culture and mass communications as a "true social science"; second, outside the academy, it facilitated fundraising efforts from government and industry sources. Questions regarding media influence on fashion became conflated with studies of voter opinions and behavior in classic works such as *The People's Choice* (1944) by Paul Lazarsfeld, Bernard Berelson, and Hazel Gaudet, and *Personal Influence* (1955) by Elihu Katz and Lazarsfeld.[5] Todd Gitlin identified this marketing orientation as an integral part of the "administrative mentality," by which he meant a research program that in general "poses questions from the vantage of the command-posts of institutions that seek to improve or rationalize their control over social sectors in social functions."[6] Or, to paraphrase Herbert Schiller, the administrative paradigm is research about those who are governed on behalf of those who govern.[7] Whether to sell soap, cultural products or politicians, the general purpose of administrative research was to understand how the media could be used to control people's behavior.

Consequently, mass communication theory and research became organized around attempting to "rationally" organize expressions of the public interest and produce quantitative measures of the "good life," such as standard of living, per capita income and even the number of radios and televisions per household. This reduction of normative questions regarding the good life and the good society to matters of consumption was taken for granted in administrative research. For the Frankfurt School, both the reduction of method and the question of the good society were unacceptable.

Daniel Czitrom divided the Frankfurt School critique of traditional mass communications research into two levels: First, it did not frame studies with the social totality in view. Second, its reduction of cultural questions to empirically verifiable categories was entirely inappropriate.[8] First, by failing to take the social totality into view, scholars working within the dominant paradigm fetishized a certain facet of social reality, resulting in an overemphasis on its actual historical impact. For the Frankfurt scholars, studying any particular facet of the social totality required interpreting the present historically as well as in terms of future potential. Unlike the functionalist "objective" claims of traditional empirical research on culture and mass communications, the Frankfurt School insisted, following Marx, that critical theory must serve the purposes of social change and not simply describe the world "as it is."

Second, the reduction of culture to empirical verifiable categories began with "the false hypothesis that the consumer's choice is the decisive social phenomenon from which one should begin further analysis."[9] Rather, studies of culture and communications had to move beyond narrow questions of individual uses of the media and their specific effects (e.g., violent behavior) to the broader issues of meaning and consciousness. Thus, for Leo Lowenthal, writing in 1950, a critical communications science would begin with the general question, "What are the functions of cultural communications within the total process of society?" and move to more specific questions such as "How are things produced under the dicta of formal and informal censorship?" and, addressing the question of resistance, "What passes the censorship of the socially powerful agencies?"[10] The difficulty in pioneering such a critical approach was twofold: such questions did not necessarily lend themselves to quantitative methods, and perhaps more important, they were not conducive to the marketing orientation underwritten by industry and government funding. Adorno encountered these constraints when he joined Lazarsfeld at the Office of Radio Research, then at Princeton, in the late 1930s. He found little room for critical social research within the Princeton Project on radio broadcasting. Adorno noted the administrative orientation of the project: "Its charter, which came from the Rockefeller Foundation, expressly stipulated that the investigations must be performed within the limits of the commercial radio system prevailing in the United

States."[11] Adorno also found himself frustrated by the pressure to translate cultural phenomena such as the "false harmony" of popular music and the corruption of symphonic music by radio broadcasting into quantifiable data.

Frankfurt School scholars were not opposed to empirical research per se; indeed they produced quite a bit of it. This is apparent from Wiggershaus's comprehensive history of the school and his extensive bibliography covering its research record.[12] Rather, Adorno complained about the tendency to prioritize empirical over theoretical work in administrative research.[13] He also had problems with the very application of empirical measures to cultural phenomena, arguing that measuring culture was "equivalent to squaring the circle."[14] While recognizing the applied utility of empirical research, Adorno rejected the view of the dominant paradigm that experimental or surveyed reactions of audiences to cultural products could serve as the primary and final sources of our understanding of cultural processes.

It is similarly difficult to "measure" the impact of the Frankfurt School within the larger field of communications research during the 1940s and 1950s. It is noteworthy that Horkheimer and Adorno's collaborative efforts on the radio project inspired Lazarsfeld to write "Remarks on Administrative and Critical Communications Research" in an effort to find common ground between the two paradigms.[15] Lazarsfeld agreed that critical theory raised important questions about the role of culture in society but believed that empirical research was still the best way to test them. He wrote:

> If it were possible in the terms of critical research to formulate an actual research operation which could be integrated with empirical work, the people involved, the problems treated and, in the end, the actual utility of the work would greatly profit.[16]

Interestingly enough, Lazarsfeld invited critical research to explore the question of how the structure of the culture industries affected media content. Specifically, he asked:

> What ideas and what forms are killed before they ever reach the general public, whether because they would not be interesting enough for large groups, or because they could not pay sufficient returns on the necessary investment, or because no traditional forms of presentation are available?[17]

These were precisely the questions Horkheimer and Adorno took up in their "Culture Industry" in 1944. However, a sustained critique of communications industry structures and practices within mass communications studies did not emerge until the late 1960s.

Summarizing the Frankfurt School's critique of the dominant paradigm, Lowenthal concluded that "[e]mpirical social science has become a kind of applied asceticism [. . .] and thrives in an atmosphere of rigidly enforced neutrality."[18] Later, C. Wright Mills characterized such research as "abstracted empiricism."[19] Their point was the same: Strict adherence to empirically oriented, administrative research served the powers that be by enhancing their ability to utilize the means of communication for purposes of social control. A critical research program, in turn, would focus on how these mechanisms work and how the structures and practices of the culture industry help reproduce the hegemony of the capitalist class.

The Political Economy of Culture

Contemporary critical approaches to the study of the political economy of communications continue in the Frankfurt School tradition by seeking to put the media within a broader historical, economic, and normative context.[20] Schiller sought to turn the dominant paradigm on its head, arguing for critical research about those who govern on behalf of those who are governed.[21]

Indeed, this was the original mission of the Frankfurt Institute when it was founded in the 1920s, more precisely, to study the history of the labor movement to assist working-class struggles. Critical political economy takes as its central task the examination of how the logic of capital shapes the structure and content of the culture industries. Questions of production had been largely ignored within the dominant paradigm. The emergence of an alternative paradigm—the "interpretive turn" in the social sciences in the 1960s—made the necessity of an institutional analysis of the relationship between economic, political, and communications systems apparent. This attention to institutional analyses was largely caused by increasing recognition that the culture industry played a significant role in suppressing social change.

Such an analysis can be found in Horkheimer and Adorno's essay "The Culture Industry." This text provides one of the earliest and most sustained critiques of the media under capitalism. In early drafts of the essay, the authors used the term "mass culture" to describe the existing media system. They finally coined the term "culture industry" in "order to exclude from the outset the interpretation agreeable to its advocates: that it is a matter of something like a culture that arises from the masses themselves."[22] They also toned down their critique of capitalism for the 1947 publication of *Dialectic of Enlightenment*. Wiggershaus notes numerous changes from the original mimeograph of 1944:

> The word "capitalism" was changed to "existing conditions"; "capital" was changed to "economic system"; "capitalist bloodsuckers" became "knights of industry"; "class society" became "domination" or "order"; "ruling class" became "rulers."[23]

He notes that such self-censorship was an Institute tradition, but these changes are especially poignant because they occurred precisely as a second anti-communist crusade was emerging.[24]

The "industrialization of culture" approach, to use Sut Jhally's term,[25] examines how cultural and intellectual creativity became increasingly commodified around the turn of the century under conditions of industrial capitalism. Industrialization, urbanization, and immigration were seen as destructive forces that undermined traditional cultural systems. This breakdown of the *"Gemeinschaft"* or "organic solidarity" created a void ultimately filled by the culture industry. Following the logic of capital, the culture industry replaced the human production of artistic and intellectual creativity and leisure in general, with a commodified product produced primarily for its exchange value rather than its use value.

The culture industry continues to prevent social change not necessarily because it disseminates a "false ideology" to the working class, but rather because it has been incorporated into an economic system driven by the profit motive. Jhally, recalling Marx, describes this process as the real subsumption of culture into the economic system. The culture industry is no longer merely an ideological mechanism for social control, but has actually become part of the system of capital accumulation.[26] Hence, the marketplace governs the production of culture and information. In the last instance, however, economic determinants have profound ideological effects since capitalist media companies are not really concerned with the "true and the beautiful," but rather with what will sell in the marketplace. Most of what they offer us, therefore, involves "an escape through pure illusion."[27] Horkheimer and Adorno wrote "The Culture Industry" just as the primary sectors of the media had become oligopolistic.[28]

From the late 1920s through the early 1950s, five vertically-integrated companies controlled the production, distribution, and exhibition of movies. Two major radio networks, NBC and CBS, dominated the radio airwaves and provided the majority of the prime-time broadcast entertainment throughout the 1930s and 1940s. The music recording industry became oligopolistic during the Depression in the 1930s. Small record companies failed as media audiences shifted their leisure spending from records to radios and theater tickets.[29] The concentration of the mass-market book trade and the rise of newspaper chains also occurred during this period.[30] In addition, the media industry had taken on a conglomerate structure, with the same companies controlling significant market shares in various media industries. For example, RCA controlled the NBC radio network, RKO pictures, RCA records, and on the hardware end, the manufacturing of RCA/Victor radio receivers and phonographs.

Horkheimer and Adorno were precisely poised to analyze a mature oligopolistic media system as they developed their culture industry approach. They recognized the ways in which oligopolies seek to create demand by convincing consumers that they are receiving what they really want. The opening paragraph of "The Culture Industry" essay states: "Movies and radio need no longer pretend to be art."[31] Media capitalists had convinced audiences that they were providing them with a legitimate service and meeting their informational and cultural needs. Anticipating the uses and gratifications theory of the mass media, Horkheimer and Adorno argued that approaching consumers in such a manner had the ideological effect of removing "any doubt about the social utility of the finished products."[32] Indeed, the capitalist class effectively extended this rationale to what had come to be seen as the facts of everyday life. As Horkheimer and Adorno put it, "It is the coercive nature of society alienated from itself. Automobiles, bombs, and movies keep the whole thing together until their leveling element shows its strength in the very wrong which it furthered."[33] Media capitalists, backed by administrative research, could therefore claim that their products responded to the rational expression of the public interest (i.e., consumer needs), which is why they were accepted with little resistance.[34]

Horkheimer and Adorno recognized what political economists have determined to be typical behavior of concentrated industries. Whether a matter of selling automobiles, consumer goods, or cultural products, the goal of oligopolistic producers is the same: to minimize risks by standardizing products and to maximize profits by creating demand through marketing and advertising. According to Simon Frith, for example, the pop music industry of the 1930s and 1940s saw its audience as manipulatable and malleable. Its goal was to create hits and offend no one, resulting in the formulaic, three-minute popular songs designed for radio play and record sales.[35] Hence, the mere formal structure of pop music itself, increasingly attuned to advertiser-supported radio broadcasting, provided Adorno with ample fodder for his attack on the music industry in his 1941 essay entitled "On Popular Music."[36]

Horkheimer and Adorno also recognized the essential role of the star system within an oligopolistic media system. The movie and music industries work hard to create stars as a form of product differentiation. Stars generally guarantee a return on investments from preconstituted audiences, as a certain number of fans can be expected to turn out for their favorite stars' latest movie, or buy their latest book or recording. Horkheimer and Adorno also noted how stars have become vehicles to promote the consumption of commodities other than media products. They argued that the boundaries between cultural products and advertising became increasingly blurred with the integration of the culture industry and other sectors of the economy. As they wrote: "The assembly-line character of the culture industry, the synthetic, planned method of turning out its products (factory-like not only in the studio but, more or less, in the compilation of cheap biographies, pseudodocumentary novels, and hit songs) is very suitable to advertising."[37] Cultural products are designed to "lend themselves to ends external to the work." Thus, "every monster close-up of a star is an advertisement for her name, and every hit song a plug for its tune."[38] The star system serves as a mechanism to raise the costs of entry into the media marketplace, since only the dominant firms can afford the high costs of advertising required to build them. Similarly, when stars became a prevalent presence in advertising they raised the entry barriers to markets for consumer goods, since only the dominant firms can afford to use them. Ultimately, advertising "strengthens the firm bond between the consumers and the big combines," while the costs of advertising "finally flow back into [their] pockets."[39]

Horkheimer and Adorno extended their structural analysis of the impact of the logic of capital on the culture industry to an analysis of media texts and their effects on audiences. They argued that because exchange value drove the production of cultural products they were necessarily stamped with the formal structure generated by the profit motive. They viewed the relationship between production and text as ultimately determined by the logic of capital. Their argument about the effects of the text on audiences, however, is more complex than it first appears. They stressed the ways in which the formal structures of media texts produce a suturing function, i.e., audiences are attracted to that which they precisely expect, as they are drawn into the form and structure of a given genre. There must be superficial deviations in the formula to keep audiences interested but never to the extent of seriously disrupting the expectations that the culture industry has generated (all in the name of "giving the audience what it wants"). This is not to suggest that Horkheimer and Adorno saw audience members as dupes. Rather, they argued, the culture industry provided escape, both when audiences became sutured into the form of the text and seduced by the fantasies provided by the narrative. "Amusement under late capitalism is the prolongation of work," they concluded, because it provides "an escape from the mechanized work process."[40] The primary means of domination by the media industry was not necessarily its ideological substance, but rather its demobilizing role.

Indeed, Horkheimer and Adorno recognized a certain self-reflexivity on the part of the audience. The closing line of "The Culture Industry" underscores this: "The triumph of advertising in the culture industry is that consumers feel compelled to buy and use its products even though they see through them."[4] The real force behind capitalist hegemony is not ideology, then, but the coercive power of capital. Capitalism guarantees itself the reproduction of a necessary number of faithful members who follow prescribed standards of conduct or face marginalization, demonization, unemployment, homelessness, institutionalization, and finally death. These threats result in the suturing of humanity into the logic of capital. Horkheimer and Adorno stressed this point when explaining the stability of the capitalist system:

> The standard of life enjoyed corresponds very closely to the degree to which classes and individuals are essentially bound up with the system [. . .] and, apart from certain capital crimes, the most mortal of sins is to be an outsider.[42]

This pressure to stay in line necessarily affects culture industry workers and is precisely what drives the reproduction of hegemonic media output. The more concentrated the media industry the more difficult it is for "outsiders" to have their voices heard.

The Culture Industry Enters the Twenty-first Century

According to Ben Bagdikian, a mere six transnational media corporations controlled most of the output of news, information, and entertainment as the United States entered the twenty-first century. This was down from an estimated fifty corporations in the early 1980s.[43] Firms such as AOL Time Warner, Bertelsman, Disney, News Corp., Viacom, and Vivendi are vertically and horizontally integrated media conglomerates with dominant market shares across media sectors, including filmed entertainment, network and cable television, recorded music, and book and magazine publishing. Their focus is on movie, record, and book blockbusters, backed by big production and marketing budgets. Horkheimer and Adorno referred to the blockbuster phenomenon as a process of "'conspicuous production,' of blatant cash investment."[44] They recognized that "[t]he varying budgets in the culture industry do not bear the slightest relation to factual values, to the meaning of the products themselves."[45] The purpose of big budgets and marketing hype is to convince audiences that they must attend to the product or end up being left out of social discourses.

The hype is extended through the synergistic practices of media conglomerates and their tie-ins with producers of consumer goods. Eileen Meehan has analyzed the synergistic practices behind the production of *Batman* (1989) and the ways in which the owner of the Batman copyright, Time Warner, utilized the character throughout a wide range of media venues, including comic books, soundtracks, music videos, animated series, and theme parks.[46] Horkheimer and Adorno were already complaining in the 1940s that the culture industry was no longer producing art for art's sake. Under conglomerate media systems, media products are deemed worthy only if they have synergistic potential. So, rather than serving the art of cinema, movies must serve the demands of the music and licensing divisions of the parent company producing a film. Contemporary musicians are forced to produce music videos in order to sell records, changing both the form and reception of music.

Horkheimer and Adorno predicted synergy would intensify with the rise of television. However, they implied that this synergistic convergence was inherent to the medium, failing to extend their own argument that the profit motive would ultimately determine the industrial organization of television. The industry immediately became concentrated, its audiences became commodified, and its content became a vehicle for the further commercialization of culture. The same profit motive is driving the structure and content of the Internet. Hence, the culture industry's capture of this new electronic frontier was predictable; it has become another means for selling audiences and commodities.[47] The synergies between AOL's Internet services and Time Warner's film, publishing, music, television, cable systems, theme parks, sports teams, and other media ventures began even before the merger was finalized.

Horkheimer and Adorno did recognize that media were interwoven with other sectors of capital, such as RCA's control of NBC and the dependence of Hollywood on finance capital.[48] They failed, however, to explore the effects of this integration on the ideological output of the culture industry. They were correct in conceding, in their day, that "the culture monopolies are weak and dependent in comparison" to the "most powerful sectors of industry—steel, petroleum, electricity, and chemicals."[49] Today the culture and information industries are no longer so weak and dependent. The capital or stock values of the leading communications companies now match those of the major industrial firms. In 1991, the Walt Disney Company replaced USX Corp. (formerly U.S. Steel) on the Dow Jones 500 Industrial Average, attesting to the integral role of media in the U.S. economy. AOL's purchase of Time Warner, approved by the Federal Communications Commission in January 2001, became the largest media merger and the third largest corporate merger to date.

The captains of industry are now also "captains of consciousness," to borrow Stuart Ewen's term.[50] The richest members of the capitalist class not only own and control basic industries but commandeer the media and communications sectors as well. An analysis of the 1991 Forbes list of the richest 400 individuals and families in the United States found that they either made their fortune from or held significant stakes in culture and information industries.[51] The Bass brothers, for example, made their fortune in oil but also owned large shares of Disney stock. Warren Buffet, listed at number 2 on the 1998 *Forbes 400* list with an estimated worth of $30 billion,[52] held significant shares of stock in Coca-Cola, American Express, Travelers Group, Wells Fargo, Gillette, Freddie Mac, Geico, International Dairy Queen, and Allied Domecq PLC, owners of the Dunkin' Donuts and Baskin-Robbins snack food chains as well as the Ballantine's Scotch, Canadian Club whiskey, and Beefeater gin liquor brands. Buffet's investments also included media companies such as the Washington Post Company and Disney.

The culture industry is further integrated into the global power structure via interlocking boards of directors. The boards of the major media conglomerates are made up of bankers, owners and directors of other Fortune 500 companies, former high-ranking government officials, and academic administrators from elite private universities.[53] Board meetings are just one site, among many, at which leading members of the capitalist class have the opportunity to articulate their common interests and organize the hegemonic projects required to protect or advance them. This is where interlocking ownership and control of the media comes to serve the interests of capital. Hence, Hans Enzensberger argued that the term "consciousness industry" better describes the primary function of the media than "culture industry".[54] What Jhally calls the "consciousness industry approach" focuses on the formal subsumption of the media within the larger social structure.[55] Rather than seeing cultural output as determined solely by the logic of capital, the consciousness industry approach focuses on the ways in which the media are used to perpetuate the hegemony of capital through direct control over media content and output.

The basic premise of the consciousness industry approach is that gaining the consent of the dominated is essential to the ruling class. The coercive nature of capitalism alone cannot guarantee its hegemony; it requires ideological work to convince subordinate classes that the system is fair, just, and "natural." Formal democratic rights guaranteed to the subordinate classes also complicate matters of class rule. The ruling class must work to articulate its particular class interests to the general interests of the citizenry as a whole. Nevertheless, the capitalist class has a clear advantage in the struggle over definitions of what policies and programs are in the "public interest." It is more organized and unified than the working class. It has the networks and resources to maintain and reproduce its hegemony. In addition, the field of struggle—whether the state or the media—is structurally tilted against subversive forces. For example, a historical study of copyright law demonstrates how the legal system tends to privilege private property rights over the rights of creators and consumers of culture and information.[56] The consciousness industry approach has been criticized for its conspiratorial overtones.[57] But the record shows that media owners have developed a variety of strategies to handle what Enzensberger called "potential troublemakers, [. . .] from the crudest to most sophisticated." The "gamut of manipulation" runs from "physical threat, blacklisting, moral and economic pressure on the one hand, [to] overexposure, star-cult, cooptation into the power elite on the other."[58] The record also shows that media owners do influence media content. They use their media outlets to influence public policy in ways that specifically benefit their own companies. They do censor or suppress works that are critical of big business or the capitalist system. There is also a tendency to remain silent on certain issues, such as the effects of media concentration, which may lead the citizenry to question the existing media structure. Finally, media owners exert their influence over the basic ideological premises upon which cultural and intellectual works are based. There are divisions of labor within the ruling class, including those who take up the role of what Marx and Engels described as "conceptive ideologists, who make the perfecting of the illusion of the class about itself their chief source of livelihood."[59] They also do the actual ideological work of articulating the interests of the capitalist class to the citizenry as a whole through the media.

Finally, Horkheimer and Adorno's culture industry approach and Enzensberger's consciousness industry approach are not incompatible. Clearly, the logic of capital and the agency of capitalists are mutual determinants of media output. The capitalist class has invested in the culture and communications sectors because they are profitable. Capitalists will also continue to pursue media ownership and control for the purposes of influencing public opinion and public policy. At the turn of the twentieth century, the transnational media conglomerates are both profitable and influential.[60] At the same time, the concentrated economic structure of the media has resulted in the increasing marginalization of oppositional voices, alternative visions, and radical opinions.

Rethinking Resistance

Enzensberger criticized Horkheimer and Adorno's culture industry approach for being too economically deterministic. In his view, their approach did not leave any space for agency on the part of artistic and intellectual workers. Rather, Enzensberger believed that the dependency of the consciousness industry on artists and intellectuals produced a weak link within the system of ideological reproduction. The consciousness industry is dependent on creators who work with ideas. For Enzensberger, this was the key to the potential autonomy of the media from capitalist hegemony. He argued: "Consciousness [. . .] cannot be industrially produced. It is a 'social product' made up by people: its origin is the dialogue."[61] Horkheimer and Adorno could not conceive of the culture industry as a site of resistance. The logic of capital ultimately determined that the output of the culture industry was affirmative of the system as a whole. In their view, then, negation of the system could only come through avant-garde art that rejected or subverted dominant cultural forms. Their escape into the realm of high culture reflected their resignation to the continued rule of capital. Their reduction of resistance to artistic works that subverted form was ahistorical. The capitalist media system, ever seeking to enclose human artistic and intellectual creativity within the commodity system, will ultimately find a way to coopt subversive expression, even that of the high culture variety.

Enzensberger, in turn, underestimated the power of capital to contain the autonomy of artistic and intellectual workers. A good example is punk rock, which emerged as a musical culture in the late 1970s as a reaction to the corporate rock being produced by the recording industry oligopoly. When the record companies brought punk into the mainstream, the result was the rise of "straight-edge punk," which rejected the excesses and cultdom that mainstream punk had come to represent. Straight-edge is now a niche market. And by the late 1980s, reggae music—originally an expression of anti-imperialism—was being used to sell Volkswagens.

If resistance is ultimately co-opted, or if the terms of resistance are defined by the culture industries as reactionary forms, the route to truly free artistic and intellectual creativity can only be the overthrow of capitalism. Marcuse concluded as much in his 1972 essay entitled "Art as Form of Reality."[62] He argued that in a truly free society the focus of art would be on "creativity, a creation in the material as well as intellectual sense, a juncture of technique and the arts in the total reconstruction of the environment, a juncture of town and country, industry and nature." For Marcuse, the creation of such an environment was dependent upon "the total transformation of the existing society; a new mode and goals of production, a new type of human being as producer, the end of role-playing, of the established social division of labour, of work and pleasure."[63] This can only occur when artistic and intellectual creativity is "freed from the horrors of commercial exploitation and beautification, so that Art can no longer serve as a stimulus of business."[64]

Raymond Williams, a contemporary of Marcuse, also concluded that culture could never be freely produced under capitalism, even that which seeks to operate outside the culture industry. With the industrialization and professionalization of artistic and intellectual creativity, the capitalist division of labor has produced the alienation of art from everyday life, something to be consumed rather than produced. Contrary to stressing audience reception as a site of resistance, Williams forcefully argued that "creation is the activity of every human mind" and therefore every human being has potential intellectual and artistic abilities that ought to be cultivated.[65] Under capitalism, this potential has been suppressed through the division of labor between producers and consumers of culture. Like Marcuse, Williams concluded that the alienation of artistic and intellectual creativity from daily life could only be resolved through the extension of public ownership of the means of communication, as well as the means of production.

Notes

1. I am using the term Frankfurt School to refer to the work of scholars associated with the Institute of Social Research, which opened at Frankfurt University in June 1924. For a discussion of the complexity of the term "school" see the Introduction to Rolf Wiggershaus, 1995, *The Frankfurt School: Its History, Theories, and Political Significance*, trans. Michael Robertson (Cambridge, Mass.: MIT Press), 1–4.

2. Max Horkheimer and Theodor W. Adorno, 1972. *Dialectic of Enlightenment*, trans. John Cumming (New York: Herder and Herder), 120–67. The essay was first produced in mimeograph form by Max Horkheimer and Theodor W. Adorno as *Philosophishe Fragmente* (New York) as an in-house publication in 1944. The work was published in German as, 1947, *Dialektic der Aufklärung. Philosophishe Fragmente* (Amsterdam, Querido).

3. V. I. Lenin, 1977, *Selected Works*, Vol. 1 (Moscow: Progress Publishers), 92–241.

4.   Daniel J. Czitrom, 1982, *Media and the American Mind: From Morse to McLuhan* (Chapel Hill: University of North Carolina Press), 142. For histories of communications theory and research see Denis McQuail, 1994, *Mass Communication Theory: An Introduction,* 3rd ed. (London: Sage Publications), 328–33; and Herbert I. Schiller, 1989, *Culture Inc.: The Corporate Takeover of Public Expression* (New York: Oxford University Press), 135–56. For a more specific discussion of critical theory and mass communication research see Douglas Kellner, 1989, *Critical Theory, Marxism and Modernity* (Baltimore, Md.: Johns Hopkins University Press).

5.   Paul F. Lazarsfeld, 1944, Bernard Berelson, and Hazel Gaudet, *The People's Choice* (New York: Duell, Sloan, Pearce); Elihu Katz and Paul F. Lazarsfeld, 1955, *Personal Influence: The Part Played by People in the Flow of Mass Communications* (Glencoe, Ill.: Free Press).

6.   Todd Gitlin, "Media Sociology: The Dominant Paradigm," *Theory and Society* 6, no. 2, (1978): 225.

7.   Herbert I. Schiller, "Critical Research in the Information Age," *Journal of Communication* 33, no. 10 (1983): 253.

8.   Czitrom, *Media,* 143.

9.   Ibid., 143.

10.   Leo Lowenthal, 1957 "Historical Perspectives of Popular Culture," *Mass Culture: The Popular Arts in America,* ed. Bernard Rosenberg and David M. White (Glencoe, Ill.: Free Press), 52, 56.

11.   Theodor W. Adorno, 1969, "Scientific Experiences of a European Scholar in America," *The Intellectual Migration: Europe and America, 1930–1960,* ed. Donald Fleming and Bernard Bailyn (Cambridge, Mass.: Harvard University Press), 343.

12.   Wiggershaus, *Frankfurt School,* 715–71.

13.   Adorno, *Scientific Experiences,* 353.

14.   Ibid., 347.

15.   Paul Lazarsfeld, 1941, "Remarks on Administrative and Critical Communications Research," *Studies in Philosophy and Social Science* 9, no. 1: 2–16.

16.   Ibid., 14.

17.   Ibid., 14.

18.   Lowenthal, *Mass Culture,* 52.

19.   C. Wright Mills, 1959, *The Sociological Imagination* (New York: Oxford University Press).

20.   For comprehensive discussions and applications of the critical political economy of communications see Oscar H. Gandy Jr., 1992, "The Political Economy Approach: A Critical Challenge," *Journal of Media Economics* 12, no. 1: 23–42; Nicholas Garnham, 1990, *Capitalism and Communication: Global Culture and the Economics of Information* (London: Sage); Peter Golding and Graham Murdock, eds., 1997, *The Political Economy of the Media* (Lyme, N.H.: Edward Elgar Publishing); and Vincent Mosco, 1996, *The Political Economy of Communication* (London: Sage).

21.   Schiller, "Critical Research," 253.

22.   Theodor W. Adorno, 1975, "Culture Industry Reconsidered," *New German Critique* 6, trans. Anson G. Rabinbach: 12.

23.   Wiggershaus, *Frankfurt School,* 401.

24. The first crusade coming at the end of World War I and epitomized by the violent suppression of labor, e.g., the Palmer Raids of the early 1920s; and the second epitomized by President Truman's Loyalty Review Program, launched the same year as *Dialectic of Enlightenment* was published (1947).

25. Sut Jhally, 1989, "The Political Economy of Culture," *Cultural Politics in Contemporary America,* ed. Ian Angus and Sut Jhally (New York: Routledge), 74.

26. Ibid., 72–73.

27. Ibid., 71.

28. See Benjamin Compaine, et al., eds., 1979, *Who Owns the Media? Concentration of Ownership in the Mass Communications Industry* (White Plains, N.Y.: Knowledge Industries).

29. Simon Frith, 1987, "The Industrialization of Popular Music," in *Popular Music and Society,* ed. James Lull (Newbury Park, CA: Sage), 59

30. On the mass-market book trade see Janice Radway, 1991, *Reading the Romance: Women, Patriarchy, and Popular Literature* (Chapel Hill, N.C.: University of North Carolina Press): 19–45.

31. Horkheimer and Adorno, *Dialectic,* 121.

32. Ibid., 121.

33. Ibid., 121.

34. Ibid., 121.

35. Frith, "Industrialization," 62.

36. Theodor W. Adorno, 1941, "On Popular Music," *Studies in Philosophy and Social Science* 9, no. 1: 17–48.

37. Horkheimer and Adorno, *Dialectic,* 163.

38. Ibid., 163.

39. Ibid., 162.

40. Ibid., 137.

41. Ibid., 167.

42. Ibid., 150.

43. Ben Bagdikian, 2000, *The Media Monopoly,* 6th ed. (Boston: Beacon Press), viii–x.

44. Horkheimer and Adorno, *Dialectic,* 124.

45. Ibid., 124.

46. Eileen Meehan, 1991, "Holy Commodity Fetish, Batman! The Political Economy of a Commercial Intertext," in *The Many Lives of Batman: Critical Approaches to a Superhero and His Media,* ed. Roberta Pearson and William Uricchio (New York: Routledge), 47–65.

47. Ronald V. Bettig, 1997, "The Enclosure of Cyberspace," *Critical Studies in Mass Communication* 14: 138–57.

48. Horkheimer and Adorno, *Dialectic,* 123.

49. Ibid., 122.

50. Stuart Ewen, 1976, *Captains of Consciousness: Advertising and the Social Roots of the Consumer Culture* (New York: McGraw-Hill).

51. Ronald V. Bettig, 1996, *Copyrighting Culture: The Political Economy of Intellectual Property* (Boulder, Colo.: Westview Press), 50.

52. Peter Newcomb and Delores Lataniotis, "The Forbes 400: The Richest People in America," *Forbes,* 12 October 1998, 168–69.

53. Peter Dreier and Steven Weinberg, 1979, "The Ties That Blind: Interlocking Directorates," *Columbia Journalism Review* 18: 51–68; Peter Dreier, 1982, "The Position of the Press in the U.S. Power Structure," *Social Problems* 29, no. 3: 298–310.

54. Hans Magnus Enzensberger, 1974, *The Consciousness Industry* (New York: Seabury Press).

55. Jhally, "Political Economy," 67–70.

56. See Bettig, *Copyrighting Culture,* specifically Chapter Six, "The Law of Intellectual Property," 151–187.

57. Stuart Hall, 1989, "Ideology and Communication Theory," *Rethinking Communication, Volume 1: Paradigm Issues,* ed. Brenda Dervin et al. (Newbury Park, Calif.: Sage), 40–52

58. Enzensberger, *Consciousness,* 14.

59. Karl Marx and Fredrick Engels, 1970, *The German Ideology,* ed. C. J. Arthur (New York: International Publishers), 65.

60. Bagdikian, *Media,* 5.

61. Enzensberger, *Consciousness,* 5.

62. Herbert Marcuse, 1979, "Art as Form of Reality," *New Left Review* 74: 51–58.

63. Ibid., 58.

64. Ibid., 58.

65. Raymond Williams, 1958, *The Long Revolution* (London: Chatto and Windus), 17.

II

ADORNO

5
Of Mice and Mimesis: Reading Spiegelman with Adorno*

Andreas Huyssen

In his recently published book entitled *In the Shadow of Catastrophe: German Intellectuals Between Apocalypse and Enlightenment,*[1] Anson Rabinbach gives us a novel interpretation of Horkheimer and Adorno's seminal *Dialectic of Enlightenment,* a work that has taken on renewed life in recent years in the context of radical postmodern critiques of European modernity and the debates about the Holocaust. Rabinbach demonstrates in admirable detail and with the help of new archival sources how anti-Semitism is much more central to the overall argument of this book than had so far been acknowledged. Key to his argument is the importance of Part V of the "Elements of Anti-Semitism," a chapter in the book that has drawn much less commentary over the years than, say, the more famous chapters on Odysseus or on the culture industry.

Rabinbach succeeds in linking Adorno's discussion of the role of mimesis in anti-Semitism to the historical and philosophical reflections on mimesis as part of the evolution of signifying systems, as they are elaborated in the first chapter of the *Dialectic of Enlightenment.*[2] Here the authors discuss mimesis in its true and repressed forms, its role in the process of civilization, and its paradoxical relationship to the *Bilderverbot,* the prohibition of graven images.[3] *Dialectic of Enlightenment* is of course part of a tradition of writing that locates the origins of Western civilization both with the Greeks and with the Jews. Thus we are not surprised to find Odysseus described as the first modern subject and the Jews as "die ersten Bürger," the first modern citizens. Mimesis is the term of mediation.

At the same time, the concept of mimesis in Adorno (and I take it that Adorno rather than Horkheimer is the driving force in articulating this concept in the coauthored work) is not easily defined, as several recent studies have shown.[4] It actually functions more like a palimpsest in that it partakes in at least five different yet overlapping discursive registers in the text: first in relation to the critique of the commodity form, its powers of reification and deception; second in relation to the anthropological grounding of human nature, which, as Adorno insists in *Minima Moralia,* is "indissolubly linked to imitation"[5]; third in a biological somatic sense as Adorno had encountered it in Roger Caillois's work, some of which he reviewed for the *Zeitschrift für Sozialforschung*[6]; fourth in the Freudian sense of identification and

---

*An earlier German version of this essay was published in Manuel Köppen and Klaus R. Scherpe, *Bilder des Holocaust* (Böhlau: Cologne, 1997), 171–90.

projection endebted to *Totem and Taboo;* and last, in an aesthetic sense and with strong resonances of Benjamin's language theory, in relation to the role of word and image in the evolution of signifying systems. It is precisely this multivalence of mimesis, I would argue, that makes the concept productive for contemporary debates about memory and representation in the public realm.

In this essay, I will focus on one specific aspect of memory discourse, namely the vexing issue of (in Timothy Garton Ash's succinct words) if, how, and when to represent historical trauma.[7] My example for the representation of historical trauma is the Holocaust, a topic on which, as we know, Adorno had provocative things to say, although he never said quite enough about it. But I do think that the issues raised in this essay pertain as much to other instances of historical trauma and their representation: whether we think of the *desaparecidos* in Argentina, Guatemala, or Chile, the stolen generation in Australia, or the post-apartheid debates in South Africa—in all these cases issues of how to document, how to represent, and how to view and listen to testimony about a traumatic past have powerfully emerged in the public domain.

I hope to show that a reading through mimesis of one specific Holocaust image-text may allow us to go beyond arguments focusing primarily on the rather confining issue of how to represent the Holocaust "properly" or how to avoid aestheticizing it. My argument will be based on the reading of a work that has shocked many precisely because it seems to violate the *Bilderverbot* in the most egregious ways, but that has also been celebrated, at least by some, as one of the most challenging in an ever-widening body of recent works concerned with the Holocaust and its remembrance. But more is at stake here than just the reading of one work through the conceptual screen of another. A discussion of Art Spiegelman's *Maus*[8] in terms of the mimetic dimension may get us beyond a certain kind of stalemate in debates about representations of the Holocaust, a stalemate which, ironically, rests on presuppositions that were first and powerfully articulated by Adorno himself in a different context and at a different time. Reading *Maus* through the conceptual screen of mimesis will permit us to read Adorno against one of the most lingering effects of his work on contemporary culture, the thesis about the culture industry and its irredeemable link with deception, manipulation, domination, and the destruction of subjectivity. While this kind of uncompromising critique of consumerist culture, linked as it is to a certain now historical type of modernist aesthetic practice, resonates strongly with a whole set of situationist and (post-)structuralist positions developed in France in the 1960s (Barthes, Debord, Baudrillard, Lyotard, Tel Quel), it has generally been on the wane in contemporary aesthetic practices. For obvious reasons, however, it has proven to have much staying power in one particular area: that of Holocaust representations where Adorno's statements about poetry after Auschwitz (often misquoted, unanalyzed, and ripped out of their historical context[9]) have become a standard reference point and have fed into the recent revival of notions of an aesthetic sublime and its dogmatic anti-representational stance.[10] But this is where the issue of public memory emerges. Politically, most everybody seems to agree, the genocide of the Jews is to be remembered (with allegedly salutory effects on present and future) by as large a public as possible, but mass cultural representations are not considered proper or correct. The paradigmatic case exemplifying this broad, though now perhaps fraying, consensus is the debate over Steven Spielberg's *Schindler's List* and Lanzmann's *Shoah*. Spielberg's film, playing to mass audiences, fails to remember properly because it represents, thus fostering forgetting: Hollywood as fictional substitute for "real history." Lanzmann's refusal to represent, on the other hand, is said to embody memory in the proper way precisely because it avoids the delusions of a presence of that which is to be remembered. Lanzmann's film is praised as something like a heroic effort in the Kulturkampf against the memory industry, and its refusal to represent, its adherence to *Bilderverbot* becomes the ground for its authenticity.[11] Aesthetically speaking, these opposing validations of Spielberg vs. Lanzmann still rest on the unquestioned modernist dichotomy that pits Hollywood and mass culture against forms of high art.[12] Looking at Spiegelman's *Maus* through the various discursive screens of mimesis, I want to argue, may allow us to approach Holocaust memory and its representations today in a way different from this earlier dominant paradigm.

Maus undercuts this dichotomy in the first rather obvious sense that Spiegelman draws on the comic as a mass cultural genre, but transforms it in a narrative saturated with modernist techniques of self-reflexivity, self-irony, ruptures in narrative time, and highly complex image sequencing and montaging. As comic, *Maus* resonates less of Disney than with a whole tradition of popular animal fables from Aesop to LaFontaine and even Kafka. At the same time, it evolved of course from an American comic book countertradition born in the 1960s that includes works such as *Krazy Cat, Fritz the Cat,* and others. At the same time, *Maus* remains different from the older tradition of the enlightening animal fable. If the animal fable (George Orwell's *Animal Farm* as a twentieth-century fictional example) had enlightenment as its purpose either through satire or moral instruction, *Maus* remains thoroughly ambiguous, if not opaque, regarding the possible success of such enlightenment. Rather than providing us with an enlightened moral or with a happy reconciliation between high and low, human and animal, trauma and memory, the aesthetic and emotional effect of *Maus* remains jarring throughout. This jarring, irritating effect on the reader results from a variety of pictorial and verbal strategies that have their common vanishing point in mimesis, both in its insidious and in its salutory aspects, which, as Adorno would have it, can never be entirely separated from each other.

Let me turn now to some of the dimensions of mimesis in this image-text. As is well-known, *Maus* as narrative is based on interviews Art Spiegelman conducted with his father Vladek, an Auschwitz survivor, in the 1970s. Spiegelman taped these interviews in Rego Park, Queens, in the house in which he grew up, and during a summer vacation in the Catskills. The subject of these interviews is the story of Spiegelman's parents' life in Poland in the years 1933 to 1944, but the telling of this traumatic past, as retold in the comic, is interrupted time and again by banal everyday events in the New York present. This crosscutting of past and present, by which the frame keeps intruding into the narrative, allows Spiegelman, as it were, to have it both ways: for Vladek, it seems to establish a safe distance between the two temporal levels; actually the tale of his past is visually framed by Spiegelman as if it were a movie projected by Vladek himself. As Vladek begins to tell his story, pedaling on his exercycle, he says proudly: "People always told me I looked just like Rudolph Valentino." (I:13) Behind him in the frame is a large poster of Rudolph Valentino's 1921 film *The Sheik* with the main actor as mouse holding a swooning lady in his arms, and the whole exercycle mechanism looks remotely like a movie projector with the spinning wheel resembling a film reel and Vladek as narrator beginning to project his story. But simultaneously this crosscutting of past and present points in a variety of ways to how this past holds the present captive independently of whether this knotting of past into present is being talked about or repressed. Thus one page earlier, Art who is sitting in the background and has just asked Vladek to tell him the story of his life in Poland before and during the war, is darkly framed within the frame by the arms and the exercycle's handlebar in the foreground. Vladek's arms, head, and shirt with rolled up sleeves are all striped, and the Auschwitz number tattooed into his left arm hovers ominously just above Art's head in the frame (I:12). Both the narrator (Art Spiegelman) and the reader see Vladek's everyday behavior permeated by his past experiences of persecution during the Nazi period. And then this first narrative framing is itself split in two. In addition to the narrative frame the interviews provide, there is yet another level of narrative time that shows the author Art Spiegelman, or rather the *Kunstfigur* Artie, during his work on the book in the years 1978 to 1991, years during which Vladek Spiegelman died and the first part of *Maus* became a great success, all of which is in turn incorporated into the narrative of the second volume. But the complexity of the narration is not just an aesthetic device employed for its own sake. It rather results from the desire of the second generation to learn about their parents' past of which they are always, willingly or not, already a part: it is a project of mimetically approximating historical and personal trauma in which the various temporal levels are knotted together in such a way that any talk about a past that refuses to pass away or that should not be permitted to pass, as discussed in the German *Historikerstreit* of the mid 1980s, seems beside the point.[13] The survivors' son's life stands in a mimetic affinity to his parents' trauma long before he ever embarks on his interviews with his father.[14] Therefore this mimetic relationship cannot be thought of simply as a rational and fully articulated working through.[15] There are dimensions to mimesis that lie outside linguistic communication and that are locked in silences, repressions, gestures, and habits—all produced by a past that weighs all the more heavily as it is not (yet) articulated. Mimesis in its physiological, somatic dimension is *Angleichung,* a becoming or making similar, a movement toward, never a reaching of a goal. It is not identity, nor can it be reduced to compassion or empathy. It rather requires of us to think identity and nonidentity together as nonidentical similitude and in unresolvable tension with each other.

    Maus performs precisely such a mimetic approximation. Spiegelman's initial impetus for conducting these interviews with his father came itself out of a traumatic experience: the suicide of his mother Anja in 1968, an event Spiegelman made into a four-page image-text originally published in 1973 in an obscure underground comic under the title "Prisoner of the Hell Planet." It is only in the latter half of the first part of *Maus* that Artie suddenly and unexpectedly comes across a copy of this earlier, now almost forgotten attempt to put part of his own life's story into the comics. *Maus* then reproduces the "Prisoner of the Hell Planet" in toto (I:100–103). These four pages, all framed in black like an obituary in German newspapers, intrude violently into the mouse narrative, breaking the frame in three significant ways: first, in this earlier work, the figures of Vladek and Artie mourning the death of Anja are drawn as humans, a fact that goes surprisingly unremarked by the mice Artie and Vladek as they are looking at these pages in the narrative of the later work. The identity of the nonidentical seems to be taken for granted in this porousness between human and animal realm. Second, the comic "Prisoner on the Hell Planet" opens with a family photo that shows ten-year-old Art in 1958 with his mother in summer vacation in the Catskills.[16] It is the first of altogether three family photos montaged into the comic, all of which function not in order to document, but in order to stress the unassimilability of traumatic memory.[17] Third, "Prisoner" articulates an extreme moment of unadulterated despair that disrupts the "normal" frame of the interviewing process, the questioning and answering, bickering and fighting between father and son. These pages give testimony of the emotional breakdown of both father and son at Anja's burial: in Art's case, it is overlaid by a kind of survivor guilt of the second degree, once removed from the original trauma of his parents. The memories of Auschwitz do not only claim Anja, they also envelop the son born years after the war. Thus Art draws himself throughout this episode in striped Auschwitz prisoner garb, which gives a surreal quality to these starkly executed, woodcutlike, grotesque images. In this moment of secondary Holocaust trauma Spiegelman performs a kind of spatial mimesis of death in the sense of Roger Caillois's work of the 1930s, which Adorno read and commented on critically in his correspondence with Benjamin.[18] Spiegelman performs a compulsive imaginary mimesis of Auschwitz as space of imprisonment and murder, a mimesis, however, in which the victim, the mother, becomes perpetrator while the real perpetrators have vanished. Thus at the end of this raw and paralyzing passage, Art, incarcerated behind imaginary bars, reproaches his mother of having committed the perfect crime: "You put me here . . . shorted all my circuits . . . cut my nerve endings . . . and crossed my wires! . . . / /You MURDERED me, Mommy, and you left me here to take the rap!!!" (I:103) The drawings are expressionist, the text crude though in a certain sense "authentic," but it is easy to see that Spiegelman's comic would have turned into disaster had he chosen the image and language mode of "Prisoner" for the later work. It could only have turned into psycho-comikitsch. Spiegelman did need a different, more estranging mode of narrative and figurative representation in order to overcome the paralyzing effects of a mimesis of memory-terror. He needed a pictorial strategy that would maintain the tension between the overwhelming reality of the remembered events and the tenuous, always elusive status of memory itself. As an insert in *Maus,* however, these pages function as a reminder about the representational difficulties of telling a Holocaust or post-Holocaust story in the form of the comic. But they also powerfully support Spiegelman's strategy to use animal imagery in the later, longer work. The choice of medium, the animal comic, is thus self-consciously enacted and justified in the narrative itself. Drawing the story of his parents and the Holocaust as an animal comic is the Odyssean cunning that allows Spiegelman to escape from the terror of memory—even "postmemory" in Marianne Hirsch's terms—while mimetically re-enacting it.

But the question lingers. What do we make of the linguistic and pictorial punning of Maus, Mauschwitz, and the Catskills in relation to mimesis? The decision to tell the story of Germans and Jews as a story of cats and mice as predators and prey should not be misread as a naturalization of history, as some have done. Spiegelman is not the Goldhagen of the comic book. After all, the comic does not pretend to be history. More serious might be another objection: Spiegelman's image strategies problematically reproduce the Nazi image of the Jew as vermin, as rodent, as mouse. But is it simply a mimicry of racist imagery? And even if mimicry, does mimicry of racism invariably imply its reproduction or can such mimicry itself open up a gap, a difference that depends on who performs the miming and how? Mimesis, after all, is based on similitude as making similar (*Angleichung* in Adorno's terminology), the production of "the same but not quite", as Homi Bhabha describes it in another context.[19] And *Angleichung* implies difference. Thus Spiegelman himself draws the reader's attention to his conscious mimetic adoption of this imagery. The very top of *Maus* I's copyright page features a Hitler quote: "The Jews are undoubtedly a race, but they are not human." And *Maus* II, right after the copyright page, begins with a motto taken from a Pommeranian newspaper article from the mid-1930s: "Mickey Mouse is the most miserable ideal ever revealed . . . Healthy emotions tell every independent young man and every honorable youth that the dirty and filth-covered vermin, the greatest bacteria carrier in the animal kingdom, cannot be the ideal type of animal. . . . Away with Jewish brutalization of the people! Down with Mickey Mouse! Wear the Swastika Cross!" *Maus* thus gives copyright where it is due: Adolf Hitler and the Nazis.

But that may still not be enough as an answer to the objection. More crucial is the way in which the mimesis of anti-Semitic imagery is handled. Here it would be enough to compare Spiegelman's work with the 1940 Nazi propaganda movie *The Eternal Jew*, which portrayed the Jewish world conspiracy as the invasive migration of plague-carrying herds of rodents who destroy everything in their path. Such a comparison makes it clear how Spiegelman's mimetic adoption of Nazi imagery actually succeeds in reversing its implications while simultaneously keeping us aware of the humiliation and degradation of that imagery's original intention. Instead of the literal representation of destructive vermin we see persecuted little animals drawn with a human body and wearing human clothes and with a highly abstracted, nonexpressive mouse physiognomy. "Maus" here means vulnerability, unalloyed suffering, victimization. As in the case of the "Prisoner of the Hell Planet," here, too, an earlier much more naturalistic version of the mouse drawings shows how far Spiegelman has come in his attempt to transform the anti-Semitic stereotype for his purposes by eliminating any all-too-naturalistic elements from his drawings.

Defenders of *Maus* have often justified the use of animal imagery as a necessary distancing device, a kind of Brechtian estrangement effect. Spiegelman's own justification is more complex: "First of all, I've never been through anything like that—knock on whatever is around to knock on—and it would be a counterfeit to try to pretend that the drawings are representations of something that's actually happening. I don't know exactly what a German looked like who was in a specific small town doing a specific thing. My notions are born of a few scores of photographs and a couple of movies. I'm bound to do something inauthentic. Also, I'm afraid that if I did it with people, it would be very corny. It would come out as some kind of odd plea for sympathy or 'Remember the Six Million,' and that wasn't my point exactly, either. To use these ciphers, the cats and mice, is actuallly a way to allow you past the cipher at the people who are experiencing it. So it's really a much more direct way of dealing with the material."[20] It is, in my terms, an estrangement effect in the service of mimetic approximation, and thus rather un-Brechtian, for at least in his theoretical reflections, Brecht would not allow for any mimetic impulse in reception. Spiegelman accepts that the past is visually not accessible through realistic representation: whatever strategy he might choose, it is bound to be "inauthentic." He also is aware of his generational positioning as someone who mainly knows of this past through media representations. Documentary *authenticity* of representation can therefore not be his goal, but *authentication* through the interviews with his father is. The use of mice and cats is thus not simply an avant-gardist distancing device in order to give the reader a fresh, critical, perhaps even "transgressive" view of the Holocaust intended to attack the various pieties and official memorializations that have covered it discursively. Of course, Spiegelman is very aware of the dangers of using Holocaust memory as screen memory for various political purposes in the present. His narrative and pictorial strategy is precisely devised to avoid that danger. It is actually a strategy of another kind of mimetic approximation: getting past the cipher at the people and their experience. But before getting past the cipher, Spiegelman has to put himself into that very system of ciphering: as Artie in the comic, he himself becomes mouse, imitates the physiognomic reduction of his parents by racist stereotype, the post-Auschwitz Jew still as mouse, even though now in the country of the dogs (America) rather than the cats. Paradoxically, we have here a mimetic approximation of the past that respects the *Bilderverbot* not despite, but rather because of its use of animal imagery, which tellingly avoids the representation of the human face. *Bilderverbot* and mimesis are no longer irreconcilable opposites, but enter into a complex relationship in which the image is precisely not mere mirroring, ideological duplication or partisan reproduction,[21] but where it approaches writing. This Adornean notion of image becoming script was first elaborated by Miriam Hansen and Gertrud Koch in their attempts to make Adorno pertinent for film theory.[22] But it works for Spiegelman's *Maus* as well. As its image track indeed becomes script, *Maus* acknowledges the inescapable inauthenticity of Holocaust representations in the "realistic" mode, but it achieves a new and unique form of authentication and effect on the reader precisely by way of its complex layering of historical facts, their oral retelling, and their transformation into image-text. Indeed, it is as animal comic that *Maus*, to quote a typically Adornean turn of phrase from the first chapter of *Dialectic of Enlightenment*, "preserves the legitimacy of the image [. . .] in the faithful pursuit of its prohibition."[23]

If this seems too strong a claim, consider the notion of image becoming script in *Maus* from another angle. Again, Spiegelman himself is a good witness for what is at stake: "I didn't want people to get too interested in the drawings. I wanted them to be there, but the story operates somewhere else. It operates somewhere between the words and the idea that's in the pictures and in the movement between the pictures, which is the essence of what happens in a comic. So by not focusing you too hard on these people you're forced back into your role as reader rather than looker."[24] And in a 1992 radio interview, he put it even more succinctly by saying that *Maus* is "a comic book driven by the word."[25]

I cannot hope to give a full sense of how the linguistic dimension of *Maus* drives the image sequences. A few comments will have to suffice. Central here is the rendering of Vladek's language taken from the taped interviews. The estranging visualization of the animal comic is counterpointed by documentary accuracy in the use of Vladek's language. The gestus of Vladek's speech, not easily forgotten by any reader with an open ear, is shaped by cadences, syntax, and intonations of his East European background. His English is suffused by the structures of Yiddish. Residues of a lost world are inscribed into the language of the survivor immigrant. It is this literally—rather than poetically or mystically—broken speech that carries the burden of authenticating that which is being remembered or narrated. On the other hand, Vladek himself is aware of the problematic nature of any Holocaust remembrance even in language when he says: "It's no more to speak." (II:113)

Spiegelman's complex arrangement of temporal levels finds its parallel in an equally complex differentiation of linguistic registers. Thus the inside narration about the years in Poland as told by Vladek are rendered in fluent English. A natural language gestus is required here because at that time Vladek would have spoken his national language, Polish. It is only logical that Vladek's broken speech only appears on the level of the frame story, the narrative time of the present. Past and present, clearly distinguished by the language track, are thus nevertheless suffused in the present itself in Vladek's broken English, which provides the linguistic marker of the insuperable distance that still separates Artie from Vladek's experiences and from his memories. Artie, after all, always speaks fluent English as his native language.

If Spiegelman's project is mimetic approximation not of the events themselves, but of the memories of his parents, and thus a construction of his own "postmemory" (Marianne Hirsch), then this mimesis is one that must remain fractured, frustrated, inhibited, incomplete. The pain of past trauma is repeated through narration in the present and attaches itself to the listener, to Artie as listener inside the text as well as to the reader who approaches the contents of Vladek's autobiographic tale through its effects on Artie. Artie as a *Kunstfigur*—the same but not quite the same as the author Art Spiegelman—thus becomes the medium in the text through which we ourselves become witnesses of his father's autobiographic narration. While this narration, gently and sometimes not so gently extracted from the survivor, aims at a kind of working through in language, it is a mimetic process that will never reach an end or come to completion, even if and when Vladek's tale catches up to the postwar period. And then there is always that other most painful obstacle to a full mimetic knowledge of the past. For the process of an *Angleichung ans Vergangene,* an assimilation to the past, is not only interrupted by the inevitable intrusion of everyday events during the time of the interviews; another even more significant gap opens up in the sense that only Vladek's memories are accessible to Artie. The memories of Artie's mother, whose suicide triggered Art Spiegelman's project in the first place, remain inaccessible not only because of her death, but because Vladek, in a fit of despair after her death, destroyed her diaries in which she had laid down her own memories of the years in

Poland and in Auschwitz. And just as Artie had accused his mother for murdering him, he now accuses his father for destroying the diaries: "God DAMN you! You . . . you murderer!" (I:159) Anja's silence thus is total. If it was Anja's suicide that generated Art Spiegelman's desire to gain self-understanding through mimetic approximation of his parents' story and of survivor guilt, then the discovery that the diaries have been burned points to the ultimate elusiveness of the whole enterprise. Artie's frustration about the destruction of the diaries only makes explicit that ultimate unbridgeable gap that pertains between Artie's cognitive desires and the memories of his parents. Indeed it marks the limits of mimetic approximation, but it marks them in a quite pragmatic way and without resorting to sublime new definitions of the sublime as the unpresentable within representation.

All of Spiegelman's strategies of narration thus maintain the insuperable tension within mimetic approximation between closeness and distance, affinity and difference. *Angleichung* is precisely not identification or simple compassion. Artie's listening to his father's story makes him understand how Vladek's whole habitus has been shaped by Auschwitz and the struggle for survival, while Vladek himself, caught in traumatic reenactments, may remain oblivious to that fact: rather than assuming continuity, Vladek's storytelling seems to assume a safe and neutralizing distance between the events of the past and his New York present. But his concrete behavior constantly proves the opposite. Artie, on the other hand, is always conscious that the borders between past and present are fluid, not only in his observation of his father, but in his self-observation as well. Mimetic approximation as a self-conscious project thus always couples closeness and distance, similitude and difference.

This dimension becomes most obvious in those passages in *Maus* II where Spiegelman draws himself drawing *Maus* (II:41ff.). The year is 1987; Vladek has been dead for five years; Art works on *Maus* II from the tapes which now have become archive; and *Maus* I has become a great commercial success. This chapter, entitled "Auschwitz (Time Flies)," demonstrates how beyond the multiply fractured layering of language and narrative time, the very pictoriality of the animal comic is significantly disrupted as well. We see Art in profile, sitting at his drawing table, but now drawn as a human figure wearing a mouse mask. It is as if the image track could no longer sustain itself, as if it collapsed under its own weight. Artie's mimicry reveals itself to be a sham. The mask reveals the limits of his project. The ruse doesn't work any longer. The task of representing time in Auschwitz itself, just begun in the preceding chapter, has reached a crisis point. This crisis in the creative process is tellingly connected with the commercial success of *Maus* I: the Holocaust as part of the culture industry. Crisis of representation and crisis of success throw the author into a depressive melancholy state in which he resists the marketing of his work (translations, film version, tv) through a fit of total regression. He avoids the annoying questions of the media sharks (questions such as: What is the message of your book? Why should younger Germans today feel guilty? How would you draw the Israelis? II:42) by literally shrinking in his chair from frame to frame until we see a small child screaming: "I want . . . I want . . . my Mommy!" (II:42) The pressures of historical memory are only intensified by Holocaust marketing, to the point where the artist refuses any further communication. The culture industry's obsession with the Holocaust almost succeeds in shutting down Spiegelman's quest. The desire for a regression to childhood, as represented in this sequence, however, is not only an attempt to cope with the consequences of commercial success and to avoid the media. This moment of extreme crisis, as close as any in the work to traumatic silence and refusal to speak, also anticipates something of the very ending of *Maus* II.

On the very last page of *Maus* II, as Vladek's story has caught up with his postwar reunification with Anja, ironically described by Vladek in Hollywood terms as a happy ending and visually rendered as the iris like fadeout at the end of silent films,[26] Artie is again put in the position of a child. In a case of mistaken identity resulting from a merging of past and present in his father's mind, Vladek addresses Artie as Richieu, Artie's own older little brother who did not survive the war, whose only remaining photo had always stared at him reproachfully during his childhood from the parents' bedroom wall, and to whom *Maus II* is dedicated. As Vladek asks Artie to turn off his tape recorder and turns over in his bed to go to sleep, he says to Artie: "I'm tired from talking, Richieu, and it's enough stories for now . . ." (II:136). This misrecognition of Artie as Richieu is highly ambiguous: it is as if the dead child had come alive again, but simultaneously the traumatic past proves its deadly grip over the present one last time. For these are the last words a dying Vladek addresses to Artie. This last frame of the comic is followed only by an image of a gravestone with Vladek's and Anja's names and dates inscribed and, at the very bottom of the page and below the gravestone, by the signature "art spiegelman 1978–1991," years that mark the long trajectory of Spiegelman's project of approaching an experience that ultimately remains beyond reach.

Much more could be said about Spiegelman's mimetic memory project, but I hope to have made the case that the Adornean category of mimesis can be made productive in a reading of Holocaust remembrance in such a way that the debate about the proper or correct Holocaust representation, while perhaps never irrelevant, can be bracketed and the criteria of judgment shifted. If mimetic approximation, drawing on a variety of knowledges (historical, autobiographic, testimonial, literary, museal), were to emerge as a key concern, then one could look at other Holocaust representations through this prism rather than trying to construct a Holocaust canon based on narrow aesthetic categories pitting the unrepresentable against aestheticization, or modernism against mass culture, memory against forgetting. This might open up a field of discussion more productive than the ritualistic incantations of Adorno regarding the culture industry or the barbarity of poetry after Auschwitz.

As a work by a member of the "second generation," *Maus* may indeed mark a shift in the ways in which the Holocaust and its remembrance are now represented. It is part of a body of newer, "secondary" attempts to commemorate the Holocaust while simultaneously incorporating the critique of representation and staying clear of official Holocaust memory and its rituals. I have tried to show how Spiegelman confronts the inauthenticity of representation within a mass cultural genre while at the same time telling an autobiographic story and achieving a powerful effect of authentication. Like many other works of film, sculpture, monuments, literature, theater, even architecture, Spiegelman rejects any metalanguage of symbolization and meaning, whether it be the official language of Holocaust memorials or the discourse that insists on thinking Auschwitz as the telos of modernity. The approach to Holocaust history is sought in an intensely personal, experiential dimension that finds expression in a whole variety of different media and genres. Prerequisite for any mimetic approximation (of the artist/reader/viewer) is the liberation from the rituals of mourning and of guilt. Thus it is not so much the threat of forgetting as the surfeit of memory[27] that is the problem addressed by such newer work. How to get past the official memorial culture? How to avoid the trappings of the culture industry while operating within it? How to represent that which one knows only through representations and from an ever-growing historical distance? All this requires new narrative and figurative strategies including irony, shock, black humor, even cynicism, much of it present in Spiegelman's work and constitutive of what I have called mimetic approximation. *Bilderverbot* is simply no longer an issue since it has itself become part of official strategies of symbolic memorializing. This very fact may mark the historical distance between Adorno, whose "after Auschwitz" chronotope with its insistence on the prohibition of images and the barbarism of culture has a definite apocalyptic ring to it, and these younger postmodernist writers and artists to whom the prohibition of images must appear like Holocaust theology. But if, on the other hand, Adorno's notion of mimesis can indeed help us understand such newer artistic practices and their effects in a broader frame, then there may be reasons to suspect that Adorno's rigorously modernist reflection itself blocked out representational possibilities inherent in that mimetic dimension. In its hybrid folding of a complex and multilayered narration into the mass cultural genre, Spiegelman's image-text makes a good case against a dogmatic privileging of modernist techniques of estrangement and negation, for it demonstrates how estrangement and affective mimesis are not mutually exclusive, but can actually reinforce each other.

Finally, there is a weaker, less apocalyptic reading of Adorno's "after Auschwitz" statements. Such a reading would emphasize Adorno's historical critique of that attempt to resurrect German culture after the catastrophe, that attempt to find redemption and consolation through classical cultural traditions—Lessing's *Nathan, der Weise* as proof of German "tolerance" of the Jews, Goethe's *Iphigenie* as proof of German classical humanism, German poetry, music, and so forth: "Healing through quotation"—as Klaus Scherpe has called it.[28] The spirit of such a critique of an official German post-Auschwitz culture is one that Adorno shares with the newer generation of artists in many countries today all of whom try to work against contemporary versions of official Holocaust culture the dimensions of which Adorno could not even have imagined yet during his lifetime. There is another sentence, less frequently quoted, but perhaps more pertinent today than the famous statement: "To write poetry after Auschwitz is barbaric." A sentence that continues to haunt all contemporary attempts to write the Holocaust: "Even the most extreme consciousness of doom threatens to degenerate into idle chatter."[29] Only works that avoid that danger will stand. But the strategies of how to avoid such degeneration into idle chatter in artistic representations cannot be written in stone.

Notes

1. Anson Rabinbach, 1997, *In the Shadow of Catastrophe: German Intellectuals between Apocalypse and Enlightenment* (Berkeley: University of California Press).

2. As is to be expected, the discussion of signification, hieroglyphs, language, and image is pre-Saussurean, pre-semiotic in the strict sense. It remains endebted to Benjamin on the one hand, and through Benjamin also to a nineteenth-century tradition of German language philosophy. But it is precisely the non-Saussurean nature of this thought that allows the notion of mimesis to emerge in powerful ways.

3. See Gertrud Koch, 1992, "Mimesis und Bilderverbot in Adorno's Ästhetik," *Die Einstellung ist die Einstellung* (Frankfurt am Main: Suhrkamp).

4. See Josef Früchtl, 1986, *Mimesis: Konstellation eines Zentralbegriffs bei Adorno* (Würzburg: Königshausen & Neumann); Karla L. Schultz, 1990, *Mimesis on the Move: Theodor W. Adorno's Concept of Imitation* (Bern: Peter Lang); Gunter Gebauer and Christoph Wulf, 1992, *Mimesis: Kultur, Kunst, Gesellschaft* (Reinbek: Rowohlt), esp. 374–422; Martin Jay, 1998, "Mimesis and Mimetology: Adorno and Lacoue-Labarthe," *Cultural Semantics* (Amherst: University of Massachusetts Press), 120–37.

5. Theodor W. Adorno, 1974, *Minima Moralia: Reflections from a Damaged Life,* trans. E.F.N. Jephcott (London: Verso), 154.

6. Theodor W. Adorno, 1983, Review of Roger Caillois, *La Mante religieuse, Zeitschrift für Sozialforschung* 7: 410–11. See also Adorno's letter to Benjamin of 22 September 1937 and Benjamin's response in his letter of 2 October 1937 in Henri Lonitz, ed., 1994, *Theodor W. Adorno—Walter Benjamin: Briefwechsel 1928–1940,* (Frankfurt am Main: Suhrkamp), 276–78, 286.

7. The literature on representing the Holocaust is by now legion. One of the richest and still influential collections of essays is Saul Friedlander, ed., 1992, *Probing the Limits of Representation: Nazism and the "Final Solution"* (Cambridge: Harvard University Press).

8. Art Spiegelman, 1986, *Maus I: A Survivor's Tale. My Father Bleeds History* (New York: Pantheon) and, 1991, *Maus II: A Survivor's Tale and Here My Troubles Began* (New York: Pantheon). Page references will be given in the text.
    The following publications were extremely helpful in preparing this essay. I acknowledge them summarily since my concern is a theoretical proposition rather than a new and differentiated reading of the text per se. Joseph Witek, 1989, *Comic Books as History* (Jackson und London); Andrea Liss, 1991, "Trespassing Through Shadows: History, Mourning, and Photography in Representations of Holocaust Memory," *Framework* 4, 1: 29–41; Marianne Hirsch, Winter 1992–1993, "Family Pictures: *Maus,* Mourning, and Post-Memory," *Discourse* 15, 2: 3–29; Miles Orvell, Spring 1992, "Writing Posthistorically. *Krazy Kat, Maus,* and the Contemporary Fiction Cartoon," *American Literary History* 4, 1: 110–28; Rick Iadonisi, Fall 1994, "Bleeding History and Owning His [Father's] Story: *Maus* and Collaborative Autobiography," *CEA Critic: An Official Journal of the College English Association* 57, 1: 41–55; Michael Rothberg, Winter 1994, "We Were Talking Jewish: Art Spiegelman's *Maus* as 'Holocaust' Production," *Contemporary Literature* 35, 4: 661–87; Edward A. Shannon, 1995, " 'It's No More to Speak:' Genre, the Insufficiency of Language, and the Improbability of Definition in Art Spiegelman's *Maus," The Mid-Atlantic Almanac* 4: 4–17; Alison Landsberg,

Spring/Summer 1997, "Toward a Radical Politics of Empathy," *New German Critique* 71: 63–86. And most recently Dominick LaCapra, 1998, "'Twas Night Before Christmas: Art Spiegelman's *Maus,*" in LaCapra, *History and Memory after Auschwitz* (Ithaca and London: Cornell University Press, 1998); James Young, "The Holocaust as Vicarious Past: Art Spiegelman's *Maus* and the Afterimages of History," *Critical Inquiry* 24, 3: 666–99.

9. For a discussion of the worst offenders see Michael Rothberg, Fall 1997, "After Adorno: Culture in the Wake of Catastrophe," *New German Critique* 72: 45–82.

10. The paradox is that when Adorno accused poetry after Auschwitz of barbarism, he deeply suspected the apologetic temptation of a poetic and aesthetic tradition, whereas much of the recent poststructuralist discourse of the sublime in relation to Holocaust representations does exactly what Adorno feared: it pulls the genocide into the realm of epistemology and aesthetics, instrumentalizing it for a late modernist aesthetic of non-representability. A very good documentation and discussion of notions of the sublime can be found in Christine Pries, ed., 1989, *Das Erhabene: Zwischen Grenzerfahrung und Größenwahn* (Weinheim: VCH Acta Humaniora).

11. Paradigmatically in Shoshana Felman's much discussed essay "The Return of the Voice: Claude Lanzmann's *Shoah,*" in Shoshana Felman and Dori Laub, 1992, *Testimony: Crises of Witnessing in Literature, Psychoanalysis, and History* (New York: Routledge), 204–283. For a convincing critique of Felman's work see Dominick LaCapra, 1994, *Representing the Holocaust: History, Theory, Trauma* (Ithaca and London: Cornell University Press) as well as ibid., *History and Memory.* The latter volume also contains a well-documented essay on Spiegelman's *Maus* that includes a critical discussion of much of the literature on this work.

12. This argument has been made very forcefully and persuasively in Miriam Hansen, Winter 1996, "*Schindler's List* Is Not *Shoah:* The Second Commandment, Popular Modernism, and Public Memory," *Critical Inquiry* 22: 292–312. For the earlier debate on the TV series *Holocaust,* a similar argument can be found in Andreas Huyssen, 1986, "The Politics of Identification: *Holocaust* and West German Drama," in *After the Great Divide: Modernism, Mass Culture, Postmodernism* (Bloomington: Indiana University Press), 94–114.

13. These were central topoi in the German debate about Holocaust memory. See the special issue on the *Historikerstreit, New German Critique* 44 (Spring/Summer 1988) as well as Charles S. Maier, 1988, *The Unmasterable Past: History, Holocaust, and German National Identity* (Cambridge, Mass.: Harvard University Press).

14. Cf. the two-page prologue initiating volume I dated Rego Park, New York City 1958 when Art is only ten years old or the photo of his dead brother Richieu that over-shadowed his childhood, but is later used at the beginning of volume II to dedicate this part of the work to Richieu and to Nadja, Art Spiegelman's daughter.

15. The category of working through has been most thoroughly explored for this context by LaCapra, *Representing the Holocaust.* LaCapra bases his approach on Freud, and he acknowledges that there cannot be a rigorous and strict separation between acting out and working through for trauma victims. While I feel certain affinities to LaCapra's general approach, I prefer not to engage the psychoanalytic vocabulary. While the psychoanalytic approach is certainly pertinent to the analysis of survivor trauma, it does

have serious limitations when it comes to artistic representations of the Holocaust and their effect on public memory. The notion of "mimetic approximation," which I try to develop through my reading of *Maus*, tries to account for that difference.

16. Significantly, the prologue to volume I that shows Artie roller-skating and hurting himself is also dated 1958, and when just a few pages and many years later Artie asks his father to tell his life's story, he is looking at a picture of his mother saying: "I want to hear it. Start with Mom . . ." (I:12)

17. With this insight and so much more, my reading of *Maus* is endebted to Marianne Hirsch's incisive essay "Family Pictures: *Maus*, Mourning, and Post-Memory." Reprinted in ibid., 1997, *Family Frames: Photography, Narrative, and Postmemory* (Cambridge, Mass.: Harvard University Press). Cf. also ibid., 1999, "Projected Memory: Holocaust Photographs in Personal and Public Fantasy," in *Acts of Memory: Cultural Recall in the Present*, ed. Mieke Bal, Jonathan Crewe, Leo Spitzer, (Hanover and London: University Press of New England), 3–23.

18. See Lonitz, *Adorno–Benjamin*.

19. See Homi K. Bhabha, 1994, "Of Mimicry and Man: The Ambivalence of Colonial Discourse," *The Location of Culture* (New York and London: Routledge), 86.

20. Interview conducted by Gary Groth, 1988 "Art Spiegelman and Françoise Mouly," in *The New Comics*, ed. Gary Groth and Robert Fiore (New York: Berkley), 190–91.

21. These are the terms Adorno uses in the first chapter of the *Dialectic* where they discuss the irremediable splitting of linguistic sign and image. Horkheimer and Adorno, *Dialectic*, 17–18.

22. Miriam Hansen, Spring–Summer 1992, "Mass Culture as Hieroglyphic Writing: Adorno, Derrida, Kracauer," *New German Critique* 56: 43–75. Koch, "Mimesis und Bilderverbot," 16–29.

23. Horkheimer and Adorno, *Dialectic*, 24. In German: "Gerettet wird das Recht des Bildes in der treuen Durchführung seines Verbots." Theodor W. Adorno, *Gesammelte Schriften* 3 (Frankfurt am Main: Suhrkamp, 1983), 40.

24. Quoted in Joshua Brown's review of *Maus I* in 1988, *Oral History Review* 16: 103–104.

25. "A Conversation with Art Spiegelman. With John Hockenberry," *Talk of the Nation*. National Public Radio, 20 February 1992.

26. An observation I owe to Gertrud Koch.

27. The term is Charles S. Maier's. See his essay, 1992, "A Surfeit of Memory? Reflections on History, Melancholy, and Denial," *History and Memory*, 5: 136–51.

28. Klaus R. Scherpe, ed., 1982, *In Deutschland unterwegs 1945–1948* (Stuttgart: Reclam).

29. Theodor W. Adorno, 1981, *Prisms*, trans. Samuel and Shierry Weber (Cambridge, MIT), 34.

6

Why Do the Sirens Sing?: Figuring the Feminine in *Dialectic of Enlightenment**

Nancy Love

[Music] is a language, but a language without concepts.
—Adorno, *Sociology of Music*

The constellation of the existing and nonexisting is the utopic figure of art.
—Adorno, *Aesthetic Theory*

The fiftieth anniversary of *Dialectic of Enlightenment* offered an occasion for rethinking the relationship between the first generation of critical theorists and contemporary feminist theory. Adorno's and Horkheimer's totalizing critique of the culture industry coupled with a seemingly archaic concept of reconciliation has obscured their shared concern with identity and difference.[1] The tendency to separate Adorno's aesthetic theory, including his sociology of music, from the critique of enlightenment further isolates them from other theories of resistance. Rolf Wiggershaus's monumental history of the Frankfurt School exemplifies this interpretive approach.[2] He identifies Adorno's and Horkheimer's two major themes in *Dialectic of Enlightenment* as: (1) the rationalization of western civilization, and (2) the relationship between humanity and nature. A "self-destructive Enlightenment," he argues, involves a "false emancipation from nature." Wiggershaus also reads the text on two levels: it includes a manifest dialectic of "reason-as-domination" and subterranean histories of "genuine Enlightenment," exemplified by aspects of Judaism and liberalism. Genuine enlightenment, Wiggershaus argues, involves resisting and softening the demands of reason-as-domination. He quotes Horkheimer: "We have to understand this development [the irresistible process of enlightenment] and we can understand it only if there is something in us which does not submit to it. . . ."[3]

Women and music are strangely absent from Wiggershaus's interpretation of *Dialectic of Enlightenment*, despite their obvious presence in the text.[4] In this article, I argue that women and music figure prominently in both of the themes and at both of the levels that Wiggershaus discusses. Patriarchy, as well as capitalism, represents

*My thanks to Thomas Dumm, Andreas Huyssen, Caren Irr, Jeffrey Nealon, Morton Schoolman, Stephen Schneck, and several anonymous reviewers for their helpful comments. This chapter is based on an article that originally appeared in *Theory & Event* 3, 1.

reason-as-domination and "woman"—like music—evokes animal/spiritual powers that civilization has not yet obliterated. However, "woman's" connection with genuine enlightenment is figured, not stated; it appears in the constellations of the text rather than its arguments. The association of "woman" with music is not, then, a simple—gender/ed—analogy. Music, especially song, instead expresses the difference(s) within and between humanity and nature.

I focus here on the presence of difference in the first excursus, "Odysseus or Myth and Enlightenment." By interpreting it as a constellation I hope to encourage similar analyses of other sections. My approach to *Dialectic of Enlightenment* is at odds with James Schmidt's claim that "to at least some degree the book is fragmentary by default rather than design."[5] Schmidt has serious doubts about readings of a book that was originally entitled and later subtitled, *Philosophical Fragments,* as a comprehensive history of the dialectic of enlightenment. I make a more modest claim: the first excursus, at least, is a carefully constructed "philosophy in fragments" that remains relevant for feminist critiques of essentialized identities.

Configuring the Feminine (and Other Identities)

Adorno and Horkheimer construct constellations in order to avoid producing texts in which criticism reverts to affirmation. Following Shane Phelan, I approach constellations first as a kind of riddle. They are "compact clusters of elements"; solving one "lights it up suddenly and momentarily." Her example is "What's black and white and re(a)d all over?"—to which children respond with delight, "the newspaper!" "The delight," she says, "comes from the shifting organization of conceptual elements that makes sudden sense out of an apparent conundrum."[6] Like riddles, constellations are constructed and, like riddles, they reveal neither deep structure nor grand theory, but "small, ordinary details of life."[7] Benjamin's metaphor—"ideas are to objects as constellations are to stars"—captures the relational aspect of constellations. But it is too abstract, too formal, too eternal, and ultimately, too Platonic for Adorno. His constellations instead "illuminate a particular historical configuration of elements."[8]

According to Phelan, this difference may reflect Jewish influences on Adorno's thought.[9] For Adorno, constellations resemble the Hebrew notion of configurations. In *Hebrew Thought Compared with Greek,* Thorlief Bohman argues that configurations should not be seen as the boundaries, outlines—or forms—of objects. Instead, they illustrate the inseparability of form and content, including language and matter, in concrete experience. In Hebrew, Bohman claims, there is no word that can be properly translated as "thing." Instead, the same term, *dabhar* or *davar,* means "'matter,' but also 'thing' and word," that is, "'the word in spoken form,'" as "'efficacious fact.'"[10] What is discussed cannot be separated—or abstracted—from our discussions of it. In the same way, Phelan claims, "the constellation is not formed by, cannot be described by, its outline or shape, its boundaries, but by its contents, by its elements and their relations."[11] It exists, it has reality, in and through our relations with it.

Adorno's configurations are, I suggest, best understood through a musical metaphor or in aural/vocal rather than visual terms. According to Adorno, music (and art, more generally) conveys meaning through action or motion. He writes: "This immanent character of being as an act establishes the similarity of all artworks, like that of natural beauty, to music, a similarity once evoked by the term muse. Under patient contemplation artworks begin to move."[12] This musical comparison suggests that Adorno's configurations are closer to compositions than constellations. Indeed, Adorno might recast Benjamin's analogy as follows: ideas are to objects as music is to sounds. The parallel to Marx is worth mentioning here. In *The German Ideology,* Marx writes, "from the start the 'spirit' is afflicted with the curse of being 'burdened' with matter, which here makes its appearance in the form of agitated layers of air, sounds, in short, of language."[13] Earlier Marx used music as an example of the relationship between subjective capacities and objective creations, one that countered the alienated objectivity of abstract thought.[14] For Adorno, configurations as compositions convey a being that exceeds knowing, or the nonidentity of subjects and objects. By invoking nonconceptuality, Adorno gives "voice" to "things" and suggests an embodied alternative to reason-as-domination.

The configuration of the first excursus is best approached through the question: "Why do the Sirens sing?"[15] First, why Sirens? As an illustration of how "woman" is figured in *Dialectic of Enlightenment,* the Sirens pose an obvious problem: they are not women but sea nymphs. They represent the allure of the "feminine" as animal/spiritual powers, or spirit in nature. As an/other—a female—Muse, they also represent a threat to narrative control. Lillian Eileen Doherty discusses similarities between Homer's sirens and the muses: They are divine females, their activity is song, they exist outside settled, i.e., male, territory, they address men individually, they claim full knowledge, and their truths and benefits are uncertain. Narrative, not sexuality, is their real power, and their song is cut short not only to exclude them, but also to evoke a totality that cannot be represented.[16]

Odysseus is Adorno's and Horkheimer's "prototype of the bourgeois individual," who individuates himself in opposition to the Sirens, by renouncing them.[17] He listens to their song while bound to the mast of his ship: "Odysseus recognizes the archaic superior power of the song even when, as a technically enlightened man, he has himself bound."[18] Adorno says, "The identical 'I' of Homer could be seen as primarily the result of a mastery of nature carried out within the individual. This new self trembles within its thing-self—a body—once the heart has been rebuked."[19] Odysseus' individuality is a grammatical fiction, a universal subject: the pronoun "I." His identity of self and word—a pronoun—masters or, at least, denies the body and with it his humanity.

By way of contrast, the Sirens might represent the association of femininity with negativity. So understood, they would illuminate the gender content of the categories—no-identity and counter-identity—from which Fred Dallmayr differentiates Adorno's nonidentity. Dallmayr defines no-identity as radical negativity, a "negation of every identity," an "erasure of identity," a "leap into . . ." nothingness. He asks, "But . . . how could anyone persist in this realm (or pretend to '*be* nothing')? Moreover, how could one honor the other's nonidentity in the absence of a recognition of the distinctness and differential relation of self and other?"[20] No identity is no being or, at best, pre-being, a not-yet presence. Here the Sirens suggest regression, a return to the repressed infantile experience of the archaic Mother.[21] Counter identity is distinguishable from no identity as "radical otherness or externality," "a leap beyond the *cogito* into a quasi-Kantian 'thing-in-itself'—a kind of objective counteridentity beyond the pale of cognition and interpretation"[22] As this noumenal realm, the Sirens reaffirm a masculine symbolic order with its dualisms—object/woman/nature versus subject/man/culture—almost intact. Adorno and Horkheimer insist that "Man as ruler denies woman the honor of individualization. Socially, the individual is an example of the species, a representative of her sex; and therefore male logic sees her wholly as standing for nature." The gendered content of no identity and counteridentity is a patriarchal construct, and they add: "Woman as an alleged natural being is a product of history which denatures her."[23] With this, they suggest that interpretations of femininity as negativity stop short. They deny not only the Sirens/"woman" but also Odysseus/"man" specific identities.

Adorno and Horkheimer note that Homer says nothing about the Sirens' fate after Odysseus passes by them. If "woman" survives only as the "other" of representation-as-domination, then *Dialectic of Enlightenment* merely replicates the reified gender relations of patriarchal capitalism. Some feminist scholars argue that Adorno's and Horkheimer's critique of "mass" culture juxtaposes the "autonomous, resistant [male] individual" to the "deafening, blinding, and numbing powers of the [feminized] mass."[24] This opposition between masculine reason and feminine "other" typifies an outer-directed patriarchal culture. Outer-directed cultures would control super/natural powers by denying and/or excluding women's inner experience and men's internal feminine and thereby preclude relational processes of self-definition for women and men.[25] According to Andrew Hewitt, Adorno and Horkheimer include women in *Dialectic of Enlightenment* only by excluding them. Women represent the possibility of exclusion as escape or "the tenuous utopian margins of the feminine." "As a *cipher* for the specific, woman is once again denied specificity."[26] Homer's women are already part of the patriarchal symbolic order. Penelope and Circe are prototypes of the wife and the whore, the binary of capitalist reproduction. Unlike the Sirens, who evoke an "other" beyond male logic, they represent women's place within it or her experience of domination. As patriarch, Odysseus also plays his gendered role. In the famous recognition scene, Penelope tests her husband's knowledge of their immovable marriage bed, built around an olive tree, symbol of sex and property. Odysseus passes the test, and Adorno and Horkheimer describe him as "the prototypical bourgeois—the with-it hobbyist."[27] Odysseus has found his way home, escaped from primal forces to the civilized world. Hewitt concludes, "Central to the analysis is not the experience of the woman [or man], but the patriarchal construct within which it becomes potentially subversive."[28]

I agree that Adorno and Horkheimer do not represent specific women (or men) in *Dialectic of Enlightenment*, but not that they are excluded. As sea nymphs, the Sirens represent something else; their songs express an/other—a body—before gender.[29] The text figures this nonidentity of individuals—male and female—with themselves and each other. Fred Dallmayr's description of nonidentity distinguishes it from no- and counteridentity, and fits the notion of configurations. He says, "the turn to nonidentity—as performed by Adorno—heralds not a retreat into indifferent vacuity but instead the encounter and contestation of distinct or differentiated identities, an encounter marked by a reciprocal transgression of self-enclosure."[30]

After Odysseus sails by the Sirens, Adorno and Horkheimer proceed to associate his nonidentical selfhood with his ambiguous name. Its spoken ambiguity—Odysseus is heard as (is homonymous with) "(O)u-deis," which means "no-body"—symbolizes the split between myth and word, and signifies the natural, physical remainder. In his encounter with the Cyclops, Odysseus survives as a subject by denying his bodily identity and imitating the amorphous. "He acknowledges himself to himself by denying himself under the name Nobody; he saves his life by losing himself."[31] His name—"No-body"—is a proper noun that is not an identical subject.

In Homer's *Odyssey*, No-body ultimately fails to disguise himself. How Odysseus is recognized—and by whom—is quite revealing. When he returns home, his old dog, Argos, knows his "voice" and, Eurykleia, his childhood nurse recognizes his "body, voice, and limbs," especially his scarred leg.[32] Penelope, the "good" wife, is not beyond testing Odysseus, not beyond the dominant, cold and calculating rationality. But Homer includes "others"—animal and female—who recognize him. About them Adorno and Horkheimer are strangely silent, a point to which I will return. They instead warn their readers that Odysseus' self-assertion as self-denial carries its own risks: "He who calls himself Nobody for his own sake and manipulates approximation to the state of nature as a means of mastering nature, falls victim to *hubris*."[33] Yet through body and sound, Argos and Eurykleia can still recognize Odysseus' non-identity with himself and others.

Bodies, Songs, and Specificity

With this, I turn to the second aspect of my question: Why do the sirens *sing?* Early in the text, Adorno and Horkheimer say, "For science, the word is a sign: as sound, image and word proper it is distributed among the different arts, and is not permitted to reconstitute itself by their addition. . . ."[34] The ensuing text emphasizes word and image over sound, as that into which sound is translated. Yet the authors insist that "the Sirens have their own quality" and that "since Odysseus' successful-unsuccessful encounter with the Sirens all songs have been affected and Western music as a whole suffers from the contradiction of the song in civilization. . . ."[35] I would suggest that through "the contradiction of the song" we can better understand the internal—as well as the external—relations between genders in *Dialectic of Enlightenment*, and hear the presence of specific women—and men—in the text.

Elsewhere, Adorno discusses sound as distinct from (though part of) music. In mass culture, music thrives only as ideology. Like "woman," music is now commodified, fetishized, objectified. Music-as-ideology whether through driving rhythms, familiar melodies, or both, has become a "mass language," a source of unconscious compliance. As "an autonomous, artistic language," music barely survives.[36] Mort Schoolman writes, music-as-art survives only in its form that evokes the spirit. Schoenberg's twelve-tone system illustrates this identity, which is not one, or a nonidentity. In the infinite, indeterminate variations of twelve-tone, everything is different, nothing is finished—paradoxically, within the ultimate rationalized system.[37] The masses can no longer hear music-as-art because of the regression of listening: their ears, like those of Odysseus' oarsmen, are stopped. Adorno insists this is not their fault, belying accusations of elitism: "The blame would not rest on the masses but on the society that has made masses of them."[38]

Only the bound Odysseus hears the Sirens' song, and he cries out. His cry and their song resound, and reveal specific human identities that words and images cannot convey. In *Dialectic of Enlightenment,* Adorno and Horkheimer need to write without concepts, and they do so by reinvoking sound—as (an)other between and within. I have written elsewhere about the differences between aural/vocal and visual imagery. Vision is a limited sense: it marks differences with hard boundaries; it fixes subjects and objects in space/time; it comes from an established standpoint; it separates seer and seen, since humans can only look outward through their own eyes. Sound is a more interactive or relational sense. It includes two subjects, a speaker and a listener; it involves a process, a movement across space in time; it is felt internally and heard externally, conveying permeable boundaries.[39]

John Shepherd characterizes the differences between musical and linguistic sound: ". . . the inherent characteristics of the *sounds* of language can have no necessary relationship to the inherent characteristics of objects as *visually* defined."[40] In other words, spoken language involves an arbitrary, cross-sensory relationship between vision and voice. With written language, even this relationship among sounds, subjects, and objects becomes obsolete. Sound ceases to be a "mediating presence," "a way of touching at a distance," and is replaced by the "safety, permanence, immutability, silence, and isolation" of vision.[41] In contrast, music—particularly song—involves a "homology" between "the sound of evocation and reference." According to Shepherd, music is a "discursive practice" that "can evoke and refer to, give life to, our corporeal existence."[42] From this perspective, musicologists' focus on the formal properties of music and the related distinction between "art" and "pop" music, are attempts to control the corporeality of music by translating it into visual representations.

There are disturbing parallels here between the process of rationalizing music and objectifying women. Shepherd claims that music and women occupy similar social spaces: "Music [like women] reaffirms the flux and concreteness of the social world at the same time that, through its categorization and packaging, it denies them."[43] As moving sound, music is more than a narrative told with lyrics and melodies. It relates more than the story of an object as a subject located in space and time. According to Jennifer Rycenga, "Music is life, because it inherently involves motion, perception, reflection, separation/connection, materiality, process, relationality—it is, at root, *involved.*"[44] This claim does not essentialize music or, by analogy, women, "because to say that the *essence* of something/someone is *a verb,* a motion, change/growth, is the opposite of the reification process that is essentialism."[45]

In Adorno's and Horkheimer's narrative, Odysseus' and the Sirens' specific identities remain in their sounds, in their cries and their songs. As "Woman," the Sirens re-present those whose bodies are unnamed but whose songs still flow forth. As "Man," Odysseus re-presents those whose bodies are inhuman and who still cry out. Yet, about their sounds Adorno's and Horkheimer's narrative is necessarily, respectfully, reticent. Reticence in narrative, they say, "is the sudden break, the transformation of what is reported into something long past, by means of which the semblance of freedom glimmers that since then civilization has not wholly succeeded in putting out."[46]

If I may be permitted a long parenthetical quotation, Adorno laments that music too now occupies "the space of possible chatter." He continues,

> It is hard to avoid observing how widespread is the faith that really unsolved and insoluble problems are solved by discussion; this explains why people flock to the ubiquitous panel sessions on culture. Akin to it is a fact which theoreticians should be the last to ignore: to many so-called culture carriers, talking and reading about music seems to be more important than music itself. Such malformations are symptoms of an ideologically normal condition, to wit, of music not being perceived as itself at all, in its truth and untruth, but solely as an indefinite and uncontrollable dispensation from dealing with truth and untruth.[47]

Adorno and Horkheimer recognize this paradox and they resist reading/speaking/writing about music. Instead, *Dialectic of Enlightenment* configures the truth and untruth of music and, with it, specific identities. Unlike sounds, words and images cannot represent male subjects or female objects, or the "other"—masculine or feminine—within us all. Language cannot translate Man/Woman into men and women, each masculine and feminine. The human, the specific, the remainder, only appears in the composition—or configuration—of their reticent narrative.

In Homer's *Odyssey*, Odysseus' encounter with the Sirens is framed to control their subversive power. Circe warns Odysseus before he passes the Sirens—a prospective account—and Odysseus provides a retrospective account of following Circe's advice. *Dialectic of Enlightenment* changes the frame. Now, Circe's warning and the story of Odysseus' unnamed body (or no-body) follow his encounter with the Sirens' song. That encounter is preceded by the story of the Hebrew God's unspoken name. In the passage between, Odysseus passes by (or bypasses?) the Sirens. Present absence hears absent presence—body and spirit momentarily resound. This new frame creates an opening in the text that was missing from Homer's original. How, readers might ask, did Odysseus know of impending danger? How did he know to lash himself to the mast, to stop his oarsmen's ears, to renounce the Sirens' song?[48] But this Odysseus—the "prototypical bourgeois individual"—already knows Homer's narrative. At least, he thinks he does. In *Dialectic of Enlightenment*, Adorno and Horkheimer give the *Odyssey* not only a new frame, but also a new meaning. Their story of Odysseus' homecoming excludes not only Argos and Eurykleia, but also Odysseus' songs of victory.[49] By reframing Homer's narrative, they omit Odysseus as the triumphant narrator of his deeds. Instead, there is laughter and, again, names: "[The] duality of laughter is akin to that of the name, and perhaps names are no more than frozen laughter. . . . Laughter is marked by the guilt of subjectivity, but in the suspension of law which it indicates it also points beyond thralldom. It is a promise of the way home."[50]

According to Adorno and Horkheimer, only a self-conscious narrative can convey the horrors of civilization, which include the "cold distancing of narration" itself. Adorno's painfully acute awareness of those horrors precluded any possibility of collective resistance. He writes, "For the intellectual, inviolable isolation is now the only way of showing some measure of solidarity."[51] Yet he also acknowledges that "the notion of culture as ideology" can itself become ideological by denying the persistence of honest communication.[52] Perhaps he and Horkheimer would agree with Doherty's statement, "I would be a Circe with a difference: one who puts the once and future reader on guard against the Siren songs of the Homeric text itself."[53] Through image and word, they remind us of sound, and sound—crying, laughing, and especially, singing—reminds us of a suffering humanity, differently embodied together.

Notes

1. References to Adorno appear (along with Derrida, Kristeva, Lacan, and Lyotard) in feminist discussions of identity and nonidentity politics, but they are seldom developed. For examples, see: Drucilla Cornell and Adam Thurschwell, 1987, "Feminism, Negativity, Intersubjectivity" in *Feminism and Critique,* ed. Seyla Benhabib and Drucilla Cornell (Minneapolis: University of Minnesota Press), 142–61; Rey Chow, 1992, "Postmodern Automatons" in *Feminists Theorize the Political,* ed. Judith Butler and Joan W. Scott (New York: Routledge), 101–117; Shane Phelan, "Interpretation and Domination: Adorno & the Habermas-Lyotard Debate," *Polity* 25, 4: 597–616.

2. Rolf Wiggershaus, 1994, *The Frankfurt School: Its History, Theories, and Political Significance* (Cambridge, Mass.: MIT Press). In his introduction to Adorno's (1997) *Aesthetic Theory,* ([Minneapolis: University of Minnesota Press], xx), Robert Hullot-Kentor writes: "After Adorno's death, interest in his writings soon dissipated, and today . . . he is regarded mainly as a historical curiosity and more likely to be diminished than admired. For over a decade, the most thorough, widely read, and esteemed history of his work—Rolf Wiggershaus's *The Frankfurt School*—dismisses him as a bitter, hyperemotional complainer, monotonously prejudiced in his views, irresponsibly protean in his thought, and unable to formulate testable hypotheses." Hullot-Kentor suggests that Wiggershaus's book "embodied a generation's rejection of Adorno echoed in dozens of similar works." (*Aesthetic Theory,* xx).

3. Ibid., 332.

4. I also have in mind articles, such as Jay Bernstein, 1999, "Adorno on Disenchantment: The Scepticism of Enlightened Reason" in *German Philosophy Since Kant,* ed. Anthony O'Hear (New York: Cambridge University Press), 305–328; Fred Dallmayr, February

1997, "The Politics of Nonidentity: Adorno, Postmodernism—And Edward Said," *Political Theory* 25, 1: 33–56; Christopher Rocco, February, 1994, "Between Modernity and Postmodernity: Reading *Dialectic of Enlightenment* Against the Grain," *Political Theory* 22, 1: 71–97; and Morton Schoolman, February 1997, "Toward a Politics of Darkness: Individuality and Politics in Adorno's Aesthetics," *Political Theory* 25, 1: 57–92. I also include my earlier (Spring/Summer 1987), "Epistemology and Exchange: Marx, Nietzsche, and Critical Theory," *New German Critique* 41: 71–95. Recent exceptions include: Robert Witkin, March 2000, "Why Did Adorno 'Hate' Jazz? *Sociological Theory* 18, 1: 145–169; Barbara Engh, 1994, "Adorno and the Sirens: Telephono-graphic Bodies" in *Embodied Voices, Representing Female Vocality in Western Culture*, ed. Leslie C. Dunn and Nancy A. Jones (New York: Cambridge University Press), 120–35.

5.   "Language, Mythology, and Enlightenment: Historical Notes on Horkheimer and Adorno's *Dialectic of Enlightenment*," Proceedings of the 1997 American Political Science Association Convention, 6.

6.   Phelan, "Interpretation and Domination," 602.

7.   Ibid., 603.

8.   Ibid., 604.

9.   Hullot-Kentor notes that Adorno's "original" German was a "Jewish language, too." He interprets Adorno's return to German as "an impulse to pick up the severed threads of what was not fascist in Germany's past and the value of which, however alloyed, he never doubted" (*Aesthetic Theory,* xix).

10.   Thorlief Bohman, 1961, *Hebrew Thought Compared with Greek* (Philadelphia: The Westminster Press), 156.

11.   Phelan, "Interpretation and Domination," 606.

12.   Adorno, *Aesthetic Theory,* 79.

13.   Karl Marx, 1977, *The German Ideology,* ed. C. J. Arthur (New York: International Publishers), 50–51. For an excellent discussion of Jewish influences on Marx's thought, see Dennis Fischman, 1991, *Political Discourse in Exile: Karl Marx and the Jewish Question* (Amherst, Mass.: University of Massachusetts Press).

14.   Marx writes, "only music can awaken the musical sense in man and the most beautiful music has *no* sense for the unmusical ear, because my object can only be the confirmation of one of my essential powers. . . ." (1975, *Economic and Philosophical Manuscripts* in *Early Writings,* trans. Rodney Livingstone and Gregor Benton (New York: Random House), 353. Drawing a parallel between Adorno and Marx, Terry Eagleton describes this alternative as a "materialist sublime." Both philosophers challenge the split between practical and aesthetic experience manifest in philosophical idealism and romantic sentimentalism. Terry Eagleton, 1990, *The Ideology of the Aesthetic* (London: Basil Blackwell), ch. 3 and 8.

15.   According to Wiggershaus, Adorno and Horkheimer had different purposes in *Dialectic of Enlightenment:* "Adorno's project involved examining the configurations of myth and modernism, nature and history, old and new, immutability and difference, decay and recovery, and proving that the ideas presented in his two monographs on the dialectic of musical progress . . . were of relevance to social theory and the philosophy of history.

For Horkheimer, on the other hand, it was a question of placing his critiques of positivism and bourgeois anthropology in a broader context and pursuing the implications of his critique of the repression of religious problems and his acceptance of Benjamin's critique of merciless progress" (Horkheimer and Adorno, 326). My interpretation of the first excursus is closer to Adorno's purposes, given its emphasis on music, nature, and sound. For a discussion of the tensions between Adorno's and Horkheimer's voices in the text, see: Rocco, "Between Modernity and Postmdoernity," 89–90.

16.   Lillian Eileen Doherty, 1995, "Sirens, Muses, and Female Narrators in the *Odyssey*" in *The Distaff Side: Representing the Female in Homer's Odyssey*, ed. Beth Cohen (New York: Oxford University Press), 85–92.

17.   Max Horkheimer and Theodor W. Adorno, 1972, *Dialectic of Enlightenment*, trans. John Cumming (New York: Seabury Press), 43.

18.   Ibid., 59.

19.   Ibid., 48.

20.   Dallmayr, "Politics," 34.

21.   As Cornell and Thurswell point out, she is not an actual mother ("Feminism, Negativity, Intersubjectivity").

22.   Dallmayr, 34.

23.   Adorno and Horkheimer, *Dialectic of Enlightenment*, 111.

24.   Chow, "Postmodern Automatons," 109.

25.   Peggy Reeves Sanday, 1981, *Female Power and Male Dominance: On the Origins of Sexual Equality* (Cambridge, MA: Harvard University Press).

26.   Andrew Hewitt, "A Feminine Dialectic of Enlightenment," 169–70. Hewitt shifts back and forth between references to "woman" and "women." This slippage suggests the difficulty of inclusion by exclusion. Cornell and Thurschwell warn of the dangers of essentialism lurking behind such interpretive moves.

27.   Adorno and Horkheimer, *Dialectic of Enlightenment*, 74.

28.   Hewitt, "Feminine Dialectic," 163.

29.   I am indebted to Engh for this point ("Adorno and the Sirens," 134). Engh interprets Adorno's distinction between "woman's" singing voice, which cannot be recorded, and "man's," which can (because his self/voice are identical) through the Frankfurt School's critique of modern subjectivity.

30.   Dallmayr, "Politics," 35.

31.   Adorno and Horkheimer, *Dialectic of Enlightenment*, 60.

32.   Homer, 1963, *Odyssey*, trans. Robert Fitzgerald (Garden City, N.Y.: Anchor Books), Book 19.

33.   Adorno and Horkheimer, *Dialectic of Enlightenment*, 68.

34.   Ibid., 17.

35.   Ibid., 59–60.

36.   Theodor W. Adorno, 1976, *Introduction to the Sociology of Music*, trans. E. B. Ashton (New York: The Seabury Press), 40.

37.   Schoolman, "Toward a Politics of Darkness," 85–90.

38.   Adorno, *Sociology of Music*, 48.

39.   Nancy S. Love, Fall 1991, "Politics and Voice(s): An Empowerment/Knowledge Regime," *differences: A Journal of Feminist Cultural Studies* 3, 1: 96.

40. John Shepherd, "Difference and Power in Music" in *Musicology and Difference: Gender and Sexuality in Music Scholarship,* ed. Ruth Solie (Berkeley: University of California Press, 1993), 54.

41. Ibid.

42. Ibid., 50.

43. Ibid., 60.

44. Jennifer Rycenga, 1994, "Lesbian Compositional Process, One Lover-Composer's Perspective" in *Queering the Pitch: The New Gay and Lesbian Musicology,* ed. Philip Brett, et al. (New York: Routledge), 284.

45. *Ibid,* n51.

46. Adorno and Horkheimer, *Dialectic of Enlightenment,* 79.

47. Adorno, *Sociology of Music,* 42.

48. I am indebted to Andreas Huyssen for raising this question.

49. For a discussion of the "kleos" or victory song, see: Sheila Murnaghan, 1987, *Disguise and Recognition in the Odyssey* (Princeton, N.J.: Princeton University Press), ch. 5.

50. Adorno and Horkheimer, *Dialectic of Enlightenment,* 77–78.

51. Theodor Adorno, 1974, *Minima Moralia, Reflections from Damaged Life,* trans. E. F. N. Jephcott (New York: New Left Books), 26.

52. Adorno writes, "Since . . . free and honest exchange is itself a lie, to deny it is at the same time to speak for truth: in face of the lie of the commodity world, even the lie that denounces it becomes a corrective. That culture so far has failed is no justification for furthering its failure. . . ." (ibid., 45). Adorno has been criticized for failing to provide a "third way" between mass culture and autonomous art, for refusing to explore the "aesthetic possibilities involved in collaborative activist and community art" (Amy Mullin, [Spring 2000], "Adorno, Art Theory and Feminist Practice," *Philosophy Today:* 16–30). In light of this passage, it seems important to note that Mullin does not discuss Adorno's remarks on musical sound, the artistic medium that arguably provides the best vehicle for collective action. On this point, see my: "'Singing for Our Lives': Women's Music and Communicative Democracy," Proceedings of the 2000 American Political Science Association Convention.

53. Lillian Eileen Doherty, 1995, *Siren Songs: Gender, Audiences, and Narrators in the Odyssey* (Ann Arbor: University of Michigan Press), 193.

7

On Doing the Adorno Two-Step

Evan Watkins

I'm assuming familiarity with the main lines of cultural studies arguments about Adorno's work on so-called mass culture, in particular the negative critiques of his elitism, his nostalgias, his masculine productionist bias, and so on. Perhaps especially during the eighties such critiques were often foregrounded within cultural studies. Adorno was made a primary example of how theorizing forged within the conditions of a broadly modernist aesthetic could go so badly wrong when attention turned instead to those cultural products that, unlike most high culture artifacts, intersected at so many levels with the complex of everyday behavior. At the same time, however, Adorno also functioned as the sign of a guilty (or at least wary) consciousness at work. For even in the midst of challenges to Adorno's analysis it was clear that the rush to discover multiple and even resistant uses of mass culture nevertheless couldn't afford to ignore entirely larger structures of ideological direction. After all neither "multiple" nor "resistant" could have much meaning unless at least certain things could be made clear about the content of that dominant direction. Thus while Adorno's premises may have seemed suspect, he could still be invoked as a suitable stand-in for an awareness that any uncritical celebration of populist alternative political currents was at best premature.

I'm assuming familiarity with these lines of argument that at the risk of a perhaps melodramatic simplification resolved themselves into a kind of Adorno two-step within cultural studies: wrong in substance, but still relevant as a reminder of the dangers of uncritical engagement. One result of this two-step was that as the conditions for doing cultural studies work changed significantly throughout the nineties Adorno was kept hanging around, often with the emphasis beginning to fall on the second rather than the first step. With the advantage of hindsight on the decades of double-focused invocations of Adorno as a metonymic presence, however, it should be possible to sketch quickly a remapping of that two-step into a series of possibilities articulated around what seems to me a central claim of Adorno's arguments. For while Adorno often seemed focused on specific cultural forms, that focus was always informed by a necessity for understanding the connections between multiple developments of mass culture and the organization of work, of labor. In other words, at some level across all his writings on mass culture, he was insistent on the relation between a capitalist wage labor organization and the specific features of mass culture that drew his attention.

Sometimes he seemed to understand that relation by means of almost a homology between cultural production and factory production. At other times, his arguments involve the relatively more complicated claim that mass culture forms must offer some kind of symbolic, compensatory promise for the psychological burdens imposed by days spent in the routinized, deskilled, repetitive operations of work. Crudely, what you get from mass culture is at least the illusion of what you're missing in your workday. Yet whichever direction his argument took, and however complicated further in elaboration, it seems to me the key to understanding mass culture for Adorno lies in the ensemble of relations that links it to the organization of labor. Taking this premise at least provisionally, without stretching the point by lengthy analysis, then allows a kind of remapping that potentially might lead to a more useful focus of attention on Adorno's work in the present.

It's possible of course to contest his assertion of connection, whether as imputed homologies of production or as involving a compensatory cultural symbolics. I think a great many earlier cultural studies' critiques of Adorno followed this path by default as it were, as they chose virtually to ignore Adorno's own insistence on connections and proceeded instead to develop direct counterclaims to Adorno's readings of specific cultural texts or to focus attention on complexities of response that escape Adorno's strictures. The emphasis, in other words, fell on a series of challenges to Adorno's conceptualization of so-called mass culture, with little attempt to rethink his assertions of connection. But given so much recent attention to the interpenetration of formerly distinct spheres of "culture" and "the economy," surely it's worth a return to the specifics of Adorno's own analysis as at least a point of departure for what might well prove to be a necessarily more nuanced and careful understanding of this assumed trajectory.

In my earlier, if brief, encounter with Adorno in *Throwaways,* my 1993 book, I tried to take a second and very different line of inquiry. Rather than directly challenging his readings of mass culture forms, I suggested we recognize his attempt at making connections, but start at the other end. The understanding of labor organization that underwrote his claims about mass culture, I argued, was seriously incomplete. What looks from the outside like routinized, deskilled, and endlessly monotonous labor doesn't necessarily seem like that when you're doing it. Much of the labor to which he refers requires an often prodigious concentration of attention on detail, and very often serious physical injury can result from letting your mind wander should you be silly enough to feel you're getting bored. Further, it seemed clear to me, to borrow the metonymies of the times, that what Rosie the riveter experienced at work was probably not quite identical to what Steve the steelworker experienced, nor was it likely the relation between "work" and "home" was the same.

Finally, Adorno's model of labor, I argued, was basically this assembly line of durable goods production, and even at the height of so-called Fordist industrial production, such labor by no means characterized most of the work of the labor force. It's a model that ignores the already burgeoning sector of multiple kinds of service work, let alone the intricacies of household labor, child rearing, black market work, piecework, and so on. Thus my point was that surely if you wanted to insist on powerful connections between the organization of labor and the realm of mass culture forms, as Adorno did, you'd have to complicate considerably not just your understanding of what people might do with the culture they consumed, but more to the point, your understanding of the conditions of work most people faced in their lives.

A third and still different line of inquiry might begin instead with an apparent paradox: if Adorno was at all correct about mass culture when he was writing, then he has to be completely wrong about any so-called mass culture in the present. Or to put it a little less elliptically, if you buy Adorno's premise that the specificities of mass culture forms exist in some intimate connection to the organization of labor, then almost nothing Adorno had to say about mass culture would hold true today, because the organization of work has changed so dramatically. In this line of inquiry, then, Adorno's texts exist as primarily a historical point of reference rather than either a source of potential insight to be mined for its relevance today, or a still-menacing example of the mistakes to be made by elitist theorists assuming a top down imposition of ideological values through so-called mass culture. One can if one wants look to Adorno for at least a roughly accurate picture of the early decades of the century, but with almost the whole work of understanding current circumstances still ahead of us.

Arguably each of these possibilities holds some promise for cultural studies work on Adorno that goes beyond that familiar two-step of past decades. And there are of course other possibilities, including most obviously an effort that begins with some radical reinterpretation of Adorno's thinking altogether. In the remainder of this essay, however, I want to pursue a line of inquiry that begins instead with what appears on the face of it as a rather surprising confirmation and extension of Adorno's understanding of determinate linkages between work and so-called mass culture. Surprising because of all things it comes from within the very midst of relatively high-level policy decisions about the direction and content of current attempts at reforming educational training programs for work skills.

The end of the eighties and the beginning of the nineties marked a period of intense concern about the preparation of an American workforce to meet the requirements of the economy in the twenty-first century. The dramatic title of the report from the Commission on the Skills of the American Workforce released in 1990, *America's Choice: High Skills or Low Wages!*, emphasized the urgency of initiating new training programs. And two years earlier, the National Alliance of Business had issued *Shaping Tomorrow's Workforce,* whose conclusions seemed remarkably congruent with the commission's findings. In 1990 as well, then Secretary of Labor Elizabeth Dole authorized a commission to establish new standards for work skills that resulted in the development of what is now familiarly referred to as the SCANS guidelines, the Secretary's Commission for Achieving Necessary Skills.

In the wake of these reports, a great many further studies were initiated, dealing with specific aspects of the process of reforming vocational training. In the context of thinking about Adorno, I want to instance in particular a passage from the introduction by the editors, Lauren Reznick and Stephen Wirt, to one of these studies, entitled *Linking School and Work: Roles for Standards and Assessment* (San Francisco: Jossey-Bass, 1996), that included essays by several of the luminaries who had served on Dole's 1990 commission. Thus as might be expected, the passage is full of a familiar urgency about educational reform, retraining workers, planning an educational system that will meet the needs of the twenty-first century, and so on. But of course there's no need to reform education unless you think something is wrong with it, and in the context of Adorno, again, it's worth reading carefully between the propaganda lines for what the authors seem to think is wrong with currently existing programs of vocational training: "For the first time since the industrial revolution, the demands being made on the educational system from the perspectives of economic productivity, of democratic citizenship, and of personal fulfillment are convergent. Today's high-performance workplace calls for essentially the same kind of person that Horace Mann and John Dewey sought: someone able to analyze a situation, make reasoned judgments, communicate well, engage with others and reason through differences of opinion, and intelligently employ the complex tools and technologies that can liberate or enslave according to use. What is more, the new workplace calls for people who can learn new skills and knowledge as conditions change—lifetime learners, in short. This is, as a result, a moment of extraordinary opportunity in which business, labor, and educational leaders can set a new, common course in which preparation for work and preparation for civic and personal life need no longer be in competition" (*Linking School and Work,* 10).

It shouldn't be difficult to anticipate any number of reasons why I've adduced this particular passage in the context of thinking about Adorno. Much of what the authors suggest about vocational education in the immediate past, as geared to molding the ideal industrial worker, also reads as a fair gloss on Adorno's own frequent comments on the routinized, deskilled, monotonous labor of industrial production. Of course the terms of critique are not Adorno's. Nevertheless, the chatter of reference to figures like John Dewey and Horace Mann serves in this passage to foreground a perception of serious deficiency not just in vocational education, but also in the whole organization of industrial labor. Neither the training nor the work itself was conducive to the education of informed, responsible, democratic citizens. Indeed, the authors go so far as to suggest that a latent contradiction existed between these democratic ideals and the realities of large-scale industrial production.

It's perhaps more significant, however, to watch what happens to the complex of ways that for Adorno characterized the symbolic promises mass culture forms made available to compensate workers for the routine boredom and disarticulated activities of their workdays. In the passage I quoted, "personal satisfaction," for example, no longer appears as a kind of endlessly deferred symbolic promise available from immersion in a world of popular music and film. It appears as a direct result of the conditions of postindustrial labor, something each of us can expect to experience in the very process of our everyday work. Likewise, the promise of wholeness, of integration, of felt connection among one's multiple activities appears as a result of work that is not only satisfying personally, but also translates seamlessly into both the qualities of a larger civic responsibility and the outcomes of a productive economic system. Finally, that most tantalizing and elusive promise of mass culture as Adorno saw it, the possibility of individual autonomy and agency expressed in a freedom of choice, appears in this passage as precisely the most valued characteristic of postindustrial workers capable of negotiating the flattened management hierarchies, diverse lifestyles and cultures, and individual performance-tuned reward systems of contemporary transnational firms. In short, more than an assertion of connection between mass culture and the organization of work, the passage limns the contours of a symbolic identity: what according to Adorno at least mass culture in the past could only promise, postindustrial work today can deliver.

Of course such descriptions of postindustrial work can seem like a kind of fairy tale, if grim enough for anyone whose so-called postindustrial labor involves data entry or working in a day-care center or scrambling across any of countless temp jobs. That is, it should be clear enough that the description owes relatively little to a close study of labor conditions for a great many, and the grand narrative of transition from industrial to a postindustrial economy functions more like an ur-myth of some phantasmal paradisial promise than a carefully considered history. What interests me immediately, however, is the migration of value adjectives: from a context that for Adorno marked the terms of mass culture and mass culture consumption, to a context where instead these adjectives function to invest conditions of work with an enormous range of cultural affect and symbolic identities, and to underwrite an elaborate imaginary of political decision making around issues of educational reform for job training. This migration from one context to another makes it important not only to recognize that the description of postindustrial labor is illusory, but also to ask what it succeeds in focusing for attention.

One obvious effect is to background a whole complex of value assumptions about labor in favor of another and quite different complex. "Personal satisfaction," again, no longer seems to result from a contemplation of the finished product or a job well done, but rather to derive from engagement with the processes of work itself. What in the past might well have appeared as an arduous, unpleasant, and perhaps even dangerous daily round of activity that at best afforded a kind of emotional payoff on completion now reappears as itself a desirable, even pleasureful activity. To extend the putative symbolic identity still further, like the process of shopping, the cessation of activity can induce a certain all too familiar emptiness, a sense that the "product"—like the purchased good—if not exactly an afterthought nevertheless is hardly commensurate with the intensities that had gone into the process.

At the same time, however, since the referent for this symbolic identity can hardly be found in a close description of actual processes of so-called postindustrial labor, then it seems important to inquire into its sources. For there is a specific history of vocational educational programs that stands behind the passage from the Reznick and Wirt volume. That is, their figure of the postindustrial worker is neither conjured out of the blue nor cynically fabricated to function merely as the lure of false promises. Beginning in the early seventies with the career education movement, vocational training in the schools began to change significantly.

Through the fifties and sixties, vocational education tracks in the secondary school system were still largely organized around the assumptions articulated most clearly by Charles Prosser in a series of texts culminating in *Vocational Education in a Democracy*, published in 1925. For not only had Prosser helped lay the foundation for that notorious division between an "academic" education for the few and a vocational education for the rest. Perhaps more important, the summary "theorems" he advanced in that 1925 book made it clear that he regarded work as imposing a double horizon of necessity to which voc ed students had to accommodate themselves. Students had to learn to scale down their expectations and values to fit the actual labor market slots most likely available to them for future employment. And they had to assimilate, as "habit," both the mental and physical motions associated with specific occupations. Certainly by the early sixties, however, these organizing assumptions were under considerable pressure from a kind of general cultural pedagogy of rising expectations from work and career that among other things increasingly emphasized the desirability of a college degree as a ticket to a rewarding career. As a result, it became more and more difficult to enforce a recognition of the labor market as imposing parameters of necessity on student expectations. Nevertheless, secondary school tracking mechanisms continued to sharply divide "college prep" from "vocational" paths, leaving teachers and counselors with the unenviable task of relentlessly having to "cool out" the expectations of "low achievers."

The career education movement in contrast laid the groundwork for a process of educational preparation where students could be encouraged to regard the working world as instead a realm of freedom where one examined the array of possible options and chose what best accommodated one's desires. Work in other words would no longer be "work" if by that one meant a realm of necessity to which, in Prosser's view at least, one must learn to accommodate oneself in the process of vocational training. In effect, within the terms of vocational training it became possible to regard the labor market as in certain respects remarkably similar to the consumer market of goods and services, as no less a realm of individual freedom and choice.

One didn't of course "choose" a career in quite the same way or on the same terms as a refrigerator or television. Nevertheless, as the idea of career choice and planning became more and more a part of the everyday curriculum of vocational tracks no less than the theorizing of educational preparation and high-level policy discussions, the centrality of individual choice (and not incidentally, the emergence of numerous studies about the psychology of career choice and motivation) identified a dramatic break from Prosser's emphasis on accommodation to the grim necessity of labor organization. In very simple and schematic terms, the career education movement marked the visible emergence of vocational training as integral to a middle-class world of expectations rather than as part of the process Prosser had envisioned of preparing a working class for an industrial economy. As a result, the labor market, again, seemed to take on something of the same dynamics as the process of consumption, where here too freedom of choice became the linking point of articulation between individual desires and, in this case, desirable career outcomes.

The broadly class terms in which I've identified the beginnings of this shift in the conditions of vocational training have a special relevance to another strand of the interwoven history behind the Reznick and Wirt statement I've quoted earlier. By the mid-nineties it was clear that one primary liberal response to the Reagan years was going to involve a crescendo of anxiety about a "disappearing" middle class in the United States. Economists like Frederick Strobel and Wallace Peterson, for example, could point to the rollback of the welfare state with its guarantees of government services. At the end of the decade, in *The Coming Class War and How to Avoid It: Rebuilding the American Middle Class,* they, like a number of others, were beginning to worry what seemed the very real possibility of a "class war" within a society increasingly polarized into haves and have-nots.

Still in mid-decade, however, the optimism so evident in the Reznick and Wirt argument had its source in the hope that the emergent conditions of postindustrial labor would lay the grounds for a new and inclusive middle-class formation organized around the democratizing of the workplace. Thus the emphasis on individual career choice (in effect the consumption of work) that had appeared within the programs of the career education movement could be made to function within this much larger political vision through the equation that drives the argument in the passage I quoted earlier: "For the first time since the industrial revolution, the demands being made on the educational system from the perspectives of economic productivity, of democratic citizenship, and of personal fulfillment are convergent." The economically productive worker is also the good citizen is also the satisfied person, the person whose consumption of work has fulfilled the conditions of personal desire.

I've sketched a complicated historical process of vocational education change very quickly here, in order to inform my initial point of departure in the recognition of how the integration of a dynamics of personal choice and consumer desire with conceptions of work and labor organization surely identifies a familiar Adorno territory. In one sense to be sure I've enlarged the scope of Adorno's inquiry into so-called mass culture forms to include a focus on the conditions of educational preparation for work. Yet it should be equally obvious that I've done so by remaining true to Adorno's insistence on determinate connections between mass culture consumption and the organization of labor. And needless to say, the class terms in which I've framed my quick sketch are hardly foreign to Adorno's analysis.

It's been the fate of Adorno and Gramsci to occupy distinctly contrasting positions within the long trajectory of cultural studies work over the last few decades. While Adorno as I suggested initially has been a figure in an ambivalent two-step that brings him into view often only to dismiss his conclusions, for better or worse Gramsci has been heroized as a founding presence. There were to be sure a great many factors at play in this respective positioning. Yet arguably, whatever the complex of factors involved, the payoff pitch has centered in on their privileged objects of textual study and perhaps even more significantly on what seems on the face of it to be the vastly different attitudes they brought to their study—a division still often marked by the values stitched into Gramsci's preferred adjectival "popular" vs. Adorno's "mass." It's worth remembering at this late date in the trajectory of cultural studies, however, that both Adorno and Gramsci in their different ways ultimately fixed their attention on the means for—and the reasons for—understanding complex social processes of transformation. For both, the interactions of texts and audiences were an avenue into this larger inquiry rather than an end in itself.

Admittedly Adorno is not often clear about the complex mediations between mass culture forms and the routines of everyday work. Nor is there any reason to assume those mediations as they exist in current conditions would become clearer simply by reinterpreting Adorno. Yet the visibility of vocational education reform in the larger context of continual "crisis" and change across the entire field of education seems to me to offer itself as an enormously significant ensemble of relations within which to pick up the threads of an Adornian analysis and continue his inquiry within the specifics of our circumstances. That is, the immediate issue is hardly the terms of judgment about Adorno, but rather what seems to me a necessity to reopen for inquiry the questions that framed Adorno's critique. For however one might feel that Adorno's assumptions often make his conclusions suspect, the extension of a consumer dynamics from so-called mass culture to the educational process of preparation for work significantly alters the stakes of understanding. Indeed, since the events of 11 September Adorno's logic seems perhaps one of the few available analytics that can grasp how "being at war" now imposes an imperative to consume rather than to ration on behalf of the nation. Likewise, if again paradoxically, scarcity now exists in the conditions for finding a job rather than in the labor power to be harnessed for a war effort.

As the many recent alarm calls about the "vocationalizing" of the university suggest, it's finally become obvious that the relations between school and work are undergoing rapid change "in" the university as well as "out there" somewhere. The reaction to this awareness, however, has all too often taken the form of a defense of textual studies that in university disciplines like English especially has then more and more come to resemble just another unfortunate version of a cultural "saving remnant," out to preserve at least some always diminishing territory from the tides of vocationalizing. Already the "return to literature" advocated by a number of university scholars, for example, has made a "passionate" language of loving texts a kind of litmus test for inclusion in the discipline. And that's of course a long familiar move by threatened fractions of a middle class: faced with the possibility of economic decline and the diminishment of social prestige, mobilize your cultural capital against it.

As a result, however, the potential thus exists for a rather different and to my mind even more debilitating version of that Adorno two-step with which I began. For in this version, Adorno's ostensibly modernist aesthetic presuppositions, so far from being the sign of a hopelessly elitist theorist at work, seem available instead to put into play as one more resource against the "reduction" of all education to the task of job preparation and the demands of the market. The second shoe can then comfortably fall into the illusion that these efforts on behalf of textual studies still somehow add up to a continuation of Adorno's "radical" critique of the whole social order of advanced capitalism. Of course in this form an Adorno two-step would have the advantage of appearing a coordinated dance rather than the ambivalent hopping around between approach and retreat of earlier cultural studies work. But it's also like tap dancing faster and faster in a smaller and smaller space. Because among other things it leaves out practically everything of importance in Adorno that might help us to understand and challenge the social processes of transformation at work in our present.

8

Maxima Immoralia?:
Speed and Slowness in Adorno*

Jeffrey T. Nealon

Prelude

If the Frankfurt School seems "dated" to many contemporary theorists, it may have something to do with the style of Frankfurt School analyses—often caricatured as heavy, labored, highly abstract, and humorless. The Frankfurt School seems slow, lumbering, a bit clumsy even. Adorno's monograph on the "irrationality" of the *LA Times* astrology column is perhaps paradigmatic here: bringing a sophisticated and ultra-serious brand of ideology critique to bear on astrology is a little like using a bazooka on an anthill. Really, shouldn't there be more levity in such an analysis? And does Adorno seriously think he's discovered something here? Isn't virtually any reader of astrology columns striken by the suspicion that "the stars seem to be in complete agreement with the established ways of life and with the habits and institutions circumscribed by our age" (Adorno, *Stars,* 59)? Can a 100-page exposé on the sinister ideology of the fortune cookie be far behind?

Difficult contemporary questions are raised by Adorno's seemingly high-handed style of cultural engagement: Does treating cultural texts so laboriously—so slowly and didactically—offer any relevant tools to intervene in the fast-world of late, later, or just-in-time capitalism? How, if at all, can the seeming slownesses of Adorno's work be adapted to confront the speeds of contemporary culture? In taking up these questions here, I want to suggest that there's an other Adorno lurking beside his finger-wagging, stony persona. I argue that it's precisely in close attention to and (re)deployment of Adorno's style that one might find a more affirmative—dare I say speedy—Adorno at work, especially in *Minima Moralia.*

My Dogma Ran Over My Karma

It is so clear that inversion or chiasmus is the dominant trope of Adorno's thinking that it scarcely seems worth mentioning—especially in *Minima Moralia,* where it's prominently on display from the very beginning. The title itself is an inversion of Aristotle's Magna Moralia or "Great Ethics"—though we should note a meta-

---

*A version of this essay appeared in the online journal *Theory & Event* 4, 3. Throughout, all Adorno references are to *Minima Moralia,* unless otherwise attributed.

inversion here at the very beginning, insofar as Aristotle's ethics (based as it is on everyday exchanges like friendship, household matters, urbanity, and commerce) is itself already an inversion of an even "greater" (that is, more metaphysical) Platonic ethics. As we open *Minima Moralia,* the inversions continue in the text's first sentence, where Adorno famously characterizes his work as a "melancholy science," in chiasmic contradistinction to Nietzsche's "joyful science" (again, itself already an inversion of idealist metaphysics). From the book's epigraph (Kürnberger's "Life is not alive") to *Minima Moralia's* most famous sentence, "the whole is false" (50) (an inversion of Hegel's dialectical dictum that only the whole is true), chiasmic reversal is all over *Minima Moralia.*[1]

It's hard not to recognize this, I suppose. But the more thorny question is, What's the upshot of Adorno's chiasms? Clearly, Adorno's is a highly performative discourse—the "form" of his thought can hardly be separated from its "content"— and it seems obvious that the interruptive and open-ended quality of chiasmus lends itself very well to a thinking dedicated to demonstrating that the whole is false: the chiasmus frustrates any kind of gathering into a unity—even the impossible unity that Hegel posits.[2] In *Minima Moralia,* it seems that the reader is meant to confront contradiction qua contradiction—on the sentence level as well as the social level.

Indeed, if the bumper sticker or the advertising slogan is ideology writ small— the keenest statement of what Adorno calls "organized tautology" (66)—then the work of ideology critique would almost have to include a kind of negative or critical moment—a chiasmic slowness that interrupts the smooth movement of tautological self-reassurance. If, as Adorno writes, the culture industry "expels from movements all hesitation" (19), then chiasmus is clearly one way of reintroducing (at the level of form and content) an ethical hesitation into the otherwise too-swift movement to a conclusion. If "the splinter in your eye is the best magnifying glass" (50), then the chiasmic fragments of *Minima Moralia* would seem to be best understood as little splintering machines, magnifying contradictions by slowing thought down, and deforming closure. And through his interruptive inversions, it seems that Adorno hopes actually to enact (rather than merely describe) his "minor ethics"; through a slowing down and breaking of ideological tautology, *Minima Moralia* hopes to "to teach the norm to fear its own perversity" (97).

Confronting the chiasmic slowdowns of Adorno's thought, one might be forced to realize, "Damn! My karma is my dogma." Or, as Adorno puts it, "relativists are the real . . . absolutists" (128).

Slower Traffic Keep Right

Okay, this makes a certain sense of Adorno's odd "method" in *Minima Moralia,* and makes him more recognizable within a series of postmodern family resemblances: this method of chiasmic interruption was, for example, the coin of the realm for American deconstruction;[3] and certainly any Lacanian would recognize these kinds of chiasmic moves, where the rock of the real is finally shown to be contradiction itself.[4] Or one might see Adorno's method as a kind of ideology critique writ small—an open-ended "minor" critique of cultural ideologies, in contradistinction to the "major" determinist critiques of the economic base.[5]

But Adorno, like a chiasmic inversion of your drunk uncle Teddy at Thanksgiving dinner, will quickly make you reconsider those postmodern family resemblances. For example, on the deconstructive move of returning rights to the nonprivileged term within an opposition, Adorno's discourse retorts: "In the end, glorification of splendid underdogs is nothing other than glorification of the splendid system that makes them so" (28). About psychoanalysis, Adorno likewise has very little kind to say: it's the complete suturing of the social to bourgeois subjective ideology—it's the karma that slows down to give your dogma a ride—and "he who calls it by name will be told gloatingly by psycho-analysis that it is just his Oedipus complex" (63). In fact, even the general project of slowing thought down to reveal its ideological contradictions seems to come under Adornian fire: "Serenity is becoming," he writes, "the same lie that purposive haste already is" (99). Indeed, Adorno will go as far as to say that irony and ideology critique are literally impossible, insofar as both presuppose some chimeric notion of the real and some fiction of aesthetic or political distance: "the difference between ideology and reality has disappeared" (211).

So if the chiasmic reversals of the melancholy science aren't attempts to highlight exclusion (not about the "underdog"); if they're not attempts to return a slowness or deliberation to thinking; if they're not exactly ideology critique either, then exactly what are they? If, as Adorno writes, his aphorisms are meant to be active—if they "are all intended to mark out points of attack or to furnish models for a future exertion of thought" (18)—why would he want to depend so heavily on the slowness of a "melancholy" science? One usually doesn't think of an ass-kicking melancholia: the Irish wake, at least as I've experienced it, hardly seems "to furnish models for a future exertion of thought," and "Danny Boy" is hardly the kind of rousing protest song that might offer "points of attack." So what exactly is the point of this melancholic slowing down?[6]

Speedball

Of course, *Minima Moralia* is not all slowness, chiasm, and slogan. Although not many people write about this, one of the things that always strikes me about Adorno is the ranting quality of his prose—the way it moves from the slowness of the chiasmic slogan to the speed of the seemingly uncontrolled rant. Take, for example, Section I #38 of *Minima Moralia*, "Invitation to the dance." The section is named after Carl Maria von Weber's piece, often touted as the first modern "dance music." For Adorno, we can only assume that this section is not going to be sweetness and light, named as it is after a music that serves as precursor to the commodified dance music that he rails against elsewhere.

Not oddly, then, this section takes up what Adorno calls "the capacity for pleasure" and its supposed cultural liberation by psychoanalysis. The screed against the commodification of pleasure is recognizably Adornian (it is in fact the sort of thing that cultural studies scholars complain about all the time in Adorno), but as you read it note (at least initially) how it's very much not a melancholy lament that works by aphoristic "slowness." Though it does begin with a slogan:

> Prescribed happiness looks exactly what it is; to have a part in it, the neurotic thus made happy must forfeit the last vestige of reason left to him by repression and regression; and to oblige the analyst, [he must] display indiscriminate enthusiasm for the trashy film, the expensive but bad meal in the French restaurant, the serious drink and the love-making taken like medicine as "sex." Schiller's dictum that "Life's good, in spite of all," papier-mâché from the start, has become idiocy now that it is blown into the same trumpet as omnipresent advertising, with psychoanalysis, despite its better possibilities, adding its fuel to the flames. As people have altogether too few inhibitions and not too many, without being a whit the healthier for it, a cathartic method with a standard other than successful adaptation and economic success would have to aim at bringing people to a consciousness of unhappiness both general and—inseparable from it—personal, and at depriving them of the illusory gratifications by which the abominable order keeps a second hold on life inside them, as if it did not already have them firmly enough in its power from outside . . . The admonitions to be happy, voiced in concert by the scientifically epicurean sanatorium-director and the highly strung propaganda chiefs of the entertainment industry, have about them the fury of the father berating his children for not rushing joyously downstairs when he comes home irritable from the office. It is part of the mechanism of domination to forbid recognition of the suffering it produces, and there is a straight line between the gospel of happiness and the construction of extermination camps so far off in Poland that each of our countrymen can convince himself that he cannot hear the screams of pain. (62–63)

This is vintage Adorno, but not a vintage that gets the same critical attention as the chiasmic, "slow" Adorno. There is, of course, a kind of chiasm at work here: the discourse of commodified happiness is the discourse of the Holocaust. But if this particular "fast" or ranting Adorno gets any critical attention at all, it is generally the stuff that gets him painted as a snob or a prude: critics of Adorno often say something like "I take the point about the Holocaust—I'm down with that—but, hey, let's not be so hasty in dismissing French restaurants and sex."

Supposedly, Adorno doesn't understand pleasure—this is, after all, the guy who said that "fun is a medicinal bath" (*Dialectic,* 140). In order to argue this position against Adorno, however, one has to ignore the immense pleasure evident on the surface of this screed. It's like a Lenny Bruce routine: it's cranky and obsessive enough to be hilarious, even while it's deadly serious. It in fact screams to be read as a kind of superego gone berserk—but that's the inversion, no? The superego isn't supposed to be berserk. If this passage is at some level an ode to the joys of "repression and regression" in the face of "fun" flashy cultural surface effects, it certainly doesn't practice what it preaches.

We could go on picking away at Adorno's supposed high-culture biases, but I'm less concerned here with the "content" of this passage than with the form—though I hope finally to show how the two are inseparable. First of all, note that the way this passage is set up, and the speed at which it makes links. It simply won't allow you to slow down, isolate, and affirm some form of "entertainment" (whether it be film, drinks, or witty banter) without being chiasmically entangled and forced to respond to the passage's other pole of engagement, the horror of the Holocaust. This passage seems to follow the Adornian "maxim that only exaggeration per se today can be the medium of truth" (*Critical Models,* 99). In fact, this kind of ranting discursive "speed" and the outrageous linkages of this passage comprise a seemingly unruly—but actually quite deliberate—inversion of Adorno's chiasmic "slowness," and as such it seems yet another crucial role for the legacy of music in Adorno's work: certainly Schönberg interrupts the reassuring flow of the popular song by slowing it down, but he also interrupts the popular song by speeding it up.

Speed and slowness are crucial composition techniques in music, and one of the primary ways in which music "means" something. In other words, in art—and recall Adorno, "Perhaps the strict and pure concept of art is applicable only to music" (223)—what something means is always inseparable from how it works, and this is in fact why immanent analysis is so important to Adorno's aesthetics and his politics. Music never allows a simple answer to the question, "What does this mean?"

I want to suggest that Adorno's "minor ethics" is a kind of "musical ethics" of speed and slowness—an ethics that does something, produces effects, over against the transcendental ethics of resentment, judgment, and condemnation. What Adorno insists about the dialectic and about aesthetics seems equally true for the discourse of ethics: you don't use it; you become it. As Adorno suggests in his work on Beethoven, we don't play music—rather, it plays us.[7] This, it seems to me, is finally what *Minima Moralia* is all about: not applying metaphysical ethical standards in a uniform way, but giving oneself over to the complexity of the situation, responding rather than handing down predetermined judgments. A symphony is no more contained in its notes than an ethics is contained in its rules.

Pot Calling the Kettle White:
An Interruptive Excursus on Adorno and Jazz

We all know the song, so just let me hum a few bars for you: Adorno has a tin ear for jazz, which he reads as a wholly commodified form; his Eurocentric high-culture biases—and, by extension, his latent anti-black racism—make him unable to hear jazz's obvious abilities to be precisely the sort of challenging music that Adorno champions in his essays on atonal composition. If he weren't such a snob or closet racist, he'd be giving it up for Monk or Bud Powell in the same breath as he's praising Schönberg.

Problem with this song: it seems to ignore that Adorno's argument is pretty much the same as, for example, Amiri Baraka's critique of jazz's commmodification in *Blues People*—where, in the famous chapter "Swing: From Verb to Noun," Baraka shows how swing has been hermetically sealed and packaged for white listening audiences. Admittedly, Adorno doesn't go out of his way to find out much about atonal jazz—he knows what he hears on the radio (Benny Goodman, the king of swing), and knows that it's flatulent and reified. And, of course, one assumes you wouldn't get very far with him arguing the merits of Cecil Taylor's piano style over Glenn Gould's—not so much because he'd disagree (though he probably would), but because he likely knew as much about Cecil Taylor as Charlie Parker knew about Gregorian chants. In any case, it's important to remember that the "jazz" that Adorno critiques is not the atonal, "free" jazz that critics like Baraka tout—Charlie Parker, John Coltrane, Ornette Coleman.

In fact the "swing" that Baraka rails against is the "jazz" that Adorno hates— and they both say pretty much the same thing about it: swing is commodified slop; it's music as noun, to be consumed, not as verb, to be responded to. Adorno calls it part of the "blind conformity of . . . radio-listeners" (36); Baraka sees it as a pillar of the "vapidity of mainline American culture" (182). Of course, nobody calls Baraka a racist—or at least no one calls him an anti-black racist—because of this critique, and he's seldom accused of being too high culture for his own good.

So a word for the future of Adorno jazz critique: if you disagree with Adorno, be prepared to tell the world what's so interesting or crucial about the swinging grooves of Fred Waring and the Pennsylvanians—or, more important yet, have something affirmative to say about the current "swing revival" and its attendant accessorizing lifestyle products. In terms of commodified whiteness, the success of the Brian Setzer Orchestra or Big Bad Voodoo Daddy seems quite a large (if noxious) confirming flower on the kudzu vine of Adorno's fifty-year-old analyses. Listening to the swing sounds of the Cherry Poppin' Daddies on so-called "alternative" radio, one might even yearn for Tommy Dorsey: as Adorno notes, "Even the outdated, inconsistent, self-doubting ideas of the older generation are more open to dialogue than the slick stupidity of Junior" (22). Close excursus. We now return to our regularly scheduled program.

Speed Kills

Speed and slowness, then, work together: if you want to know what an aphorism "means," Adorno urges you to read it according to "its tempo, compactness, density, yet also by its tentativeness" (100). As in music, one extreme (slowness) doesn't "mean" anything except in relation to the other (speed); and that relation must always be worked out immanently, in terms of a specific piece or situation and its social contexts. If slowness is primarily interruption of tempo or rhythm, then speed is primarily linkage to other cadences. And one might say that for Adorno there's no shortage of haste in contemporary culture, but there's certainly not enough speed. The slogan, for example, is always "false," until it's introduced into a larger field of multiple social and theoretical linkages. Or as Adorno writes, "the statement that things are always the same is false in its immediateness, and true only when introduced into the dynamics of totality" (235)—again, plenty of haste or "immediateness," but not enough speed or cultural "dynamics." Speed and slowness are dialectical elements of composition, but as extremes they allow no simple (or even complex) sublation. They enact the "dynamics of totality."

Speed and slowness are, at some level, another set of names for Adornian mediation, but as musical terms they importantly have no essential or immediate link with the individual ("karma") or the whole ("dogma"), and as such they comprise the watchwords for an ethics that doesn't dictate, but rather works through and modulates extremes in a dialectical way. As Adorno writes in *Three Studies,*

> for Hegel, mediation is never a middle element between extremes, as since Kierkegaard, a deadly misunderstanding has depicted it as being; instead, mediation takes place in and through extremes, in the extremes themselves. This is the radical aspect of Hegel, which is incompatible with any advocacy of moderation. (9)

Given this sense of dialectic, Adorno's can never be an ethics that advocates any kind of moderation or the giving of crackerbarrel advice; his is not a dialectical or chiasmic slowing down for the sake of edification.[8] As he recalls about the leisure industry, the imperative to slow down is "a formula borrowed from the language of the nursing home, not of exuberance" (217). Oddly enough, then, "exuberance" seems to be a key animating principle of the melancholy science.

So the project of an Adornian minor ethics is not solely to limit, slow down, or truncate a too-hasty move tototalization. Certainly, such a slowing down is one effect of *Minima Moralia,* but the text itself demonstrates that there is no privileged or final way to produce "ethical" effects: slowing thought down would always have to be dialectically combined with speeding it up in other registers, in order to establish the fluid dynamics of a complex, concrete singularity.

In and of itself, however, the dialectic is not a privileged mode of inquiry—just as chiasmus or inversion is not a trope that necessarily guarantees anything in the realm of ethics. As I suggest above, the Adornian dialectic is a performative, rather than a constative, discourse. In other words, the dialectic "is" something only insofar as it produces effects; learning from the music that is a kind of template for the dialectic, the philosophical question "What does it mean?" will always be subordinated to the ethical question "What does it do?" Think here of Adorno's interest in the slogan: Is the slogan a rightist or a leftist tool? For Adorno, this is the wrong question. Better, one might ask, "What slogan? Uttered by whom? What effects does it produce?" The slogan itself is neither here nor there; however, "Slogans . . . are the index of their own untruth" (*Critical Models,* 41) precisely insofar as they attempt to downplay and simplify their own dynamic cultural interactions and linkages. Nike's slogan "Just do it!," for example, seems to index its own untruth pretty quickly: "Don't do it without the proper accessories!"

Dialectic for Adorno is finally not an ontological or epistemological discourse. As he argues, "Just as the dialectic does not favor individual definitions, so there is no definition that fits it" (*Hegel,* 9). The dialectic is too "fast" to be defined; in fact it is nothing other than a complex modality of speed, linkage, response.

As Adorno sums up the work of dialectic in *Minima Moralia,* he insists

> limitation and reservation are no way to represent the dialectic. Rather, the
> dialectic advances by way of extremes, driving thoughts with the utmost conse-
> quentiality to the point where they turn back on themselves, instead of qualify-
> ing them. The prudence that restrains us from venturing too far ahead in a
> sentence, is usually only an agent of social control, and so of stupefaction. (86)

It is this insistence on the "driving" "extremes" of thought—the speed of
linkage—that propels the both the sentence and the dialectic forward, that projects
thought and forces it to move both forward and back upon itself. Speed, rather than
slowness, finally seems to be the immeasurable measure of dialectical ethics in
Adorno.[9]

Indeed, following this dialectical path, it seems best to describe his thought as
both a *Minima Moralia* (a "minor" ethics of melancholia or originary loss), as well as
a kind of "maxima immoralia": an anti-ethics that proceeds by "venturing too far
ahead" of transcendental and ideological certainties—an ethics of speed, affirmation,
and futurity.

Speed as Hope

Inevitably, the question posed to the "slow" or "chiasmic" Adorno is the question of
hope: sure, you can slow down ideological closure, frustrate totalization, keep open
questions, relentlessly reveal the contradictions of capital, but how is that any kind of
effective intervention? How does that interruption offer any hope to change things?
In an already hopelessly contradictory society, to insist on contradiction and chiasmic
impasse seems kind of like pissing in your wishing well.

In trying to answer such questions, Adorno will often write in a Benjaminian
vein: "No other hope is left to the past than that, exposed defenselessly to disaster, it
shall emerge from it as something different. But he who dies in despair has lived his
whole life in vain" (167). Certainly, one could argue, Adorno's insistence on slowness,
contradiction, and chiasmus has an upshot in a kind of paradoxical Benjaminian
"hope," something like the "messianism without messianism" that dominates
Derrida's recent thought.[10] And, of course, such interruption is key to any post-
Holocaust thinking, which must honor the dead precisely by standing in the way of
any kind of "final solution." This hesitation itself is a kind of hope.

But I'd like to end by suggesting another kind of hope in Adorno, not the hope
of slowness as interruption, but the hope engendered by speed as linkage. Adorno
insists throughout his minor ethics that the ethicist is inexorably caught up in the
situation that she's diagnosing; as he insists, "The detached observer is as much
entangled as the active participant. . . . This is why the very movement of withdrawal
bears features of what it negates. It is forced to develop a coldness indistinguishable
from that of the bourgeois" (27). I'd argue that what Adorno here calls "coldness" is
akin to what I'm calling "speed," the necessity of linkage. If one always learns from

Adorno that "there is no way out of entanglement" (28), one also learns that such entanglement inexorably calls for critical response. Active, engaged praxis within existing conditions is the first and last principle of Adornian ethics.

Gillian Rose concludes her book on Adorno by arguing that "his 'morality' is a praxis of thought, not a recipe for social or political action" (148). While I take her point (Adorno's ethics doesn't offer dogmatic courses of action), I think that the provocative quality—the speed—of his minor ethics is precisely a kind of recipe, or, as I suggest above, even a musical score: a set of organized potentials that must be performed, responded to, acted out. The recipe or musical score presents a set of provocations that must be modified—sped up or slowed down—in the process of "enacting" them at a specific time or place; even if you follow the recipe, the cake is never the same twice, just as the *Goldberg Variations* are different in each performance. And, more important, such a notion of difference can't merely be explained away by the individual idiosyncracy of the cook or the performer; difference is always wrapped up and manifest in the complexities of social and contextual response. You don't get to write the recipe or the musical score, but nevertheless it doesn't simply control you. You have to respond to it.

Certainly, the chiasmic Adorno shows us how negation or withdrawal is a response; but in the end Adorno also shows us that such withdrawal or slowness isn't effective until it is dialectically coupled with an "extreme" movement of speed or affirmation. Critique is effective and ethical only insofar as it's "forced to develop a coldness indistinguishable from that of the bourgeois"; cultural criticism is called not only to interrupt or critique, but literally to forge multiple linkages. As Adorno argues concerning cultural critique, "Repudiation of the present cultural morass presupposes sufficient involvement in it to feel it itching in one's own finger-tips, so to speak, but at the same time the strength, drawn from this involvement, to dismiss it. This strength is by no means of a merely individual nature" (29).

In the end, or from the beginning, this necessity of involvement or response— this ethical "strength" of continued engagement, this coldness of future linkages—is what one might call the legacy of hope as speed in Adorno. While the slowness of chiasmic reversal ruins thinking as totalization and thereby offers its own kind of future hope, the movements of speed as linkage offer another kind of open-ended ethical "hope" in his texts: the tools for reinscribing culture elsewhere. As Adorno writes in one of his last essays, "Thought is happiness, even where it defines unhappiness" (*Critical Models*, 293). And we learn from Adorno that it's never too late for such a speedy critical intervention. "Hurry up, please. It's time."[11]

Notes

1. For more on chiasmus and Adorno's style, see Jameson (*Late Marxism*, 5–12), Rose (*Melancholy*, 11–26), and Jay (*Adorno*, 56–81).

2. Adorno of course has much to say about "Hegel, whose method schooled that of *Minima Moralia*" (16). According to Adorno, however, dialectic "is distorted in Hegel:

with serene indifference he opts once again for liquidation of the particular. Nowhere in his work is the primacy of the whole doubted" (17). Hence, "the whole is false" (50).

3.   See, for example, Culler's *On Deconstruction:* "attempts to reverse and thus displace major hierarchical oppositions of Western thought open possibilities of change that are incalculable" (158).

4.   See, for example, Zizek: "Lacan's point is not that full self-consciousness is impossible since something always eludes the grasp of my conscious ego. Instead, it is the far more paradoxical thesis that this decentered hard kernel which eludes my grasp is ultimately self-consciousness itself" (*Tarrying,* 66).

5.   Most cultural studies analyses fit within this rubric—attempting to move away from a base-superstructure model of capital's relation to culture. As Grossberg writes, cultural studies "rejects analyses that . . . operate as if capital determines [culture] in a mechanical way from start to finish" (10–11).

6.   A potential link, which will remain unexplored here: Melancholia is certainly about loss, but it's unacknowledged loss in Freud—precisely its distinction from mourning, which has a more defined (lost) object. So melancholia, as Judith Butler points out (*Bodies,* 233–36), has a privileged link to performativity as rage—it can be seen as an "acting out" over a loss that can't even really be named. To paraphrase Leonard Cohen, the melancholic can't forget, but doesn't remember what.

7.   Adorno insists that the bad dialectician is like the bad musician—using the dialectic instead of working through it: "The harm is done by the thema probandum: the thinker uses the dialectic instead of giving himself up to it. In this way thought, masterfully dialectical, reverts to the predialectical stage: the serene demonstration that there are two sides to everything" (247).

8.   Again, one learns this from Hegel, who insists that "philosophy must beware of the wish to be edifying" (6).

9.   Slowness, we might note, is already a particular modality of speed, though not vice versa.

10.   See, for example, *Specters of Marx.*

11.   This quotation is William Burroughs' rewriting or inversion of T. S. Eliot's famous line from "The Waste Land." Eliot suggests a kind of passive, apocalyptic waiting: Eliot's line, "HURRY UP PLEASE ITS TIME," longs for some mystical force to hurry up the time of this "IT," a coming revelation. Burroughs's rewriting, "Hurry up, please. It's time" (*The Western Lands,* 258) suggests a much more positive sense of deployment or praxis—now is the time to do something. In addition, Burroughs's active rewriting of Eliot comprises the final words of "the old writer who couldn't write anymore because he had reached the end of words" (258) in Burroughs's final novel, *The Western Lands;* as such these words are a kind of Burroughsian farewell to words, a final and always-resonating call for action. See Murphy (200) for more on this Burroughsian rewriting.

Refences

Adorno, Theodor W. 1998. *Critical Models: Interventions and Catchwords.* Translated by Henry W. Pickford. New York: Columbia University Press.

————. 1993. *Hegel: Three Studies.* Translated by Shierry Weber Nicholsen. Cambridge, Mass.: MIT Press.

————. 1974. *Minima Moralia: Reflections from a Damaged Life.* Translated by E. F. N. Jephcott. New York and London: Verso.

————. 1994. *The Stars Down to Earth and Other Essays.* Edited and Translated by Stephen Crook. New York and London: Routledge.

Adorno, Theodor W., and Max Horkheimer. 1972. *Dialectic of Enlightenment.* Translated by John Cumming. New York: Continuum.

Baraka, Amiri. 1963. *Blues People: Negro Music in White America.* New York: William Morrow.

Burroughs, William. 1987. *The Western Lands.* New York: Penguin.

Butler, Judith. 1993. *Bodies that Matter.* New York, Routledge.

Culler, Jonathan. 1982. *On Deconstruction.* Ithaca: Cornell University Press.

Derrida, Jacques. 1994. *Specters of Marx.* Translated by Peggy Kamuf. New York: Routledge.

Grossberg, Lawrence. 1997. *Bringing It All Back Home: Essays on Cultural Studies.* Durham, N.C.: Duke University Press.

Hegel, G. W. F. 1977. *Phenomenology of Spirit.* Translated by A. V. Miller. Oxford, Eng.: Oxford University Press.

Jameson, Fredric. 1990. *Late Marxism: Adorno, or, The Persistance of Dialectic.* New York and London: Verso.

Jay, Martin. 1984. *Adorno.* Harvard University Press.

Murphy, Timothy. 1997. *Wising Up the Marks: The Amodern William Burroughs.* Berkeley: University of California Press.

Rose, Gillian. 1978. *The Melancholy Science: An Introduction to the Thought of Theodor Adorno.* London: Macmillan.

Zizek, Slavoj. 1993. *Tarrying with the Negative: Kant, Hegel and the Critique of Ideology.* Durham, N.C.: Duke University Press.

III

BENJAMIN, HORKHEIMER, MARCUSE, HABERMAS

9

The Negative History of the Moment of Possibility: Walter Benjamin and the Coming of the Messiah

Richard A. Lee Jr.

The moment of the emergence of modernity is the moment of the emergence of history—modernity is, essentially, historically self-conscious. One of the central problematics of modern philosophy has been to place the movement of history (and its goal or end) within history itself such that the emergence of modernity coincides with the movement of history itself.[1] The insertion of the movement and end of history within history requires that history be reconceived on the basis of the notion of progress. Only if history itself is progress can its movement and especially its end be seen as an intra-historical event and not an extra-historical intervention by God.

What Lukács says of Kant also applies retrospectively to pre-Kantian modern philosophy: the goal of history is not itself historical.[2] Modernity begins along with history because it is only through history that modernity can claim its difference from premodern philosophy. History is the mode of legitimation of modernity—and that legitimation comes through the notion of history as progress. Progress, however, without an intra-historical goal threatens itself.

The problem of the extra-historical goal of history ought not to be separated from the extra-historical emergence of the notion of history as progress, which begins in modernity. The initial claim of legitimacy, i.e., that we are no longer medieval, was not originally a historical claim because it was itself the condition for the possibility of history. It is not until the extra-historical origin of modernity can be made historical that the goal of history, formerly seen as extra-historical, can be made historical. That is, it is not until the gesture of separation (to be modern is not to be medieval) is turned into a narrative of history (history has moved, unfolded, progressed to modernity), that modernity will recognize its need for history as a mode of legitimation.

This point recedes into the background of the analysis of the Enlightenment found in *Dialectic of Enlightenment*. Horkheimer and Adorno open their analysis with a gesture that already forces history out of the analysis: "Enlightenment, in the sense of progressing thought, has always pursued the goal of taking fear from humans and setting them up as masters."[3] Immediately, the analysis shifts away from the "progressing" of thinking and toward domination. This is not to deny that domination of nature is not central to modernity, nor even to deny that domination of nature itself becomes a legitimation claim. Rather, it is to point out that the domination itself is understood by the Enlightenment to be progressive. The move toward domination has the effect of making historical determination difficult to understand because the very heart of the notion of history has been left behind. Enlightenment begins with Odysseus. I will return to this point shortly.

To be sure, the legitimation through history begins only negatively. For thinkers like Bacon and Descartes, history as progress functions as a way to separate themselves from the past—particularly the Middle Ages—and also as a methodological test. Progress is the test that the Middle Ages, indeed the entire tradition of philosophy, failed and therefore it is the motivation for a new method. It plays no more positive function than that. Yet if history is to be a mode of legitimation, it cannot do so externally. If modernity succeeds because of progress, then modernity must take its place within history.

But Descartes merely uncovered the historical rupture that is modernity. He did not attempt to think the movement of history according to which modernity appears out of history but in relation to it. That is, he did not think about the way in which modernity stands as the culmination of history. This task was taken up by Kant. In his essay, "What Is Enlightenment," as well as his "Idea for a Universal History from a Cosmopolitan Point of View," Kant struggles with the notion that history has a movement that can be detected and captured for our own benefit. The movement that Kant detects in history is the movement of reason, or, at the very least, the movement toward reason. The "Idea for a Universal History" traces a history that leads toward the development of the capacities of creatures to their fullest. At the pinnacle of this development is the faculty of reason in humans. This history leads, naturally as it were, to the development of a universal civic society. Thus what Descartes saw as merely epochal uniqueness, Kant sees as historical progress. While Kant charts the movement of history in terms of progress, he does not pay attention to the mechanism or the motor that drives history.[4] The failure of Kant's theory of history, as we have seen Lukács point out, is that it is ahistorical.

The notion that reason plays itself out in history in successive moments of consciousness's greater self-realization is Hegel's contribution to the modern concern with history as progress. This succession of moments moves dialectically. This dialectical movement of history overcomes Kant's problem—it reinserts that which moves history back into history. It is the becoming self-conscious of Spirit, Hegel tells us in his introduction to the *Lectures on the Philosophy of History,* that provides the dialectical movement of history. Thus, the very becoming of this self-consciousness not only moves history, it is itself historical. Thus, from its beginning, modernity contains as its essential moment a theory of history as progress. Because modernity is the self-consciousness of the movement of history, it alone is able to move history toward its goal. In Hegel, progress comes to be seen as the necessary progress of Reason toward freedom, or, seen from another side, the progress of Spirit's quest for self-consciousness.

I do not want, nor is there space, to open the debate about just how Hegelian Marx's dialectic is. I cannot answer here the question about what it means to turn Hegel on his feet or on his head or on any other bodily appendage. We can notice without running the risk of opening that debate, however, that Marx certainly indicates that modernity is not only the culmination of a kind of logic already present in elementary barter systems of exchange, that modernity is not only the historical moment in which capitalism appropriates the fruits of the labor of the proletariat, but also that modernity is the moment that makes possible the overcoming of the contradictions of capitalism. The age-old question about why the revolution was successful in Russia when it was the most backward economy in Europe raises the Marxian problematic most clearly. Can we move from feudalism directly into socialism? It is not only a question of the movement of history leaping over what seems to be a necessary stage. It is also a question of the progress that production has in fact made under capitalism. It is only in modernity that the possibility of satisfying the material needs of all arises. Marx too needs progress. But Marx never seemed to realize that history as progress is the mode of legitimation of modern bourgeois thinking.

The critique of this bourgeois thinking and culture was perhaps the main focus of the Frankfurt School. Adorno's constant insistence that critique never contain a positive moment is precisely an insight into the way in which modernity and bourgeois culture have become enmeshed. Yet Adorno too, as we have seen, never addressed the central function of the theory of history in modernity. He never provided a negative dialectical theory of history. Without a critique of the theory of history as progress, no critique of modernity can be successful. We can now see that *Dialectic of Enlightenment* raises the very problem of history because of the absence of history in the text. If bourgeois culture can be pushed back all the way to Odysseus, i.e., if the history of western culture from the Odyssey until today is the dialectic of enlightenment and myth without a positive moment, then history itself has become a problem. How can we talk about "historical determination" when we seem to have lost that very determinateness that the dialectic gave to history? Yet Adorno still raises the possibility of "redeeming the hopes of the past." What are the temporal-historical conditions that make "hope" and "past" possible?

If we take seriously the power and possibilities of critique that lie within a negative dialectic, then Adorno can be seen as pointing the way toward a successful theory of history that would simultaneously undercut the legitimacy of modernity through its notion of history: it must be dialectical and it must not contain within itself a positive moment—only such a theory of history will not produce a nostalgic reference to premodern society. I want to explore whether we can see Benjamin's theory of history as an answer to this call—even in the face of Adorno's critique that Benjamin's theory contains "undialectical positivities."

The Negative Dialectics of History

From his earliest writings, Walter Benjamin was intensely interested in the notion of history, both as it stands in bourgeois culture and as it ought to be presented in opposition to bourgeois culture.

> There is a conception of history which puts its faith in the infinite extent of time and thus distinguishes quickness or slowness with which people and

epochs advance along the path of progress. . . . The following remarks, in
contrast, consider a definite condition in which history appears to be concentrated into a single focal point. The elements of the ultimate condition do not
manifest themselves as a formless tendency towards progress, but rather are
deeply rooted in every present as the most endangered, most disparaged and
derided creations and thoughts. The historical task is to disclose this immanent
state of perfection and make it absolute, to make it visible and dominant in the
present . . . it can only be grasped in its metaphysical structure, as with the
Messianic Kingdom . . .[5]

In this essay from 1915, many of the elements of Benjamin's later theory of
history and of the historical task that ought to be taken up are present. There are three
aspects of this theory, already present in this early text, that I would like to explore: (1)
the relation of the present to the past within the notion of history as progress; (2)
history as an "absolute moment" that presents itself to the present only as "dangerous"; and (3) the role of the messianic in the theory of history.

The Past as Past for the Present

In this early essay, as well as in a fragmentary sketch for his *Trauerspeil* text, Benjamin
is concerned about the way in which the past can appear to the present through
history. Benjamin distinguishes the conception of time that belongs to mechanics
from the conception of time that belongs to history: "It should not be thought that
time is nothing other than the measure with which the duration of a mechanical
change is measured."[6] Rather, for Benjamin, the time of history is such that the
fulfillment of a moment, of a "happening" is empirically undetermined, it is an
"Idea." "This idea of fulfilled time is called in the Bible, in which it is the dominant
historical idea, 'messianic time'."[7]

In his earlier writings, Benjamin seems to argue that the time of history is the
transcendental condition for the possibility of events happening. History is not
merely the collection and connection of events that have happened, history, for
Benjamin, carries with it a relation to fulfillment or redemption. In his "Tragedy and
Mourning-Play," the notion of fulfillment is proper only to historical time. "In any
case, the idea of fulfilled historic time is not to be thought like the idea of individual
time. This determination, which naturally changes the sense of fulfillment entirely, is
that which differentiates tragic time from messianic."[8] Benjamin does not, however,
consider fulfilled time as a real historic possibility. For Benjamin, fulfilled time
pertains only to the messianic. Just how we should understand the messianic remains
unclear. We will say more about this in a moment.

This relation between fulfillment and history is made most explicit in Benjamin's "Theses on the Philosophy of History." "The past brings with it a secret index,
through which it is related to redemption."[9] The theory of history as progress claims
that the past is redeemed in the present because each past moment finds its possibilities fulfilled in the present. This is, in its essence, what progress means. Each
moment is in a sense incomplete because it finds its completion, its fulfillment, only

in a future moment. Yet this relation to the past is, for Benjamin, an obliteration of the past. It makes the past a handmaiden of the present. In short, progress is the story told by the victors. It is a story in which events, happenings, and moments are singled out as "greater" than others. From the point of view of progress, any moment is empty and interchangeable; the moment can only become fulfilled through an event that the present endows with its own significance. The past exists only for the present—i.e., only for the victors of the present. "The idea [*Vorstellung*] of the progress of humanity in history is not to be detached from the idea of its progression running through a homogeneous and empty time."[10] The theory of history as progress, then, presupposes the kind of time that Benjamin, in "Tragedy and Mourning-Play," had called "mechanical." Progress is the theory of history that pays attention only to the quasi-mechanical change, and names this change "improvement." Such a notion of history, however, destroys the past. It makes of the past only a stage on the way toward the present. Thus, Benjamin's theory of history is one in which the past opens up not as fulfilled in the present, but as pointing toward a redemption of its own as an absolute moment.

The Past as an "Absolute Moment" and the Task of History

As an antidote to the conception of history as progress, Benjamin proposes a notion that opens up the "moments" of the past in a different way. He wants to free the past from its redemption in and through history. "Only as a picture which flashes up in a moment of its recognizability, never to be seen again, is the past to be grasped."[11] When the moment merely "flashes up" it refuses to be set in the series of stages that is progress. In fact, when one allows the moments of the past to "flash up" in this way, the past itself becomes dangerous—dangerous to our story of history told from the point of view of the victors; dangerous for the present itself. It is this moment of danger that Benjamin refers to as the "coming of the Messiah." This, then, shows the proper task that the historian and the theoretician of history must take on.

From his understanding of the relation of the past to the present, Benjamin derives the task that we must take on in relation to history. This "must" may be moral, but it derives from the claim the past makes on us. This is the very opposite of history conceived as progress in which the present makes claims on the past. "For there is a secret agreement between past generations and our own. For our existence on the earth was expected. For it is for us as for every generation which came before us, that we are endowed with a *weak* messianic power, to which the past has claim."[12] The claim that the past makes on us is a claim for liberation. We are asked to redeem the past. But such redemption, as we have seen, comes not through or in history—understood as progress—but in a picture of the past as a moment of danger. This "true" picture of the past, however, merely "flits by."

The view of history that takes account of the past's claim on our weak messianic power is called, problematically, "historical materialism." The historical materialist must not be confused with the "dialectical materialist" who is still held captive by the notion of progress. Rather, the historical materialist is the one whose only interest is in the moments of the past that are full of possibilities that are never realized in any present. This is the danger of the "absolute moment" of the past. It calls into question our own present, it pulls the historical ground out from under the present, and demands that it, too, become a moment of infinite possibility. The task, then, of the historical materialist is to recall the past, to picture the past as a moment of infinite possibility—not of potentiality that has been actualized in some present. This is the "moment of danger" that the historical materialist recognizes. This is the grasp of the past in which the past appears only negatively—in an Adornian sense. For in Benjamin's sketch of our task, the past must always remain unfulfilled in our present. The reality of the absolute moment is such that no future actuality fulfills the possibilities contained in the moment. History as progress lacks the power to fulfill such infinite possibility. Only the coming of the Messiah can redeem the past.

Messianic Time

In this light, Benjamin's reflections on the "coming of the Messiah" are far from a deferral of history until its end. To be sure, for Benjamin the Messiah means the end of history in the sense of its destruction, not in the sense of its intra-historical fulfillment. "The Kingdom of God is not the telos of historical dynamism; it cannot be set as the goal. Seen historically, it is not the goal, but the end."[13] This means that history can in no way lead up to the coming of the Messiah, cannot work toward bringing it about. But it also means that history does not wait for the Messiah to come. The Messiah, to be sure, completes all historical happening, but the completion comes not through history but from its end, its destruction.

This conception of the coming of the Messiah allows Benjamin to open history up to the notion of the "moment" we analyzed above:

> Materialistic historiography, on the other hand, is based on a constructive principle. Thinking involves not only the flow of thoughts, but their arrest as well. Where thinking suddenly stops in a configuration pregnant with tensions, it gives that configuration a shock, by which it crystallizes into a monad . . . In this structure [the historical materialist] recognizes the sign of a Messianic cessation of happening, or, put differently, a revolutionary chance in the fight for the oppressed past.[14]

The coming of the Messiah opens history up to a new kind of historiography. Without the idea of the Messiah, Benjamin's notion of history loses an important mechanism. For it is only when Benjamin can think the total destruction of history as a possibility that haunts every moment that he can open up the moment from its servitude to the past and to the future seen as the site in which history will be redeemed.

When viewed from the point of view of Messianic time, history becomes imbedded in the present as the "moment of the now." This moment always bears within itself a relation to the Messianic, it is "shot through with chips of Messianic time." Since the Messianic is freed from the movement of history itself, the moment is similarly freed from the movement of history and appears as a monad in which there is a cessation of happening, in which the movement of history is brought to a stop and faces the danger of its own destruction.

The idea of Messianic time and the "coming of the Messiah" does not function in Benjamin's thought as apocalyptic in the sense that it has no relation to the present and to the movement of history. It is not something that we simply wait for. Rather, it is an idea that fundamentally changes our conception of history and gives us a "weak Messianic power" through which we can attempt to redeem the past. Thus, "redemption" means grasping the past as a "now" whose possibilities are not actualized in any present. The notion of history and the type of historiography that Messianic history opens is that of the moment or the monadic now. It is the idea of the coming of the Messiah that allows Benjamin to see the moment, the now, as a moment of infinite possibility that is never reduced to any actuality. And only a conception of history such as this opens the metaphysical space where revolutionary action makes sense. Revolution is always messianic in that it is always tied to a now freed from its past and open to an infinite horizon in the future.

Adorno's critiques of Benjamin notwithstanding, his theory of history seems to be the only one possible within a negative dialectics. The coming of the Messiah is the only way to move toward a redemption of the hopes of the past. This is not a sign of "defeatism" on Benjamin's part. Rather, it is a sign that even in the theory of history, "objects do not go into their concepts without remainder."[15] The coming of the Messiah is a sign of the temporality of revolution. This event is always historical only in the sense that it can redeem the hopes of the past. It is never historical in the sense that it is the culmination of history. The angel of history sits on its ashes.

History and Critique/Benjamin and the Frankfurt School

Benjamin is certainly not alone among philosophers in turning toward history as a form of critique. In the twentieth century, for example, Michel Foucault stands out as an example of a thinker for whom history calls into question the necessity of the present. Yet Benjamin is unique in that his theory of history, and his practice of cultural reading based upon it, attempts to be materialist through and through.[16] Yet unlike a Marxist materialist dialectic of history, Benjamin's dialectic works to undo the very notion of progress. For Benjamin, materialism refers not to the mechanism by which history progresses, but to one of the dialectical sites in culture in which messianic history can operate. Benjamin's notion of dialectic operates much like that of Adorno: it refers to the relationship between an element and its societal/cultural whole—it is "at a standstill." Yet unlike Adorno's critical practice, Benjamin's is both more material and more historical, or rather is situated at the site of a material object read in relation to society and the history of its victors.

Benjamin's messianic history places his version of cultural critique somewhere between the practice of the central members of the Frankfurt School and the practice of cultural studies. Like critical theorists, Benjamin is constantly aware of the relation between any form of cultural production and the social whole in which it is produced. For him, culture and its objects are not immediately sites of resistance. Yet, unlike the usual practice of critical theory, Benjamin's materialist Messianism leads him to treat the products of culture—and especially popular culture—as sites where the culture comes into contention with itself, as sites where the material residue of a culture contests the constellation of ideas that make up that culture.

Notes

1. Reinhart Koselleck has argued that the Protestant claim that the end of the world was at hand and that the hastening of the end could be brought about through human activity results in the notion that the Christian apocalypse becomes a historical event rather than an extra-historical ending of the human world. See his essay "Vergangene Zukunft der frühen Neuzeit" in Reinhart Koselleck, 1989, *Vergangene Zukunft* (Frankfurt: Suhrkamp), 17–37.

2. Georg Lukács, 1968, 1971, *History and Class Consciousness*, trans. Rodney Livingstone (Cambridge, Mass.: The MIT Press), 49. In the philosophy of history of the Kantians, history "must be seen as the instrument, senseless in itself, by means of which timeless, suprahistorical, ethical principles are realised."

3. Max Horkheimer and Theodor W. Adorno, 1997, *Dialektik der Aufklärung*, vol. 3, ed. Rolf Tiedemann, *Gesammelte Schriften*, (Frankfurt am Main: Suhrkamp), 17.

4. In the second half of his *Critique of Judgment*, §83 of the Critique of Teleological Judgment, Kant presents an argument that is quite similar to the one in his "Ideas for a Universal History," with the exception that in the *Critique* he argues that the movement of history arises out of social and economic inequality whereas in the latter essay the movement of history is thought of in terms of human "unsocial sociability."

5. Walter Benjamin, 1977, "Das Leben der Studenten," vol. II.1, in *Gesammelte Schriften*, ed. Rolf Tiedmann and Hermann Schweppenhäuser, (Frankfurt: Suhrkamp), 75.

6. Benjamin, "Trauerspiel und Tragödie," in ibid., 134.

7. Ibid.

8. Ibid., 134.

9. Walter Benjamin, 1974, "Über Den Begriff der Geschichte," in *Gesammelte Schriften*, ed. Rolf Tiedemann and Hermann Schweppenhäuser (Frankfurt: Suhrkamp Verlag), 693.

10. Ibid., 701.

11. Ibid., 695.

12. Ibid., 694.

13. Benjamin, "Theologico-Political Fragment," in ibid., 203.

14. Thesis 17.

15. Theodor W. Adorno, 1973, *Negative Dialectics*, trans. E. B. Ashton (New York: Continuum), 5; Theodor W. Adorno, 1970, *Negative Dialektik*, ed. Rolf Tiedemann, *Gesammelte Schriften* (Frankfurt: Suhrkamp), 17.

16. While it would take me far afield here, I would argue that Benjamin's *Arcades Project* is an example of his theory of history borne out in practice. Here, I just want to indicate how, for him, the material basis (and more particularly the material detritus) of a culture provides the site in which messianic history can be practiced.

10

The Frankfurt School and the Domination of Nature: New Grounds for Radical Environmentalism

Kevin DeLuca

My aim in this essay is modest. I want to suggest that the domination of nature, a concept introduced by Max Horkheimer in the 1940s and later developed by a student of Herbert Marcuse's, William Leiss, is a potential keystone concept for environmental theory and practice.[1] In my discussion, I am purposefully excluding mainstream environmentalism, which has been rightly dismissed with the adjectives shallow, market, beltway, institutional, Band-Aid, and reformist. In short, mainstream environmentalism is hopelessly compromised, constrained, and circumscribed by the tenets of industrialism. Instead, I want to focus on two branches of radical environmentalism, social ecology and deep ecology, that have adopted positions that place them at loggerheads and leave them stuck when considering the central issue of humanity-nature relations. The domination of nature is a useful lever by which to dislodge them.

This dislodging is necessary on both theoretical and practical grounds. At the simple level of coalition building, the radical environmental movement does not benefit from protracted debates that sink to the level of personal insults and splinter the movement. For instance, social ecology founder Murray Bookchin took the occasion of the first national Green conference in the United States to associate deep ecology with "eco-fascism" and to lambaste its supporters as "eco-brutalists" and nature worshipers. Those attacked responded in kind. Writer and patron saint of Earth First!, Ed Abbey, wishing to live up to Bookchin's description, challenged him to a fistfight. Christopher Manes dismissed Bookchin's four decades of work as so ineffectual that social ecology, instead of sweeping the world, has "succeeded only in sweeping the halls of the Institute for Social Ecology."[2] In this essay I propose to start with an extended discussion and critique of the concept of the domination of nature as theorized by Horkheimer and Leiss. Then I will note the presence or, more aptly, absence of Frankfurt School thought in environmental circles, sketch the positions of deep ecology and social ecology, discuss why they are stuck, and suggest why the domination of nature would be a useful bridge concept. Although the aim of this essay is modest, the potential ramifications are not. In focusing on the Frankfurt School's work on nature, I am suggesting a necessary engagement of environmental studies/politics with cultural studies, an engagement that promises to be both painful and productive.

Reason and Nature: The Need for a Reconciliation

The domination of nature and instrumental reason, two key elements in the articulation of progress,[3] are central to the thought of critical theorists working in the tradition of the Frankfurt School. Max Horkheimer and Theodor Adorno,[4] working in the United States in exile from Germany during World War II, found themselves trying to explain how the dream of the Enlightenment, freedom from fear and sovereignty over nature, had turned into the nightmares of the twentieth century so that "the fully enlightened Earth radiates disaster triumphant."[5] The horrors of the twentieth century could not be blamed on any external barbaric horde but arose from within the heart of Western civilization. To explain this endemic barbarism, or the reversal of the Enlightenment, Horkheimer and Adorno turn to the relationship of Western civilization to nature, which they conceptualize through the notion of the domination of nature: "world domination over nature turns against the thinking subject himself"[6] for it requires "a denial of nature in man for the sake of domination over nonhuman nature and over other men. . . . As soon as man discards his awareness that he himself is nature, all the aims for which he keeps himself alive—social progress, the intensification of all his spiritual and material powers, even consciousness itself—are nullified."[7]

This is an interesting turn because civilization and nature are often treated as separate spheres that experience only tangential contact, yet Horkheimer and Adorno's analysis rests on the interconnection of nonhuman nature and humanity, an interconnection at the root of Western civilization's return to barbarism. For, as Horkheimer elaborates,

> The human being, in the process of his emancipation, shares the fate of the rest of his world. Domination of nature involves domination of man. Each subject not only has to take part in the subjugation of external nature, human and nonhuman, but in order to do so must subjugate nature in himself. Domination becomes internalized for domination's sake.[8]

Horkheimer and Adorno also cite the rise of instrumental reason and the eclipse of objective reason as being partly responsible for the madness of the twentieth century. For Horkheimer, instrumental reason is used by the individual as a means to ends, usually self-preservation, which it cannot theorize. Instrumental reason strips the world it encounters of any intrinsic meaning and reduces everything to a tool or means for its own use. By contrast, objective reason is inherent in the world and helps reconcile human wants with the larger order or environment. It theorizes ultimate ends and views the world and nature as having intrinsic worth. "The theory of objective reason did not focus on the coordination of behaviour and aim, but on concepts . . . on the idea of the greatest good, on the problem of human destiny and on the way of realization of ultimate goals."[9]

Horkheimer does not argue that instrumental reason is inherently evil and objective reason good, but rather that a balance is needed and the present age has experienced the rise of instrumental reason and the eclipse of objective reason, with disastrous results. Humanity now lives in a world of shrewder means and witless ends.[10] The task of critical theory, according to Horkheimer, is to prepare for (but not announce) a reconciliation of reason and nature.[11] This call, however, has received no sufficient response and Horkheimer's analysis reaches a dead end for three related reasons. He sees the domination of nature as primary to the reversal of the Enlightenment, rather than instrumental reason; he collapses his distinction between instrumental reason and objective reason into an analysis of reason in general; and he extends the meaning of domination of nature too far, so that any human action in nature would seem to constitute domination.

An extended quote from Horkheimer's essay "On the Concept of Philosophy" in *Eclipse of Reason* illustrates these three problems:

> If one were to speak of a disease affecting reason, this disease should be understood not as having stricken reason at some historical moment, but as being inseparable from the nature of reason in civilization as we have known it so far. The disease of reason is that reason was born from man's urge to dominate nature, and the "recovery" depends on insight into the nature of the original disease, not on a cure of the latest symptoms. The true critique of reason will necessarily uncover the deepest layers of civilization and explore its earliest history. From the time when reason became the instrument for domination of human and extra-human nature by man—that is to say, from its very beginnings—it has been frustrated in its own intention of discovering the truth. This is due to the very fact that it made nature a mere object, and that it failed to discover the trace of itself in such objectivization, in the concepts of matter and things not less in those of gods and spirit one might say that the collective madness that rages today, from the concentration camps to the seemingly most harmless mass-culture reactions, was already present in germ in primitive objectivization, in the first man's calculating contemplation of the world as a prey.[12]

In this passage Horkheimer collapses his distinction between objective reason and instrumental reason. Reason has always, by its very nature, objectivized the world and reduced it to a means. Reason has never seen the world as having intrinsic worth. All reason has always had the characteristics of instrumental reason. Furthermore, reason is not only secondary to the domination of nature, it is born from the domination of nature. Reason, indeed civilization, are mere offshoots of humanity's "urge to dominate nature." This assertion by Horkheimer has two consequences. Horkheimer, who has always argued for the necessity of historically specific analysis, provides an ahistorical analysis of reason. All reason, all civilization, has always dominated nature. If domination of nature and instrumental reason have always been central to all reason, Horkheimer cannot account for the wide cultural variations with regard to the domination of nature. Even more important, he cannot account for the acceleration of the negative effects of the domination of nature in the twentieth century, "the collective madness that rages today." Thus, Horkheimer's call for the reconciliation of reason and nature rings hollow. If "the sole way of assisting nature is to unshackle its seeming opposite, independent thought,"[13] yet reason is born from the urge to dominate nature, nature (and consequently civilization) seems doomed. If all reason and civilization are tainted by the disease of reason, there is no answer to the reversal of the Enlightenment but faith or despair. Finally, Horkheimer seems to extend the meaning of the domination of nature so that any human action or objectivization constitutes domination. However, objectivization per se is not the problem. Objectivization only becomes a problem when it is the dominant or sole way of perceiving the world.

In short, Horkheimer (and Adorno) sought to explain the collective madness of the twentieth century, the reversal of the Enlightenment, through the domination of nature and the rise of instrumental reason. Their analysis is significant because they saw the root of Western civilization's problems to be humanity's relation to nature— the domination of nature. Also, they saw the need for a balance between instrumental reason and objective reason. They argue that the rise of instrumental reason, particularly as the reason of modern science, prevents the theorization of ultimate ends to guide civilization rationally and thus contributes to the reversal of the Enlightenment. But Horkheimer's analysis falls short when he collapses the distinction between instrumental reason and objective reason and theorizes all reason to have the characteristics of instrumentality and to be born of humanity's urge to dominate nature. If all reason (and thus civilization) is tainted by the disease of the domination of nature, then Horkheimer's analysis seems not only to criticize the reversal of the Enlightenment but to make Enlightenment impossible. Thus his call for a reconciliation of diseased reason and nature seems contradictory and useless. If all reason is diseased, the history of civilization is a dead end. Horkheimer does leave a glimmer of hope with the modest qualifier "so far." This is reminiscent of the Dr. Seuss fable of ecological catastrophe, *The Lorax,* wherein all hope for the post-apocalyptic landscape is invested in the word "unless." "So far" suggests that "the nature of reason in civilization" and "man's urge to dominate nature" are not immutable essences, instincts, but historical practices and that the future is not the stage for the playing out of an already written script but a realm of excess, the site of possibilities that exceed the horizon of the known.

Domination of Nature

Writing thirty years after Horkheimer and Adorno first wrote about the domination of nature and instrumental reason, Leiss took up the concept of the domination of nature at a time when it was first becoming evident that human-made environmental problems threatened civilization, Leiss furthered Horkheimer and Adorno's analysis by retaining the idea that the domination of nature is at the root of social problems but shifting emphasis to domination of non-human (external) nature and then focusing on the idea that the domination of nature is also at the root of environmental problems.

Leiss, in his book *The Domination of Nature,* traces the history of the idea of the domination of nature. His book is particularly useful because he perceives the idea of the domination of nature as being involved in a dynamic historical process. Neither the element—the domination of nature—nor the articulations into which it has entered have remained static. The history of the domination of nature is traced by Leiss, and others, most notably Lynn White Jr. in "The Historical Roots of Our Ecological Crisis," to the Judeo-Christian tradition and the book of Genesis: "Be fruitful and multiply, and replenish the earth and subdue it: and have dominion over the fish of the sea and over the fowl of the air and over every living thing that moveth upon the earth" (Genesis 1:28). As Leiss notes, initially the domination of nature was constrained by the religious articulation in which it arose (this is similar to Horkheimer's "objective reason"):

> Man's will is not the highest principle in heaven or on earth, but instead is checked and limited by ethical norms established independently of it. Similarly, the surrounding world of nature has a purpose entirely apart from its function as the basis of human activity: it is a divine creation and therefore sacred.[14]

Domination of nature, then, was constrained in an articulation involving God, humanity, humanity's place in the hierarchy of beings, and nature as both material provider and divine creation. The breakdown of this articulation allows the full realization of the domination of nature in the discourse of progress.

Leiss cites the work of Francis Bacon as the point at which the religious articulation constraining the domination of nature started to be dearticulated. Bacon was working within a religious context but was able to carve out a niche for science. "For man by the fall fell at the same time from his state of innocency and from his dominion over creation. Both of these losses however can even in this life be in some part repaired, the former by religion and faith, the latter by arts and sciences."[15] Dominion over creation through science promised material wealth. Bacon not only legitimated science in a religious context, he separated scientific knowledge and moral knowledge, facts and values, the scientific world and the everyday life-world, instrumental reason and objective reason.

> For Bacon and his contemporaries religion had provided the means for understanding science as a human activity . . . religion supplied the link uniting scientific activity with everyday action in the life-world. But the overwhelming success of the marriage between industry and the new science, and the growing social authority of the novel scientific methodology, spelled inevitable defeat for the traditional scheme of religiously based ethics.[16]

The rise of instrumental reason and the consequent waning of religion freed the domination of nature. Nature became separated into two spheres: "intuited nature experienced nature of everyday life," the unthematized background, and "scientific nature . . . abstract universal, anathematized nature,"[17] thematized nature. As modern science, characterized by instrumental reason, grew in importance, its abstract and universal view of nature as a "silent, colorless universe of matter in motion"[18] became the definition that counted. "When something becomes a thematic concern, however, deliberate attention is focused on it; through a process of abstraction a certain aspect of experience becomes the subject of special interest, other aspects being simultaneously overshadowed and devalued."[19] When science, through instrumental reason, focused on a mathematical nature, other aspects of nature—sacred nature, nature with intrinsic worth, and nature as the background of everyday life, faded in importance. Dominion over a universe of matter in motion, mere stuff, entails different possibilities of action than dominion over a sacred, divine creation.

Whereas religion once linked the scientific world and the everyday life-world, they became linked by technology in the modern worldview. The "connection between the progress of modern science and the multiplication of material benefits in everyday life that have been extracted from the environment . . . [is] a connection constituted in practice by technology."[20] The domination of nature becomes ensconced in a new articulation. This articulation, which has historically been called progress, has been the hegemonic articulation from the Enlightenment through modernity to our time. Central to this articulation is the relation of instrumental reason and nature. Instrumental reason has emptied nature of any intrinsic meaning, leaving it a universal, abstracted storehouse of resources to be used for material needs. However, the promise of progress has not been fulfilled. Instead, disenchanted nature seems to lead to environmental disaster.

Leiss recognizes the need to dearticulate the grand design of progress. He realizes that the linkage of domination of nature, instrumental reason, and technology is contingent, not inherently necessary: "The form of rationality that characterizes the modern natural sciences is instrumentalist in a specific sense, but this does not mean that it is inherently bound to technology as an instrument of domination. What constitutes the historical connection between scientific rationality and the progress of domination over nature is a specific constellation of social forces."[21]

Leiss argues that a first step to a dearticulation of progress is an account of the historical function of progress. This is true enough and his book is a good first step, exposing the antagonisms that constitute the limits of progress. For Leiss, the next step is to provide a new articulation such that progress focuses on "*ethical or moral development* rather than scientific and technological innovation."[22] It is at this point that Leiss's analysis falters. Problems occur in Leiss's account of the domination of nature when he uses the concept "domination of nature" to refer to an element within a larger discourse or hegemonic articulation and to refer to the larger hegemonic articulation itself domination of nature is both an element in various articulations with a history Leiss traces back to Genesis, and a grand design elaborated from this key element.

As an element,

> So long as Christianity remained a vital social force in Western civilization, the notion of man as lord of the earth was interpreted in the context of a wider ethical framework. [The decline of religion led to the] identification of mastery over nature with the results of scientific and technological progress. . . . By themselves neither capitalist industry nor the science of mechanics nor machin-

ery are necessarily related to the idea of mastery over nature, and likewise this idea by itself cannot serve as an explanation for the development of those phenomena (either in isolation or in terms of their interrelationship) throughout modern history.[23]

Unfortunately, Leiss does expand the element domination of nature into an explanatory hegemonic articulation or

> grand design which came to be known as the domination of nature. Through a collective social enterprise, extending over many generations and paced by the march of science and technology, the human species would fulfill its destiny by gaining complete control over the forces of the natural world, appropriating to the full its resources for the satisfaction of human needs.[24]

Such a double usage inflates the importance of the domination of nature, minimizes the importance of other elements and the linking of elements, and does not allow for a theorizing of the relation of element and articulation. Such an expanded conception of domination of nature subsumes instrumental reason, foreclosing the possibility of theorizing a new way of thinking or new ethic for humanity-nature relations. The result is to see the domination of nature as the key element in this grand design that leads to the social and ecological problems of the twentieth century. Therefore, against Leiss' intentions, the domination of nature comes to acquire an aura of being natural, ahistorical, and unavoidable. Actually, though, the *linkage* of the domination of nature, instrumental reason, and technology is what is key to this grand design or articulation. Later on, Leiss refers to this grand design as the "doctrine of continuous progress"—a more apt name.[25] For the purposes of this work, the domination of nature is to be understood as an element in the grand design or articulation known as progress: humanity, by dominating nature through the use of instrumental reason (formal reason and technique) and technology (the relation of technique and social forms) will achieve security.

Leiss has rightly argued that the domination of nature is a historical concept that in different contexts or articulations has served different purposes. For Leiss, the domination of nature is not inherent in all reason as it is for Horkheimer. Horkheimer and Leiss can account historically for the catastrophic social and environmental problems of the twentieth century by arguing that the linkage of the domination of nature, instrumental reason, and technology, freed from any constraining context such as that once provided by religion, allows the full realization of the adverse effects of dominating nature. Leiss' historical analysis of the element domination of nature allows him to get beyond the transhistorical notion of domination in reason that muddies Horkheimer's analysis. What Leiss's analysis shows is that domination of nature is not the key element in progress. Domination of nature constrained in a religious articulation or by objective reason does not result in catastrophes like those of the twentieth century. The rise of instrumental reason is the key, the element that allows the full realization of the domination of nature. Leiss recognizes as much when stating that the key element of a new articulation would be liberation of nature, which would entail liberation of human consciousness or reason. In other words, what is primary to rearticulating progress is a development of human reason that transcends instrumental reason. Such a reason would then constrain the domination of nature in an articulation that allows for a mutually beneficial humanity-nature relationship or would perhaps lead to a different sort of relation between humanity and nature that is not based on domination. This is not, at present, a clear articulation, but it is the domain in which we must seek to construct such an articulation.

Since Leiss did not focus his critique on instrumental reason, he is not able to theorize the emergence of a new thinking that transcends instrumental reason. As Leiss acknowledges, "The present secular context requires a very different interpretation, namely, one in which mastery of nature is understood as an advanced stage in human consciousness wherein intelligence is able to regulate its relationship to nature (internal and external) in such a way as to minimize the self-destructive aspects of human desires."[26] Leiss knows what is needed but cannot get there from his analysis of the domination of nature. A theorization of instrumental reason is needed. Leiss understands the historical idea of progress, but he doesn't consider the dynamism (the dialectic of Enlightenment) that undermines goals, so he doesn't investigate the concept of reason. Thus, Leiss cannot conceptualize (and go beyond) instrumental reason, yet such a theorization of instrumental reason is what is needed. Indeed, Leiss puts forth, in a later essay entitled "Caring for Things" in *Under Technology's Thumb*, a philosophy of caring as a new ethic for humanity-nature relations, human-human relations, and human-inanimate objects (or ideas) relations, to transcend the domination of nature. However, the same problem remains for Leiss: how to get from the domination of nature to caring. What Leiss writes about the work of the Frankfurt School is apropos for his own work: "At the core of the human effort to dominate nature is 'instrumental rationality,' the critique of which forms an important subsidiary theme in their thought."[27] The problem in both Horkheimer's and Leiss's work is that the critique of instrumental reason is secondary to that of the domination of nature, but defining reason and civilization through the domination of nature renders the critique unable to theorize an alternative. An analysis focusing on instrumental reason is necessary to clear the way for the theorizing of a reason that can be the core of a new ethic for humanity-nature relations.

To summarize this section, Horkeimer and Adorno sought to explain the collective madness of the twentieth century, the reversal of the Enlightenment, through the domination of nature and the rise of instrumental reason. Their analysis is significant because they saw the root of Western civilization's problems to be humanity's relation to nature—the domination of nature. While Horkeimer and Adorno were concerned with how domination of nature leads to the domination of other people and self-domination, Leiss focuses on domination of nonhuman nature in an effort to show how such domination lies at the root of the world's environmental problems. Leiss has rightly argued that the domination of nature is a historical concept that in different contexts or articulations has served different purposes. For Leiss, the domination of nature is not inherent in all reason as it is for Horkeimer. Leiss can account historically for the catastrophic social and environmental problems of the twentieth century by arguing that the linkage of the domination of nature, instrumental reason, and technology, freed from any constraining context such as that once provided by religion, allows the full realization of the adverse effects of dominating nature. Leiss's historical analysis of the domination of nature allows him to get beyond the transhistorical notion of domination in reason that muddies Horkeimer's analysis. Leiss' elaboration, then, extends critical theory and provides the grounds for critical ecology.

Deep Ecology, Social Ecology, and the Frankfurt School

These grounds are unoccupied. Reflecting a larger disjoint between social theory and environmental thought, scant attention has been paid to the environmental possibilities in critical theory. The few exceptions tend to trace a depressing trajectory from Horkeimer and Adorno through Marcuse to Habermas and they lament, as Robin Eckersley does, the failed promise of the Frankfurt School. It is a depressing trajectory for it moves from Horkeimer and Adorno's critiques of the domination of nature and instrumental reason to Habermas's deeply anthropocentric communicative reason.[28] The early work of the Frankfurt School has suffered one of two fates in environmental circles: benign neglect or hasty disparagement. The former has been its fate in deep ecology circles. Deep ecology, often viewed as the philosophical grounding for the radical environmental action group Earth First!, is an eclectic collection of philosophical, spiritual, mystical, and emotional insights and intuitions loosely united in their rejection of anthropocentrism and adoption of bio/ecocentrism. "Eclectic" may be too kind a descriptor. Though based on the work of Norwegian philosopher Arne Naess, deep ecology skips across traditions as diverse and contrary as Zen Buddhism, Christianity, ecology, Native American beliefs, and twentieth-century physics. In the book *Deep Ecology,* philosophers Bill Devall and George Sessions mention as some sources of deep ecology: Saint Francis, Martin Heidegger, Fritjof Capra, Gary Snyder, Rachel Carson, Lao Tse, Aldo Leopold, Dogen, Aldous Huxley, Henry David Thoreau, Chief Seattle, and John Muir. When stirred together, the resulting mush is hardly comprehensible. Still, from its ecocentric perspective emerges the generally accepted first premise that all life has intrinsic value. As expressed in the first plank of the deep ecology platform, "The well-being and flourishing of human and nonhuman life on Earth have value in themselves (synonyms: intrinsic value, inherent worth). These values are independent of the usefulness of the nonhuman world for human purposes."[29]

Planks two and three basically reiterate number one, while the remaining five planks argue for the need to reduce human impact on the material world by drastically reducing population and consumption. In short, deep ecology can be seen as reversing the culture/nature dichotomy at the root of Western civilization and privileging wilderness. This position can be summarized in the bumpersticker "Save the planet, kill yourself." When stated so baldly, some problems become obvious. First, it is not likely to be a platform with mass appeal. Further, in vilifying a universalized humanity and valorizing an idealized wilderness, deep ecology just reifies the culture/nature dichotomy at the root of environmental problems. This is typified by the attitude of Earth First! co-founder Dave Foreman, who declares, "I resolutely stand with John Muir on the side of the bears in the war industrial society has declared against the Earth."[30] Since humans have always already been part of nature, picking either side in "the war" is suicidal. Instead of being reversed, the dichotomy needs to be displaced.

The Frankfurt School, with its theorizing of the domination of nature as involving the intractable interconnection of humans and nature in a shared fate, provides a first step on the path to rethinking humanity-nature relations. Deep ecology, in constructing a universal humanity as the villain, neglects the many examples of exploitation of humans by humans. Given the histories of colonialism and patriarchy, it is more than a little cruel as well as obtuse to suggest that all peoples under the label of an abstract and universal "humanity" are equally culpable for the ecological crises facing the world. It also does not account for the disproportionate impact upon the environment of industrialized peoples. Quite clearly, the linkage of the domination of nature with instrumental reason and technology makes a qualitative as well as quantitative difference in relation to the impact humans can have on their environment. In other words, the industrial United States has had an impact on the North American continent (and the planet) in ways and to a degree unimaginable by the indigenous inhabitants. As mentioned, the Frankfurt School's formulation of the domination of nature points out that such domination necessarily entails the domination of humans, thus suggesting that analysis requires attention to the social aspect of the domination of nature in its contextual and historical specificity.

Finally, too often deep ecology dismisses reason as evil. This sort of clear-cut approach to thinking is as damaging to thought as it is to forests. Though writing in a different context, Horkheimer warns against such a reaction and eloquently states the case for embracing reason and nature:

> The equating of reason and nature, by which reason is debased and raw nature exalted, is a typical fallacy of the era of rationalization. Instrumentalized subjective reason either eulogizes nature as pure vitality or disparages it as brute force, instead of treating it like a text to be interpreted by philosophy that, if rightly read, will unfold a tale of infinite suffering. Without committing the fallacy of equating nature and reason, mankind must try to reconcile the two.[31]

Social ecology does pay attention to the social aspect of the domination of nature, but to its loss it pays scant attention to the work of the Frankfurt School. Murray Bookchin, the leading light and perhaps only light of social ecology, treats the Frankfurt School with hasty disparagement. In a recent revision of his book, *The Philosophy of Social Ecology,* Bookchin makes a point of noting, "I have excised favorable references to the Frankfurt School."[32] He has left in the unfavorable references, however, dismissing the work of the Frankfurt School as "fashionable commodities" that have too easily fostered postmodern views.[33] In specific reference to Horkheimer and Adorno's *Dialectic of Enlightenment* and Adorno's *Negative Dialectics,* Bookchin concludes that they "were little more than mixed farragoes of convoluted neo-Nietzschean verbiage, often brilliant, colorful, and excitingly informative, but often confused, rather dehumanizing and, to speak bluntly, irrational."[34] Bookchin's major problem with Horkheimer and Adorno is that they trace the root of environmental and social problems to humanity's domination of external nature. Bookchin reverses the analysis. As he writes, "the very *idea* of dominating nature stems from the domination of human by human. This hierarchical mentality and system has been extended from the social domination of people."[35] Bookchin's perspective arises out of his privileging of humanity as evolution's highest achievement. An unrepentant Hegelian, Bookchin views humanity as "nature becoming aware of itself"[36] As Bookchin expounds, "This marvel we call 'Nature' has produced a marvel we call homo sapiens. . . . Natural evolution has conferred on human beings the capacity to form a 'second' or cultural nature out of 'first' or primitive nature. Natural evolution has not only provided humans with the ability but also the necessity to be purposive interveners into 'first nature,' to consciously change 'first nature' by means of a highly institutionalized form of community we call 'society.'[37] For Bookchin, then, humanity is the "unique . . . rational statement of nature's creativity and fecundity . . . the embodiment of nature's own thrust toward self reflexivity."[38]

Bookchin's deeply anthropocentric and avowedly humanistic position is problematic for radical ecological thought. (As an aside, Bookchin's teleological interpretation of evolution is mere wishful thinking or arrogant projection, not ecology or evolutionary biology.) More important, his call for conscious human intervention in natural evolution, far from challenging the domination of nature, would seem to require it. Further, his privileging of humanity and second nature over first nature reinstantiates the culture/nature dichotomy in its traditional hierarchy. Given the premise of eliminating all hierarchies that is at the heart of social ecology, the perpetuation of this most basic of hierarchies is troubling. Finally, even taking Bookchin on his own terms, there is no reason to assume that a human society organized along egalitarian and nonhierarchical lines will necessarily guarantee benign and nonexploitive relations with the nonhuman world. Internal human organization is not determinative of humanity-nature relations. In theorizing human-nature relations, the examples of deep ecology and social ecology make clear the dangers of assuming a dichotomy and focusing on one pole to the neglect of the other. The Frankfurt School's theorizing of the domination of nature, though not without its flaws, is crucial for getting at the intractable interconnections that entwine humanity and nature. It can be the keystone necessary for bridging the chasm separating deep ecology and social ecology, thus enabling an analysis of the environmental crisis that encompasses social and ecological dimensions.

The work of Horkheimer and Adorno remains one of the wellsprings of cultural studies. It is also a remarkably prescient diagnosis of humanity's troubled relation to nature and the consequences. Given the emergence and significance of both cultural studies and environmental studies and politics in the closing decades of the twentieth century, it is puzzling and disturbing that their interactions have been haphazard at best and antagonistic too often. Although a history of the interactions between cultural studies and environmental studies and politics is not possible in the present space, two important books typify the tenor of the (dis)engagement and offer me an opening for proposing a more fruitful engagement.

In 1995, environmental historian William Cronon edited the volume *Uncommon Ground: Rethinking the Human Place in Nature*. The major premise of the collection is that not only nature but wilderness is a social construction. The bulk of the essays trace various constructions of nature and wilderness in national parks, theme parks, and shopping malls. Notably, what might be understood as conventional environmental politics is hardly mentioned. Science and scientists are also scarce. This collection is not an anomaly. The perspective of the participants is succinctly summed up in the theme of Alexander Wilson's *The Culture of Nature*: "Nature is a part of culture."[39] The reversal of the dominant position in the nature/culture dichotomy is significant. Nature does not ground and circumscribe culture, but rather nature is a subset within the larger category of culture. People are not part of nature; nature is part of the human world. The roots of this perspective in what we now call cultural studies arguably reach back to Marx: "For that matter, nature, the nature that preceded human history, is not by any means the nature in which Feuerbach lives, it is nature which today no longer exists anywhere (except perhaps on a few Australian coral-islands of recent origin) and which, therefore, does not exist for Feuerbach."[40] Nature is declared dead (if it ever existed). Bereft of existence, nature remains a rhetorical resource for politics (as Raymond Williams suggests) and a cultural concept for social analysis.

In diminishing nature, cultural studies can no longer take it seriously. It becomes a site of play, a sideshow, just another text, not a central problematic. Toiling in the living rooms of television on behalf of race, class, gender, and sexual identity, cultural studies hardly notices nature aside from the occasional vacation in the fields of nature (as embodied in a chain store at a mega-mall) and neglects environmental politics as a site worthy of study. What Susan Davis writes of communication scholars specifically also applies to cultural studies scholars generally: "while communication scholars have extensively tracked the representations of violence, races, genders, and professions in the mass media, it is striking that they have not given such categories as nature, wilderness, or the environment more than the most rudimentary analysis."[41]

Blithe declarations of "the end of nature" have provoked a reaction, part of which is collected in *Reinventing Nature: Responses to Postmodern Deconstruction*, edited by Michael Soule and Gary Lease. The tone of hysterical defensiveness is neatly captured in the opening paragraph of the preface:

> This multidisciplinary volume is a response to certain radical forms of "postmodern deconstructionism" that question the concepts nature and wilderness, sometimes in order to justify further exploitive tinkering with what little remains of wildness. An eminent European colleague warned us not to publish this work because, he said, the deconstructionists feed on controversy. Perhaps he is right, but we feel that the threats to nature are now so grave that the prudent course is to directly challenge some of the rhetoric that justifies further degradation of wildlands for the sake of development.[42]

Besides the palpable sense of panic, this quote reveals a defensiveness that short-circuits thinking. Soule and Lease freely accuse "postmodern deconstructionsists" of being in league with the resource exploitation industries, as if Derrida is a consultant with Exxon-Mobil or Cronon heads up a division of Weyerhauseur.[43] The fear is understandable, but wild accusations need to be replaced by a serious consideration of the challenges of postmodernism and an open engagement between environmental studies/politics and cultural studies.

This is what the Frankfurt School offers. Surely, Donna Haraway is right and when she suggests, "The certainty of what counts as nature, a source of insight and promise of innocence, is undermined, probably fatally. The transcendent authorization of interpretation is lost, and with it the ontology grounding Western epistemology."[44] Still, conceding that does not warrant displacing nature from the center of social theory. In maintaining humanity-nature relations as the central problematic for industrial society, the Frankfurt School is echoing environmental thinkers and marking a trail for cultural studies. Thoreau's dictum, "In wildness is the preservation of the world" is elaborated by ecologist Aldo Leopold: "Wilderness is the raw material out of which man has hammered the artifact called civilization. Wilderness was never a homogeneous raw material. It was very diverse, and the resulting artifacts are very diverse. The differences in the end-product are known as cultures . . . wilderness gives definition and meaning to the human enterprise."[45]

This sentiment is not alien to the roots of cultural studies. Marx himself, who perceptively noted that external nature is "not a thing given direct from all eternity, remaining ever the same, but the product of industry and the state of society, and, indeed, in the sense that it is a historical product,"[46] also acknowledged, "Man *lives* from nature, i.e., nature is his *body,* and he must maintain a continuing dialogue with it if he is not to die."[47] Nature is not just the grounds for basic existence for Marx, but, in a perspective similar to Leopold's, is also the grounds for cultural existence: "The worker can create nothing without *nature,* without the *sensuous external world.*"[48] In other words, even a historicized nature remains a privileged sphere, maybe not a source of ontological certainty but also not just another text, akin to romance novels, video games, *Star Trek,* and Madonna. For both cultural studies and environmental studies and politics to remain intellectually vital and politically relevant, in order to intervene in the crucial questions of our time, they need to place the nature-humanity problematic at the center of their projects.

Notes

1.   I am indebted to Ian Angus for his expertise in Critical Theory and for his comments on earlier drafts of this essay. He is an extraordinary teacher and thinker.

2.   Christopher Manes, 1990, *Green Rage: Radical Environmentalism and the Unmaking of Civilization* (Boston: Little, Brown), 156.

3.   The discourse of progress can be defined as: humanity, by dominating nature through the use of instrumental reason (formal reason and technique), and technology (the relation of technique and social forms) will achieve security.

4.   Though I refer to Adorno when mentioning the co-authored *Dialectic of Enlightenment,* my analysis is primarily concerned with Horkheimer's thought.

5.   Max Horkheimer and Theodor Adorno, 1972, *Dialectic of Enlightenment* trans. John Cumming. (New York: Herder), 3.

6.   I do not correct or add to the sexist language used by some of those quoted in this work for the reason that such sexist language is not merely a matter of terminology but is often of theoretical significance. For example, when Horkheimer writes on "man," often his analysis is of men and he extends his insights to include all people in Western society, though he pays little attention to the experience of women. The dominance of the patriarchal family and the conception of woman as nature were part of Horkheimer's (and his society's) thought. In my own work I try to avoid sexist terminology and sexist thinking, though probably not with complete success.

7.   Horkheimer and Adorno, *Dialectic of Enlightenment*, 26, 54.

8.   Max Horkheimer, 1947, *Eclipse of Reason* (New York: Oxford LTP), 93.

9.   Ibid., 5.

10.   Ibid., 97.

11.   Ibid., 126.

12.   Ibid., 176.

13.   Ibid., 127.

14.   William Leiss, 1974, *The Domination of Nature* (Boston: Beacon Press), 34.

15.   Bacon as quoted in ibid, 49.

16.   Ibid., 134.

17.   Ibid., 135–36.

18.   Ibid., 132.

19.   Ibid., 136.

20.   Ibid., 140.

21.   Ibid., 208.

22.   Ibid., 193.

23.   Ibid., 35, 93.

24.   Ibid., xi.

25.   Ibid., 184.

26.   Ibid., 197.

27.   William Leiss, 1974, "Critical Theory and Its Future," *Political Theory* 3: 330–49.

28.   These exceptions include: Vincent DiNorcia, 1974–1975, "From Critical Theory to Critical Ecology," *Telos* 22: 86–95; Joel Whitebrook, Summer 1979, "The Problem of Nature in Habermas," *Telos* 40: 41–94; Robin Eckersley, 1992, *Environmentalism and Political Theory* (Albany: State University of New York Press); Andrew Dobson, 1993, "Critical Theory and Green Politics," in *The Politics of Nature*, ed. Andrew Dobson and Paul Lucardie (New York: Routledge); Andrew McLaughlin, 1993, *Regarding Nature: Industrialism and Deep Ecology* (Albany: State University of New York Press); and Michael Dion, Summer 1998, "A Typology of Corporate Environmental Policies," *Environmental Ethics* 20: 151–62. For a more optimistic assessment of the trajectory through Habermas, see John Dryzek, 1990, "Green Reason: Communicative Ethics for the Biosphere," *Environmental Ethics* 12: 195–210; and Steven Vogel, 1996, *Against Nature: The Concept of Nature in Critical Theory* (Albany: State University of New York Press).

29. Naess, Arne, 1995, "The Deep Ecological Movement," in *Deep Ecology in the 21st Century,* ed. George Sessions (Boston: Shambhala): 68.

30. Dave Foreman, 1991, "Second Thoughts of an Eco-Warrior," in *Defending the Earth: A Dialogue Between Murray Bookchin and Dave Foreman* ed. Steve Chase (Boston: South End Press): 107.

31. Horkheimer, *Eclipse of Reason,* 125.

32. Murray Bookchin, 1995, *The Philosophy of Social Ecology: Essays on Dialectical Naturalism* (New York: Black Rose Books): ix.

33. Ibid., 102, 183.

34. Ibid., 175.

35. Murray Bookchin, "Where I Stand Now," *Defending the Earth, 131.*

36. Murray Bookchin, 1987, *The Modern Crisis* (New York: Black Rose Books), 20.

37. Ibid., 21.

38. Bookchin, *Philosophy of Social Ecology,* 140.

39. Alexander Wilson, 1992, *The Culture of Nature: North American Landscape from Disney to the Exxon Valdez* (Cambridge, Mass.: Blackwell): 12.

40. Karl Marx, "The German Ideology," in *The Marx-Engels Reader,* ed. Robert Tucker, (New York: W.W. Norton), 171.

41. Susan Davis, 1997, *Spectacular Nature: Corporate Culture and the Sea World Experience* (Berkeley: University of California Press), 10.

42. Michael Soule and Gary Lease, eds., trans. S. Ryazanskaya. *Reinventing Nature: Responses to Postmodern Deconstruction* (Washington, D.C.: Island Press), xv.

43. Wilderness activist and Earth First! co-founder Dave Foreman and leftist/Marxist journalist Alexander Cockburn specifically make such charges, with Cockburn accusing Cronon of occupying an academic chair that places him in Weyerhauseur's pocket.

44. Donna Haraway, 1991, *Simians, Cyborgs, and Women: The Reinvention of Nature* (New York: Routledge), 152–53.

45. Aldo Leopold, 1949/1968, *A Sand County Almanac* (New York: Oxford University Press), 188, 200.

46. Marx, "German Ieology," *Marx-Engels Reader,* 171.

47. Karl Marx, 1975, "Economic and Philosophical Manuscripts," in *Karl Marx: Early Writings* ed. Quintin Hoare. Trans. Gregor Benton. (New York: Vintage Books), 328.

48. Ibid., 325.

11

One-Dimensional Symptoms: What Marcuse Offers a Critical Theory of Law*

Caren Irr

If the central problem of cultural studies is the interpretation of practices of culture in relation to social history and stratification, then clearly cultural studies requires a critical theory of law. Contemporary American culture, after all, depends heavily on legal authority; many producers of culture not only take law as subject matter but also send their products through a filter of lawyers before distributing them to the consuming public. In a famously litigious society, libel statutes and the politics of legitimate representation, along with copyright and trademark law, can play a determinate role in cultural production.

Often the relationship between particular works of culture and the law is simple and direct. For example, when developing films, the Disney corporation negotiates contracts with its employees and with independent producers, setting conditions for the corporation's appropriations of traditional and modern cultures. Whether establishing contractual rights to previously published works (such as *Bambi* or Stravinsky's *The Rite of Spring*) or claiming access to unprotected general ideas in the public domain (such as the nerd stereotype used in *Honey, I Shrunk the Kids*), Disney relies on the law to outline the parameters of legitimate cultural production.[1] Similarly, Disney uses the law to protect its intellectual property after production and to control the means of its circulation. For instance, in 1990, Disney sued Carl Powell, a small-time souvenir vender in the District of Columbia, for his purveying of "mouse-face" tee-shirts and other paraphernalia representing Donald Duck, Huey, Duey, Louie, Pluto, Goofy, and Roger Rabbit.[2] Both before and after Disney works become available to the public, then, the law mediates the production-consumption circuit. This mediation is especially obvious in the case of industrial cultural production such as Disney's but arguably occurs in more artisanal styles of production as well.

To account specifically and critically for the role of the law in culture requires that cultural studies see law itself as a formation. Law is not reducible to policy questions; it is not simply the result of a series of pragmatic choices or the passive reflection of ideological imperatives. Nor is law immediately reducible to the interests of economically dominant segments of society—though clearly there is an affinity

*Thank you to Evan Watkins for his comments on this essay and David Bottorff for his excellent bibliographical research.

between economic and legal power. Instead, law is in part what it says it is: a semiautonomous institution governed by a rationality with its own traditions and history. Without losing all sight of the political and economic features, a critical theory of law will attend to this institution's specificity and then proceed to integrate an analysis of law with an account of its relationship to culture.

Cultural studies, in other words, needs a critical theory of the law in order to describe accurately the dynamics of culture. Such a theory should attend to law per se and not treat law as an allegory for other concerns, if it is to account well for the industrial character of contemporary culture. Finally, such a theory must be *critical* and *theoretical* so it may recognize the role of law in culture without losing sight of the social totality and the uneven distribution of the benefits of law across the totality. Toward this end, this essay outlines a critical theory of the law derived from the Frankfurt School, especially Herbert Marcuse's *One-Dimensional Man.*

Critical Theory and the Law

In his comprehensive intellectual history, *The Frankfurt School: Its History, Theories, and Political Significance,* Rolf Wiggershaus offers a serious and helpful definition of critical theory. The "common task" of critical theorists, he asserts,

> . . . was to produce a theory of society as a whole, a theory of the contemporary era, whose subject would be human beings as producers of their own historical forms of life—forms of life which had, however, become alienated from them.

Such a theory, he continues, "had to be both rational and, at the same time, had to offer the right word, the word which would break the spell under which everything . . . lay."[3] Despite the fact that Max Horkheimer—as director of the Frankfurt Institute for Social Research—is in many senses the hero of Wiggershaus' study, in this definitive passage he paraphrases Marcuse instead. "Critical thought," Marcuse wrote in *One-Dimensional Man,* "strives to define the irrational character of the established rationality . . . and to define the tendencies which cause this rationality to generate its own transformation."[4] In other words, as Marcuse usefully emphasizes, critical theory is a rational exposé of the systemic irrationality of contemporary society, and its own rationality aims toward a spell-breaking transformation of that irrationality.

The vital elements of critical theory's super-rationality, then, are these:

1. Critical theory begins with "human beings as producers of their own lives"; when a master-slave dialectic is at work, this means beginning with the point of view of the slave and attributing productive force to the active participants and not, for instance, to metaphysical inevitabilities.
2. Critical theory produces "a theory of society as a whole"; it ambitiously refuses to attribute causality to only one terrain of human production and

seeks instead to capture the several and mobile ongoing processes that together constitute the social totality. Societies are wholes for critical theory—unfinished, complex, and inorganic—but wholes nonetheless.

3. Critical theory understands "forms of life" as "alienated" from human beings; that is, it identifies and explores the contradictions structuring social totalities. In particular, critical theory foregrounds contradictions between the subjective world of cultural producers and their results, and reading subjectivity symptomatically becomes a precondition for any experientially validated accounts of the totality.

4. Finally, critical theory seeks "the word which would break the spell." It not only offers an alternative rationality, critical theory also attributes transformative power to the word, the concept, or the theory—specifically the power to strengthen alternatives already latent within the contradictory social totality.

Overall, there is what we might call a strong ascetic flavor to critical theory. It seeks to overturn everyday or socially dominant perceptions with a negative critique based on the primary forces involved in the production of life and aiming toward a vision of totality and a unifying transformation of that totality. The negative or ascetic moment in critical theory (or, in Marcuse's vocabulary, the Great Refusal) is powerful and ultimately positive, and it is not cause for disavowals of the type preoccupied with the Frankfurt School's so-called pessimism. The ascetic moment is directly and logically linked to the promise of utopian transformation. Understood in social terms, the ascetic moment begins with the point of view of the slave or what Wiggershaus more broadly calls "those who were exploited and humiliated" (6). This starting point insistently and critically recalls the facts that liberal social theory obscures, and without this element critical theory shifts toward the Freud side of its Marx-Freud synthesis. Unless the ascetic moment acquires social content at some point, critical theory has a tendency to interpret the negative as Thanatos or some other nonsocial metaphysical principle.

It is this point of view—that of the exploited and humiliated producers of human life—that Marcuse helps us retain for a critical theory of the law. This contribution supplements excellent existing work on the law in the Frankfurt School tradition. Though I can only briefly survey this work here, the Frankfurt School offers enormous (and largely untapped) resources for philosophically and sociologically sophisticated theories of the law in modern industrial societies.

Some recent scholarship on the Frankfurt School has explored the problem of law in critical theory. For instance, William Scheuerman has argued for the important contributions of Franz Neumann and Otto Kirchheimer to legal theory.[5] Engaged in a dialectics of influence with the far right political theorist Carl Schmitt, Kirchheimer and Neumann developed substantial totalizing theories of modern states. Others have drawn attention to work such as Friedrich Pollock's theory of "State Capitalism"; Pollock's analysis unifies discussion of Soviet planning and Keynesian economics, ultimately arguing that the profit motive is subordinate to the power motive.[6] Rather than opposing totalitarian political forms to democratic ones, Pollock identifies both totalitarian and democratic political forms as alternative methods of asserting power over economic planning. Although he definitely asserts the necessity of employing political means for social and economic transformation, Pollock situates "politics" within the context of a social totality.

The consequences of this macrological approach for a critical legal theory are several. Pollock's analysis produces a useful openness to historical interpretation. Treating politics, law, and the state in the context of social totality means understanding that the relative position of law with respect to other institutions will vary over time, as the social totality shifts in its shape and structure. As opposed to a static functionalist model, critical theory following Pollock suggests that law may have become more determinate in the postwar period.

In Pollock's analysis, however, there is a tendency for the problem of law in particular to be fused with the problems of the state and politics more generally. These then tend to become affiliated with an interests approach to power; that is, forms of capitalism ("private" vs. "state") are differentiated according to the ways they mediate the interests of "the ruling group." (78). Remaining too long at the macrological level, Pollock's analysis retains the negative moment only in its more speculative passages, when considering the potential for reconciling political and economic liberty in a state capitalist system. Similarly, Andrew Arato argues that Pollock replaces a critique of political economy with a critique of politics, while omitting the cultural focus that would allow for some forms of resistance; the law, on this account, would likely prove simply one more tool of domination.[7]

By way of contrast, the project on the authoritarian personality in which Adorno, Erich Fromm, Marcuse, Pollock, and others participated sought to offer a micrological approach to the state and, indirectly, the law. Using empirical research techniques to explain the appeal of fascist state authority, Adorno et al. concluded that authoritarian state structures were the social correlative of sadomasochistic family structures, especially those in which an overly dominant paternal figure required the ongoing, resentful dependence of sons (Wiggershaus 148–56). Here, critical theory's emphasis on contradiction was crucial; though law and the state appear in this study sometimes as noncontradictory effects of the conflicted individual psyche, this work in social psychology rhymes with and complements some of the participants' contemporaneous thinking more specifically devoted to the law.

For example, in Horkheimer and Adorno's famous account in *Dialectic of Enlightenment* of Odysseus tying himself to the mast, we find a discussion of law sensitive to the institution's internal contradictions.[8] They famously read *The Odyssey* as a site of the proleptic emergence of the bourgeois subject. By constraining himself physically but leaving his ears open to the Sirens' song, Odysseus reveals himself to be a lawyer. He escapes the world of myth (which is governed by repetition—i.e., the undifferentiated application of the law), by taking literally the command that he give himself over to the song. He takes this law at face value by keeping his ears open, not attempting to hide from the law's application; yet he also avoids the law's effects by making himself *more* subject to the law, by overcompensating, by overdramatizing his subjection as one bound to the ship that carries him. Since he is entirely subjected, he is not steering, and the ship does not crash when he is overcome by the Sirens' song. Using a typical lawyer's trick then—following the letter of the law (which demands subjection)—Odysseus escapes the effects of the law and becomes the prototypical bourgeois subject; Odysseus becomes the subject who makes the law work to his own purposes.

In other words, we find with Horkheimer and Adorno an analysis of the literalism of rights discourse that insists we recognize its involvement with the spread of instrumental reason. The separation of ends and means, letter and spirit, leader and those led in the episode from the *Odyssey* is for this generation of the Frankfurt School the prototype of the bourgeois "coldness" that is (a) inverted but not overcome by de Sade's transgressive Juliette, (b) totalized by the culture industry, and (c) met by its own barbaric Döppelganger in fascist anti-Semitism. The literalism of rights discourse, in other words, despite all its appeals to political contestation also testifies to the rise of Weberian technocracy, a structure that addresses inequality for the purposes of crisis management, not its principled eradication.

Many readers have deplored Horkheimer and Adorno's tendency in this text to read the Enlightenment as inevitably tending to resolve its contradictions in a regression to absolute barbarism, but we might note here that even very sympathetic readers point to the need to continue developing the dialectic outlined here.[9] Contradiction as a social logic—however elegantly and subtly explored—may itself require historical situating; we may well, for instance, wish to situate Horkheimer and Adorno's preoccupation with Odysseus' perspective while recalling other contradictions that it overshadows, such as the blind physicality of the rowers. Brought together, in their unresolved combination, these two perspectives may allow us to sort out the irrational elements of contemporary law from its latent alternatives.

The consequences of the third element of critical theory (the transformative "word") for analysis of law have been most thoroughly explored by Jürgen Habermas. Building on his theory of communicative action, in *Between Facts and Norms* (1992), Habermas argues that a theory of law adequate to contemporary pluralist societies will recognize the necessity of deliberative democracy. Opposing the "normative defeatism" of sociological accounts of law as an institution constrained by external power, Habermas outlines a positive concept of the public sphere and its ability to negotiate the competing demands of complex societies. He refers, for instance, to the active concept of political participation that motivates civil disobedience and concludes that such participants' perspectives are vital and effective means for an "uncoerced articulation of social interests."[10] That is, when counterbalanced by a responsible mass media and an active deliberative citizenry, constitutionally guaranteed legal discourse can—on Habermas's account—successfully transform not only its own terms but also its neighboring domains in the social world. Cautiously optimistic (rather than exuberantly utopian), Habermas presents legal discourse as a post-metaphysical alternative to the failures of moral and ethical reason. On his account, the "word," when subjected to public scrutiny and empirical, historical qualification, is an already extant and promising alternative to the opportunistic reign of "fact" (e.g., the market) and the culturally variable appeal of universalist "norms" (e.g., religion or human rights). Communication breaks the magic spell of metaphysics for

Habermas and enlivens the mutually dependent grounds of social integration: law and public discourse.

In developing a synthetic theory that attempts to integrate sociological and normative accounts of law, Habermas is in part responding to his critics. Significant among his American critics have been feminists who draw attention to the sociological limits to the law's assumption that participants have equal standing.[11] In particular, feminists have questioned the efficacy of communication in a public sphere to which women and others have socially restricted access and in which they are routinely misrecognized and disrespected. In answer to these charges, Habermas restates the need for "all those affected [to] have an effective opportunity to voice their demands for rights on the basis of concrete experiences of violated integrity, discrimination, and oppression" (426). Public participation of the oppressed and exploited becomes, in his theory, a precondition for securing the guarantees of an independent private life. Beginning with intersubjective public articulations, Habermas' commitment to the transformative power of the word thus places itself fundamentally at odds with those public articulations that begin with the constraints of an alienated private life—whether understood as family or personal identity. Populations whose experiences of exploitation or expression are specifically constituted by prejudicial access to the public sphere are located in, but not central to, this version of a critical theory of the law.

All three of these approaches—Pollock's, Adorno's, and Habermas's—present important elements of a critical theory of law, but all will benefit, I assert, from a complementary commitment to the perspective of "the slave." A critical theory of law will want to work not only from the sociological exterior or the internal and contradictory perspective of practitioners or idealistic theoreticians. In what follows, employing Marcuse's historical approach to the drives, I make a case for understanding the law from the point of view of its "objects," those internal but nondominant participants whose concerns often appear in the form of cathexion rather than reason.

Reading Marcuse

Since the 1960s, Marcuse's work has been read in one of two ways. On the one hand, it has often been seen as a dated celebratory rhetoric of sexual liberation: "When you read Marcuse now, he seems out of another time: 'Express your sexuality and there will be peace on earth.' But what we call liberation can turn out to be shattering— forget monogamy, intimacy, family. And what happened? We all ended up on psychiatrists' couches."[12] This reading of the "happy" Marcuse stresses the utopian potential of Eros as described in *Eros and Civilization.* Some defend the "happy" Marcuse as an inspiring hermeneut, or as the proponent of an ideology critique of Freud who nonetheless proposes libidinal politics as a model for social transformation in general. His exploration of "pleasure" is seen as offering resources for the exploration of high and middlebrow culture.[13] Others, however, reject the Marcuse of *Eros and Civilization,* citing an overvalorization of the subject as a site of possibility and a prematurely optimistic reading of nature—and even death itself—as a recoverable site of nondominated social relations.[14] In essence, it is the interpretive stress that Marcuse's synthesis of Marx and Freud in *Eros and Civilization* places on the moment of truth within actually existing repressive civilizations that is the target of negative readings of the "happy" Marcuse.

In his own 1966 "political preface" to *Eros and Civilization,* Marcuse supports these latter readings, asserting that he had "neglected or minimized. . . the 'social engineering' of the soul" characteristic of affluent, postscarcity societies.[15] This observation marks an important shift to the "sad" or ascetic Marcuse of *One-Dimensional Man.* Centrally concerned with the successful irrationality of repression or Thanatos, this work makes the "happy" reading difficult to sustain. Thus, for intellectual biographers such as Douglas Kellner who stress the later Marcuse, he turns out to be too sad, too pessimistic, not sufficiently concerned with the agency of the individual of social subject; he is charged with underplaying the structural contradictions that fueled the new social movements of the 1960s.[16] In other words, the "sad" Marcuse is too Adornian for some members of the 1960s generation, as well as for the mainstream media, and those of the Fromm school who seek psychological adjustment within a society based on control. Paradoxically, orthodox Communists seem sometimes to agree on this point with the psychoanalysts.[17]

At the same time, some find even the "sad" Marcuse not sad enough. In this spirit, thorough-going American anti-Communist interpretations join poststructuralist attacks on the dialectic.[18] From both angles, even the "sad" Marcuse retains an unduly positive trace of faith in version of Enlightenment progress.

Rather than affirm either of the dominant readings of Marcuse's work, I want to point here to the fundamental assumptions that they both share. Both accept a notion of Marcuse as one who adopts a general tone or emotional attitude in response to an empirically documentable (and thus contestable) historical situation. That is, all views either accept or reject his portrait of social conditions and then move on to agree or disagree with the response to those conditions that they take Marcuse to be recommending. This fundamental separation between "attitude" and social conditions can only occur at the expense of downplaying one of Marcuse's central points: that the drives themselves (attitudinal responses naturalized as temperament) are historical and social in character. This is the basic synthesis underlying both *Eros and Civilization* and *One-Dimensional Man,* and taking it seriously means that there is, structurally speaking, no possibility of distinguishing the empiricist account of social conditions from an emotional response to it. Furthermore, it is this primary attention to the sociological features of the unconscious that make Marcuse's version of critical theory especially useful for a critique of law. Marcuse identifies social features of the "slave" subject's psychology, especially in relation to technology. Then he reads several institutional discourses for the effects of social psychology. As a dialectical mediating structure, technology figures prominently in Marcuse's work and I will ultimately want to read this figure as a correlative for the law.

One-Dimensional Man includes many passing references to law, generally negative in tenor. Marcuse describes a nation's laws as a mere reflection of the power of a dominating group: "The U.S. Congress, assembled in session, the Central Committee, the Party, . . . are tangible and effective entities over and above the component individuals. They are tangible in the records, in the results of their laws" (205). At other times, the concept of the law has a more metaphysical connotation, recalling an idealist philosophy to which Marcuse opposes his own: "The linguistic syndrome of 'loveliness,' 'aesthetic sense,' and 'desert landscape' evokes the liberating air of Nietzsche's thought, cutting into Law and Order" (216). Similarly, Technics is described as having a "Logos" (236), and the transformative capacity of technology is only realized when this Logos is overcome, releasing a wilder and self-consciously irrational act of refusal. As even these few examples illustrate, the concept of law recurs in central and significant contexts for Marcuse, joining together sociological, philosophical, and normative themes. To understand the significance of these passing references, however, requires a broader view of the themes of Marcuse's text.

One-Dimensional Man proposes a critical theory of discourse as a social symptom rather than a site of signification. In producing his second-generation Frankfurt School thesis on the one-dimensionality of advanced industrial society, Marcuse not only synthesizes the theoretical work of Marx and Freud. He also situates the versions of Marx and Freud that were handed down to him, as it were, in the postwar institutions of white-collar labor and consumer society. Analyzing the ideological conditions these institutions presuppose, Marcuse reads their one-dimensional discourses symptomatically and thus registers the work of these institutions and discourses in a fundamentally contradictory situation. He identifies at the outset the totalizing irrationality of one-dimensional society (the "peaceful production of means of destruction" [ix]), uncovers the contradictory social logic that sutures subjects to this situation, traces the stultifying effects of this collapse into one-dimensionality in the intellectual arenas that ought to provide alternatives, and finally locates traces of genuine alternatives elsewhere. Throughout this analysis, the most valuable element for our purposes is Marcuse's transformation of the problem of the consciousness of the "exploited and humiliated."

Marcuse's transformation of the problem of slave consciousness is bound up with his analysis of the arts. Perhaps the best known chapter of *One-Dimensional Man* is "The Conquest of the Unhappy Consciousness: Repressive Desublimation," in which Marcuse works out the primary synthetic move of his project: the claim that that desire is historical—or, to put it somewhat more evocatively, that "[t]he music of the soul is also the music of salesmanship" (57). Carrying on the legacy of Horkheimer and Adorno's critique of the culture industry in *Dialectic of Enlightenment,* Marcuse argues that it is not only mass culture of the mid-century that is industrialized, standardized, and reified; "high" culture, too, is integrated into the hegemonic happy consciousness, into the mystified acceptance of "salesmanship." While surrealist art of the 1920s and 1930s offered a certain "aesthetic incompatibility" with respect to the hegemonic society (on the basis of its articulation of the unsatisfied desires that project a different erotic future), in the structurally different situation of Marcuse's present, this two-dimensionality has subsequently been flattened; "the Great Refusal is in turn refused" in the face of the spread of technological rationality (64).

The result of this dialectical turn, for Marcuse, is that both critical distance (or exteriority) and artistic alienation (or interiority) collapse, so that neither the institutions of avant-garde art nor the psychic stance of the artist-critic offers potential for desublimation, for the release of erotic energies in conflict with the reality principle. The conquest of social life occurs to such an extent that both the basic drives are reorganized around the Happy Consciousness. This latter happiness "arranges games with death and disfiguration in which fun, teamwork, and strategic importance mix in rewarding social harmony" (for instance, in the RAND Corporation's nuclear threat scenarios); desublimation, in other words, acts to further repression (80). Eros and Thanatos ultimately serve the same master, rather than contradicting each other. As a result, the artist is not the primary site of affective resistance for Marcuse in *One-Dimensional Man* (though the aesthetic dimension never entirely loses its capacity for negative critique for Marcuse).

Since such a critique confronts head on both liberal and radical faith in the autonomy of culture, education, and consciousness as sites of resistance, it is perhaps not surprising that this chapter has been the most influential part of Marcuse's study in the post-1960s United States. It has also been taken as a prophetic account of the implosion of movement culture.[19] By arguing that culture and the psyche are almost entirely integrated with domination, Marcuse's account of repressive desublimation leaves us in a situation requiring the treatment of so-called liberated desires as false consciousness or false needs. To say the least, this cynicism does not sit comfortably with the more naïvely utopian impulses of the 1960s, let alone with a developmental-ist approach to the culture of consumption—i.e., with the mode of triumphalism that assumes individuals and cultures require a consumerist delirium of desire in order to combat the logic of scarcity. In those contexts, Marcuse's analysis sounds overly ascetic and thus also opposed to the insights of a contemporary cultural studies regarding the resistant or compensatory pleasures involved in consumption.

What I want to stress, however, is that we miss the point when we focus exclusively on Marcuse's scathing critique of Happiness. His larger and more impor-tant concern is the historical character of *all* desire. By examining a transformation in the relationship between desire and domination in advanced industrial societies (such that the two are more integrated than had previously been the case), Marcuse is of course berating a society in which indulging one's desires or even formulating them has become a motor of domination, not resistance to it. But also and more important he is demonstrating how, from the point of view of the manufactured psyche of the one-dimensional society, the historical character of desire as resistance changes.

As a consequence, romanticizing the psyche and its processes as some sort of undiscovered or dark continent is no longer effective for Marcuse. In fact, such romantic tendencies themselves become explicable symptoms of domination. The symbolists and surrealists were "breaking the spell of the things that are," he writes; their "word refuses the unifying, sensible rule of the sentence" (68–69). But, for Marcuse, theirs was an opportunity provided by the historical conjuncture of psycho-analysis as a technical vocabulary and the conditions of Taylorized mass production, together with a phase of imperialism that began to demystify the fetishistic qualities of the European art object while this object still had enough residual "aura" to be temporarily transferred to mass-produced cups and saucers, bicycle parts, postcards, and chests of drawers. With this historical proviso in mind, the transformed situation of culture and desire in the one-dimensional society is not so much a loss as another specific conjuncture, containing its own not entirely realized possibilities. The artist or intellectual might be able to recover a claim to a nondominated point of view as the historical situation changes, but she or he is not necessarily central at all (or any) points in time. It is to the position of other sorts of producers of human life that Marcuse turns.

In "The New Forms of Social Control" and "The Closing of the Political Universe," Marcuse traces the larger social context in which the production of human life takes place. In particular, he attends to the development of new "needs," especially the need for identification via commodities, as it comes to supplant the demand for "rights and liberties" that characterized earlier stages of industrial society (1). The production and temporary satisfaction of these false needs operate as forms of containment of forces previously directed toward the state, Marcuse argues, because they institutionalize an empiricist and technical rationality that is at its base irrational. By producing further goods and affluence within the logic of industrialization, technical rationality reinstitutes its control, redirecting a social need for peace, for instance, to the massive and irrational production of war in the form of nuclear weapons. The Welfare State and the Warfare State merge, on this logic, into total administration, and public life is cast into the role of debating more and less efficient methods of administrating the dominant mode of irrationality. In contrast to Habermas, Marcuse does not see the public sphere as a likely terrain for the self-actualization of dominated groups.

Public life is constrained because underlying these forms of social control are dramatic transformations in the organization and character of labor. Mechanization, on Marcuse's account, "assimilate[s] productive and non-productive jobs," so that divisions between white- and blue-collar labor diminish and are transferred to forms of status and consumption (25). Furthermore, as class autonomy and self-identification in the workplace shrinks and identification with the machine increases, political conflict between classes is contained; the working class's political integration and the dependence of both blue- and white-collar laborers on administration per se allows the continued and contradictory production of massive human, technological, and military waste along with the production of containment. For Marcuse, the political consequences of this situation include the necessity of historicizing the subject of social change; on his analysis, coalitions of students, intellectuals, the homeless, racial minorities, and Third World migrants are in a better position for political action than the structurally integrated working class and the artists. Critical theory does not know ahead of time, as it were, where the point of view of the dominated subject will be found, so it should seek its historically constituted subjects at the margins, among those whose desires are organized by social engineering as necessarily unhappy.

In other words, for Marcuse, a necessary precondition to re-theorizing the critical capacity (or lack thereof) of culture is a historically particular analysis of political and economic structures of domination as they have been transformed in the administered society. In producing this account, Marcuse relies heavily on contemporaneous sociology of the white-collar class and American suburbia, but he synthesizes the work of C. Wright Mills, Vance Packard, William H. Whyte, David Reisman, and others rather than simply lifting their conclusions out of context. In their accounts of the changing tastes and consumption habits of the new middle classes, the "white-collar" sociologists described postwar marketers' and employers' systematic reproduction of the popular temperaments and lifestyles they preferred. While producing an essential and influential account of the manufactured character of social norms, this scholarship did not focus on the history of desire and sometimes devolved into elitist critique of the intellectual and cultural barrenness of the middle brow.[20] On the other side of the equation, in their accounts of transformations of the social psychology, late Freudians such as Fromm tended to rigidify normal social relations.[21] Against both tendencies, Marcuse asserts the historical particularity and processual character of the one-dimensional happy norm.

What saves Marcuse's analysis, however, from the charge that it prematurely assumes that marginal subjects (students, migrants, minorities, etc.) are unproduced or permanently outside norms is, I think, the following: he locates their presence not in reified desiring consciousnesses but rather in part in discourse and "thought" or, as we might say today, the media. Throughout the bulky middle of *One-Dimensional Man*, Marcuse identifies constitutive habits of one-dimensional discourse— particularly the suppression of contradiction as unempirical, but also including a stress on scientific neutrality, and the therapeutic function of anti-metaphysical philosophy. Available in a germinal form in these analyses are the tools for a historically nuanced and dialectical critique of the discourse of the law, a critique that functions critically only if it reveals the law's situation with respect to the social totality—that is, to the mechanized workplace, the transformation of social identities, and the historical technologies of psychic life. We find some tools and pointers for analyzing the law not as a site of signification, but as a site of social labor. In a Marcusean vein, we learn to attend to the law as the language of "administration" without slipping into objections produced by a reification of desire as something and also as a technology that has been the target of strong cathexions. We learn, in other words, to seek after those elements of the law that appear "unlovely and disorderly from the logical point of view," since they "may well comprise the lovely elements of a different order, and may thus be an essential part of the material from which philosophic concepts are built" (216).

These "unlovely and disorderly" elements have an affiliation with certain ghostly universals: "The hypostasized whole resists analytic dissolution" (207). The whole persists and accompanies its own parts for Marcuse. This enduring "whole" is his figure for what he calls the true consciousness of members of a group, class, or society: "true . . . consciousness . . . would synthesize the data of experience in concepts which reflect, as fully and adequately as possible, the given society in the given facts" (208). Experientially or emotionally endorsed metaphysical concepts such as Consciousness, Beauty, Justice, or Happiness register for Marcuse the "divided world in which 'that which is' falls short of, and even denies 'that which can be'" (209). Academically disreputable appeals to universals, in other words, are to be read symptomatically as evidence of utopian social desire. These ghostly universals are the traces of the perspective of the dominated.[22]

Marcuse makes clear at a number of points in *One-Dimensional Man* that his interest in these ghostly universals should not be translated into an affirmation of primitivist fantasies. He is not seeking a regression to some historically prior Gestalt but rather a transcendent project that negates present conditions while preserving and improving on them. The point of view of the dominated, in other words, may not always present itself in obviously political or critical terms; it is rather to be read out of projects that include among their effects a powerful and improving negative moment.

In the case of the law, then, Marcuse's theory suggests that it will be essential to differentiate between the universal claims inherent in the discourse itself (those elements Habermas identifies as a normative morality) and the ghostly universals invoked by a subordinated population's experiences of law. A popular metaphysics of law, in other words, provides a crucial element for critical theory, especially when supplementing a critical reading of the techniques of domination and instrumental rationality that preoccupy the discourse.

Often, this popular metaphysics is strongly affective; it identifies law as a site of social power and often reads the law through a sociological lens. In this metaphysics, show trials, such as the O. J. Simpson case, become social allegories, and the "technicalities" of law mere tricks for the wealthy (or persons otherwise unfairly advantaged) to get "off the hook" on which others hang. "Justice" and "rights" remain in these popular conspiracy theories universals with important negative potential. A rigorous critical theory of law would need to account for the powerful affect attached to these universals and do its best to locate their capacity for refusal. Where official accounts of law routinely diminish or exclude affect from their considerations, a critical theory will want to treat seriously what is clearly a common and significant popular experience of the law: tremendous frustration resulting in the expression of longing for greater justice. In the context of a critical theory attentive to the contradictory and potentially transformative character of the unfinished and complex social totality, such an account of the law could significantly alter our concept of the cultural work accomplished by this social institution. That is, reading marginal subjects' affective relation to the law as a social symptom can lead us to reverse the tone of Marcuse's passing references to the law in *One-Dimensional Man*. Although often serving as a dystopian figure, the law also serves in this text the crucial function of attracting a utopian universalist imaginary.

Conclusion

Returning to the Disney cases with which we began, we can briefly test a Marcusean critical theory of law. In *Boosey & Hawkes v. The Walt Disney Company* (1998), for instance, the British music company that owned the rights to Stravinsky's "Rite of Spring" contested Disney's use of selections of the work in the globally distributed videotape and laser disc versions of the motion picture *Fantasia*. The ownership of cultural works available through new technologies and in transnational marketplace was thus at issue. Ultimately, after a series of appeals, Disney triumphed.

When allegorizing this case, we could conclude that the ghost of the modernist composer has met his match in the form of corporate genius Michael Eisner whose half-billion-dollar-a-year salary and vicelike grip on *Fantasia's* dancing hippopotami force the public realization of the hidden correspondences between the totalizing impulses of high art and the global homogeneity of American mass media.[23] Or we could decide that Disney's superior resources and long history of underhanded victories in the American courts made it possible for them to roust the British in an assertion of cultural imperialism soon to be exported around the globe.[24] Or, we might express satisfaction at seeing the individualism of the grand *auteur* being displaced and dispersed by the cryogenically preserved pseudo-populist creator of the Mouse; perhaps the recent high tech export of *Fantasia* allows space for multicultural recoding of the film's dicey equations of races and species through the critical distance of high fan culture.[25] That is, even the bare bones of the disputes over this multimillion-dollar property prompt certain allegorical readings that treat it as a microcosm of global controversies over who owns culture and what they own. Each of these readings invokes strong affect and the ghostly universals powering those affects should be explored for their critical promise.

At the same time, Marcuse's attention to forms of social control reminds us to attend something crucially important taking place in this case at another level. In addition to being a case about the cultural content of dancing hippopotami in tutus and so on, this case is also an exercise in affiliating reason with property. *Boosey & Hawkes v. Walt Disney* shows us the labor of the law, how it invents and distributes itself well outside the boundaries of the state. To see how this process works and what its consequences might be for the culture industry, we need to look a bit more closely at the modes of reasoning that the courts employed, and in so doing Marcuse's technologies of reading are indispensable.

Of course, at one level, *Boosey & Hawkes v. Walt Disney* is much like many court cases. Legalese turns complicated factual and theoretical questions into clunky noun phrases that sediment reasoning into a series (or several layers of series) with confusing internal relationships: "Defendant, licensee of right to use Stravinsky's musical composition, . . . appeals from district court's grant of declaratory judgment that its license did not authorize distribution" and so on. To read this document, we must treat its legalistic language denotatively and not necessarily sequentially. We need to know what a "declaratory judgment" is, then how that is granted, and what an appeal of the grant would be, before we can come to some appreciation for this court's dismissal of the appeal of the grant of declaratory judgment. We must assume that these terms mean the same thing each time they are used (or else accuse their authors of amphibole), and we must accede to the court's practice of treating previous decisions as conclusive judgments, rather than historically specific instances. That is, it is essential to this mode of legal reasoning that precedent be specific and binding.

These general conditions apply to almost any instance of case law one encounters, so it is useful to recall the kind of labor they symptomatize. First, *Boosey & Hawkes v. Disney* is clearly an instance of what Marcuse would call administered reasoning. Guilt, disturbance, and affective involvement are banished to the margins by the transformation of specific acts into technical procedures. Furthermore, precedent distributes anonymity through "official" language. It is not only the particular actors in this case who are recoded in terms of their formal roles (defendant, licensee, plaintiff, assignee, counsel, judges, etc.); it is also the past itself that is depersonalized, ripped from "context," and stripped of specificity by means of legal citation. Reduced to a "rule" or a procedural indicator, the logic of precedent obviates consideration of so-called first principles, intentions, or effects. Its function is to perpetuate efficiency of administration; it is inherently technocratic, orderly, and—in Marcuse's vocabulary—Happy. Its version of equality is strictly formal, in that it pretends not to notice who the players are or how different the world in which something like "contract" rose to prominence is from our own.

Furthermore, two particular issues in this case teach us how the particular institutional constraints and negotations of labor are working themselves out at present in terms of globalizing intellectual property. First, in this case we find the Court of Appeals applying a somewhat more markedly methodological argument than is often used. In attempting to resolve the "new use" question—that is, the question of whether contracts cover the use of technologies that did not exist at the time the contract was made—the 2nd Court of Appeals writes that "new-use analysis should rely on neutral principles of contract interpretation rather than solicitude for either party . . . What governs . . . is the language of the contract" (487). In these phrases, the courts are explicitly sidelining any question having to do with the intent of the authors of the contract—not out of any poststructuralist dispersal of the metaphysics of the subject, but rather for pragmatic reasons: "intent is not likely *to be helpful* when the subject of the inquiry is something the parties were not thinking about" (488; emphasis added). The "language of the contract" is what is appealed to here as a final source of authority, though this supposedly neutral premise slips quickly into a defense of the status quo. Disney's claim to rightful new uses of Stravinsky's copyrighted materials is upheld on the grounds that to read the contract otherwise would deviate "from the most reasonable reading of the license" (488). Favoring the intentionless language of the contract, then, in this case results in the court upholding the kind of "reasonable reading" that conforms to standard corporate practice. In Marcuse's terminology, we find that the task of the court is to reconcile conflict into one dimension, the Happy Consciousness of one-dimensionality by making all "language" "reasonable"—that is to say, subject to the usual exercises of power.

The second specific issue *Boosey & Hawkes v. Disney* introduces has to do with the question of foreign copyright. As suggested above, this is the sole issue on which the Court of Appeals apparently ruled in favor of Boosey & Hawkes. By vacating the dismissal of the foreign copyright claims, the Court of Appeals overturned the district court's decision that infringement cases would have to be tried separately in every country in which Boosey & Hawkes wanted to stop Disney's sale of the videocassette. This earlier decision was overturned on two grounds: according to the 2nd Court of Appeals, the previous decision did not pay proper attention to the questions of (1) whether an alternative forum with jurisdiction over this case exists and (2) which forum would be most convenient and most just. Here, the waters are murky. While the earlier decision rested on the assertion that the difficulties and inconveniences involved in adjudicating foreign law would be too great for the American courts, the 2nd Court of Appeals disagreed, ruling (1) that the lower court had failed to consider whether the case could actually be decided in foreign copyright courts and (2) that the "trial would be more 'easy, expeditious and inexpensive' in the district court than dispersed to 18 foreign nations," since access to witnesses, evidence, and other resources is simplest to achieve in New York where the plaintiffs launched the case (491).

In other words, in *Boosey & Hawkes v. Walt Disney,* the concentration of cultural capital in the United States becomes grounds for American courts to gather to themselves the right to rule on issues of foreign law. Putting this part of the ruling together with the previous one, we find in this case authorization for American courts to make decisions concerning the non-U.S. distribution of intellectual property owned and disputed by citizens of other nations. On the basis of "convenience" (that is, an administrative pragmatics resulting from cultural, political and economic hegemony), American law seizes the right to serve as the medium in which challenges to that hegemony are evaluated.

This legal assertion of a right to global social control underwrites Disney's efforts in the content of its productions to engineer a global affect. After all, Disney recently launched the world premiere of *Fantasia 2000,* an "extravaganza of sight and sound, which combines six new animated segments and insterstitials with three returning favorites from the bold 1940 classic."[26] Accompanied by a one-week "World Tour" of the London Philharmonic Orchestra and a special New Year's Eve screening at the Pasadena Civic Auditorium (complete with 2,000 "special guests" and a gala party), *Fantasia 2000* was clearly expected to prove a highly profitable commodity. (In fact, the expectation of profitability extended, too, to the formal structure of the work; the segmentation of the structure of *Fantasia 2000* had as one of its explicit principles the goal of minimizing labor costs: "contrary to what some believe," asserted Thomas Schumacher, executive vice president of Walt Disney feature animation and theatrical production, the short segment structure "allows us to keep the production staff very lean very small."[27]) In this context of high cost and high publicity invested in a "classic" property, it was clearly crucial for Disney that they retain uncontested global rights to Stravinsky's piece in order for this expensive property to retain its value. Whether or not it was the "intent" of the courts, their "language" has clearly not interfered with Disney's goal in any substantial way. Disney and the courts in this instance work toward the same end: the legitimation and ownership of a machinery of affect.

While recognizing that partnership, however, we can learn from Marcuse to listen as well to Stravinsky (who famously objected to *Fantasia's* "execrable" musical performance and the "unremitting imbecility" of the animation).[28] Ironically, the avant-garde composer's expression of aesthetic disdain can recall through its high level of affect the traces of the social world. Rather than simply affirming Stravinsky's view however, a critical theory of the law will not curse (or celebrate) the law for its role in the commodification of high culture. Instead, it will demonstrate the discursive closures of the law (its one-dimensionality) while also treating affective responses to those closures seriously and symptomatically. A critical theory of the law will learn to read cases through their effects (in this case, the shoring up of American legal hegemony) *and* through their conditions of possibility. In this discussion of *Boosey & Hawkes v. Disney,* we have only suggested these conditions, but perhaps it will be sufficiently disorderly and Marcusean to close by suggesting that we find in this case and in the many crises in contemporary intellectual property law indications of a major and anxiety-producing restructuring of relations between culture and economy. From analysis of this sort, a critical theory of the cultural work accomplished by law will sketch the emerging global social totality—in which culture as an alienated commodity becomes more prevalent. It will identify contradictions between, say, high and low cultural traditions and regional or national cultural patterns. It will seek among these contradictions traces of alternative models for global cultural development. And, finally, it will at all points strive to counterbalance the law's account of its own reason with the often affective traces of those most severely disabled by the law and the totality of which it is one administrative element.

Notes

1. *Twin Books v. Disney* 83 F.3d 1162 (1996); *Boosey & Hawkes v. Disney* 145 F. 3d 481 (1998); *Kouf v. Disney,* 283 U.S. App. D.C. 111 (1990). Also, for a useful discussion of the Disney corporation's strategic use of the courts as a tool for maintaining a high rate of profit, see Douglas Gomery, 1994, "Disney's Business History: A Reinterpretation" and Jon Lewis, 1994, "Disney After Disney: Family Business and the Business of Family" in *Disney Discourse: Producing the Magic Kingdom* (New York: Routledge), 71– 105.

2. 283 U.S. App. D.C. 111 (1990).

3. Rolf Wiggershaus, 1994, *The Frankfurt School: Its History, Theories, and Political Significance* (Cambridge, Mass.: MIT Press), 6. All further references to this work will appear in the body of the essay.

4. Herbert Marcuse, 1964, *One-Dimensional Man* (Boston: Beacon Press), 227. All further references to this work will appear in the body of the essay.

5. See William Scheuerman, ed., 1996, *The Rule of Law Under Siege: Selected Essays of Franz L. Neumann and Otto Kirchheimer* (Berkeley: University of California Press) and William Scheuerman, 1994 *Between the Norm and the Exception* (Cambridge, Mass.: MIT Press).

6. See Friedrich Pollock, 1982, "State Capitalism" in *The Frankfurt School Reader,* ed. Andrew Arato and Eike Gebhardt. (New York: Continuum), 78.

7. Arato, "Political Sociology and Critique of Politics" in ibid., 24–25.

8. Max Horkheimer and Theodor Adorno, 1944, *Dialectic of Enlightenment,* trans. John Cumming (New York: Continuum).

9. See Fredric Jameson, 1990, *Late Marxism* (New York: Verso), a study that is essentially a mediation on reformulating or reclaiming Adorno in the context of postmodernism/late capitalism.

10. Jürgen Habermas, 1992, *Between Facts and Norms* (Cambridge, Mass.: MIT Press), 386.

11. See for example, Nancy Fraser, 1992 "Rethinking the Public Sphere: A Contribution to the Critique of Actually Existing Democracy" in *Habermas and the Public Sphere,* ed. Craig Calhoun (Cambridge, Mass.: MIT Press), 109–142.

12. Judith Butler, quoted in James Atlas, "The Loose Canon: Why Some Scholars think *Hustler* Deserves a Place Beside 'Hamlet.'" *New Yorker,* 29 March 1999: 64.

13. See Caudhill in *Legal Studies as Cultural Studies,* and Fredric Jameson, 1980, *The Political Unconscious* (Ithaca: Cornell University Press): 73. For more recent readings, see Martin Hipsky, Fall 1994, "Anglophil(m)ia: Why Does America Watch Merchant Ivory Movies?" *Journal of Popular Film and Television* 22: 98–107; Carolyn Lesjak, Spring 2000, "Utopia, Use, and the Everyday: Oscar Wilde and a New Economy of Pleasure" *ELH* 67, 1: 179–204.

14. For a pointed comparison of Marcuse's "positive" side with Adorno's "negative" critique, see Wiggershaus, *Frankfurt School* 496–504.

15. Herbert Marcuse, 1955, 1966, *Eros and Civilization: A Philosophical Inquiry into Freud* (Boston: Beacon Press), xi.

16. See Douglas Kellner, 1984, *Herbert Marcuse and the Crisis of Marxism* (London: Macmillan), 267–75.

17. See Barry Katz, 1982, *Herbert Marcuse and the Art of Liberation* (New York:Verso), 174–77; Erich Fromm, 1955, *The Sane Society* (New York: Rinehart); and Kellner, *Herbert Marcuse,* 269.

18. See the informative discussion of Marcuse's reputation in Peter Monaghan, 31 July 1998, "Giving a 1960s Cultural Icon His Due," *Chronicle of Higher Education.* This essay and a number of others mark the publication of new editions (and new volumes) of Marcuse's writings by Routledge, edited by Douglas Kellner.

19. See for example, Paul Breines, 1970, "From Guru to Spectre: Marcuse and the Implosion of the Movement" in *Critical Interruptions: New Left Perspectives on Herbert Marcuse,* ed. Paul Breines. (New York: Herder & Herder), 1–21.

20. C. Wright Mills, 1951, *White Collar* (New York: Oxford), David Riesman, 1953, *The Lonely Crowd* (New York: Doubleday); Vance Packard, 1961, *The Status Seekers* (New York: Pocket); William H. Whyte, 1956, *The Organization Man* (New York: Simon & Schuster).

21. Wiggershaus, 265–73.

22. Russell Jacoby identifies the ghosts in Marcuse's theory of language with slang, graffitti, and situationist cartoons (see "Reversals and Lost Meanings" in *Critical Interruptions,* 63); I want to emphasize here the ways in which "concepts" such as those of the law can become the people's ghostly, mutilated language.

23. This is basically the approach taken by Richard Pollak in, 25 August 1997, "Pop Invades Classical Space: Can Disney Save Classical Music from a Mickey Mouse World?" *The Nation:* 36.

24. See Kennedy Wilson, 16 September 1998, "A Mickey Mouse War," *The* (Glasgow) *Herald:* 23.

25. This has become a not unpopular reading, as Moya Luckett reveals in "*Fantasia:* Cultural Constructions of Disney's 'Masterpiece'" in *Disney Discourse,* 214–36.

26. "Disney's *Fantasia 2000* Makes Big Screen Bow in Millennium with Exclusive Engagements at IMAX Theaters," *Business Wire* 9 February 1999; "Disney's *Fantasia 2000*

Starts the Millennium Celebration with Live Worldwide Symphony Tour," *Business Wire* 9 February 1999.

27.   Judy Brennan, "Coming, Sooner or Later; Disney's Been Working on a Re-Release of *Fantasia* Since 1990," *Los Angeles Times* 19 August 1997: F1.

28.   Quoted in Wilson, "A Mickey Mouse War," 23.

12

The *Öffentlichkeit* of Jürgen Habermas: The Frankfurt School's Most Influential Concept?

Thomas O. Beebee

Undoubtedly the best-known member of the Frankfurt School's "second generation," Jürgen Habermas immediately became a major figure with his second book, *Struktur-wandel der Öffentlichkeit* (*Structural Transformations of the Public Sphere*, hereinafter *SdÖ*), published in 1962.[1] Habermas began this study as a *Habilitationsschrift* (a kind of second dissertation) under Theodor Adorno at Frankfurt. The work used empirical evidence to show both how *Öffentlichkeit* had functioned in the early modern period, and also how it had been gradually attenuated under capitalism. The most widely accepted English translation of *Öffentlichkeit* is "pubic sphere," but this essay will show why such a translation is only partly successful. I will use the German term throughout this essay. The book's thesis supported Adorno and Horkeheimer's idea of the "totally administered" society, but also departed significantly from that idea by upholding discursive reason as an antidote to the *pharmakon* of instrumental reason—a distinction that would become fundamental to Habermas's theory of communicative action. While the bulk of critical reaction has confronted the more developed aspects of Habermasian theory, none of his theoretical terms has become part of the critical vocabulary to the extent that *Öffentlichkeit* has.[2] This paper will explore the concept's complex birthing out of the critical theory of the Frankfurt School, trace its adoption by a larger community, and probe the viability of its application to the cultural dynamics of the twenty-first century.

Öffentlichkeit, the Frankfurt School, and the 1960s

SdÖ contradicted the thinking of the leader of the *Institut für Sozialforschung*, Max Horkheimer, whose philosophy had proven less and less compatible with Adorno's in the context of the postwar Federal Republic. Habermas himself has described the diverging attitudes of his mentors: "Intuitively, Horkheimer entrusted a rational potential to developed capitalist societies that he had long despaired of in theory. Adorno, in turn, in his analysis of 'late capitalism,' held fast to ideas that dovetailed with the framework of a negativistic philosophy of history. . . . [T]he older Hork-heimer was not only highly conventional in his cultural criticism; he became conser-vative generally."[3] Habermas's study was too radical for Horkheimer's tastes.

Habermas withdrew it and placed it instead with Wolfgang Abendroth, a labor historian at Marburg University, and one of the few academic professors in Germany at the time who was also a practicing socialist.

Habermas has described *Öffentlichkeit* most simply as "a realm of social life in which something approaching public opinion can be formed."[4] The abstraction and flexibility of this definition show why *Öffentlichkeit* has become so widely used a term. For one thing, the realm of social life is deliberately not specified, because it will change according to historical circumstance. Habermas documents how media such as newspapers and forums such as coffeehouses and salons fulfilled the function of the public sphere in early modern Europe. Later in the wake of industrialization, these media became too excessively aligned with commercial interests to provide the free exchange of viewpoints necessary for the formation of public opinion. We can speculate about whether interactive media such as the Internet might constitute such a sphere today. *SdÖ* may be considered one of the original rethinkings of the Frankfurt School by one of its pupils. Like other fertile theoretical concepts, the term *Öffentlichkeit* has taken on a life of its own far beyond the intentions of its author. A bibliography compiled by Arthur Strum in 1994 lists hundreds of works that use the concept of public sphere.[5] This fragmentation of the idea's reception raises the question of whether a public sphere can be identified today.

Just because *SdÖ* displeased Horkheimer, one should not assume that it delighted Adorno. Habermas has said in an interview that he does not think Adorno ever read a single one of his books.[6] Although Habermas used empirical analysis to supplement Adorno's mostly theoretical model of the collapse of subjectivity in the era of late capitalism, the former's insistence on the concept of *Öffentlichkeit* in the face of this collapse itself contradicted the master's thinking.[7] Habermas's original intention in *SdÖ* had been to use history (e.g., the development of a "bourgeois public sphere" of political expression from the late seventeenth through the mid-nineteenth centuries) to critique the present—specifically, the lack of a "public sphere" in German politics after 1933. To use William Outhwaite's formulation, "it is not too far-fetched to see *SdÖ* as a social-scientific remake of Horkehimer and Adorno's *Dialectic of Enlightenment*. Just as the enlightenment critique of myth turned into another myth, the principle of the bourgeois public sphere . . . turns into what Habermas calls a manipulated public sphere in which states and corporations use 'publicity' in the modern sense to secure for themselves a kind of plebiscitary acclamation."[8] Thus, the relationship of Habermas to Adorno reminds one of Aristotle's philosophy as a response to Plato: a pupil equal to his teacher in talent had produced a significantly divergent work within the same general frame of inquiry. The divergence in viewpoints between master and pupil did not diminish the friendship between Adorno and Habermas; nor did the German press's playing off the two scholars against each other at the time of the student demonstrations in the late 1960s. In Habermas's recollection, Adorno had protected him against his real opponent at the school, Max Horkheimer. In 1969, the last year of his life, Adorno wrote in a letter to Alfred Sohn-Rethel that he was "very good friends and also completely in solidarity [with Habermas] in terms of the things going on here."[9] It is true that during this period the leftist Habermas considered *Öffentlichkeit* to be as much endangered from "fascism of the left" as from the combination of conservative political and bureaucratic structures and mass media he had identified in his book.[10]

The "things going on" were the student demonstrations that so embittered Adorno's last years. The solidarity between the two thinkers seems ironic, for *SdÖ* was serving as an inspiration for these demonstrations, as young people attempted to create, through public use of reason and unreason, the *Öffentlichkeit* Habermas had shown to be lacking in the Federal Republic. Though *Strukturwandel der Öffent-lichkeit* reads much more ponderously than *Soul on Ice* or *Steal This Book,* and though on the other hand its pronouncements are less mysterious and oracular than those of Jacques Lacan's seminars that inspired French radicals, it struck a chord with German students of the late 1960s, who were demanding more open and democratic institutions, and who were becoming increasingly frustrated with Adorno's apolitical stance vis à vis events in the Federal Republic. In an interview with Habermas, Detlef Horster provides a typical testimonial of someone who came into contact with *SdÖ* as a student: "Your book on the public sphere was very disillusioning for the belief in the democracy of the younger generation. At least it turned my political orientation completely upside down. For me, the only alternative left then was the Socialist German Alliance (SDS)."[11] One of the triggering factors for the student demonstrations was the formation in 1966 of a "Grand Coalition" between the Christian Democrats and the Social Democrats, leaving the Federalists as the only opposition party, with less than ten percent of seats in parliament. This situation reminded many of the Nazi *Gleichschaltung* (elimination of opposition) from the Reichstag after 1933. Feeling that neither parliament nor the media could function as a public sphere, students attempted to open alternative sites through strikes and demonstrations.

Eventually, Habermas would attack Adorno's thought directly, placing his mentor virtually in the camp of the French poststructuralists in the lectures of *Der philosophische Diskurs der Moderne* (*The Philosophical Discourse of Modernity*). Adorno and Horkheimer, no less than Michel Foucault, reduce the rational content of modernity:

> The *Dialectic of Enlightenment* does not do justice to the rational content of cultural modernity that was captured in bourgeois ideals (and also instrumentalized along with them). I am referring . . . to the universalistic foundations of law and morality that have also been incorporated (in however distorted and incomplete a fashion) into the institutions of constitutional government, into the forms of democratic will formation, and into individualist patterns of identity formation.[12]

While Habermas's corrections to Adorno have frequently been analyzed, his early concept of *Öffentlichkeit* has rarely been central to these analyses. The notion of *Öffentlichkeit* seems intended to ameliorate Adorno's idea of the "total reification" of contemporary society.

If we think of language as composed of first-person, second-person, and third-person relationships, then Adorno's theory of the dialectic of enlightenment posits that the third-person realm of instrumental rationality penetrates the sphere of the first-person, such that all subject pronoun *I*s are suspect. Adorno sees, for example, the state of epistolary exchange in the twentieth century as a symptom of the disappearing subject: "In a societal configuration in which each individual is reduced to the level of a function, no one has the right to talk about herself in a letter as though she were still the untouched individual which the letter says she is: the 'I' in the letter is always something of a mirage."[13] As if responding to Adorno, *SdÖ* provides the contrasting model of a genuine subjectivity that publicizes itself through the medium of the letter: "People developed their subjectivity in writing letters. This subjectivity, as the innermost domain of the private, is always related to the public" (*SdÖ* 113–14; "Briefe schreibend entfaltet sich das Individuum in seiner Subjektivität. . . . Diese, als der innerste Hof des Privaten, ist stets schon auf Publikum bezogen."). Habermas and Adorno are referring to different historical periods, so their different conclusions do not necessarily imply a contradiction in method. Like Adorno, Habermas recognizes the dialectic of private and public, but he does not assume their identity.

From the point of view of literary history, Habermas was continuing the best traditions of the Frankfurt School, which were to produce theoretical models that allowed the investigator to tie formal aspects of the literary work to the life-world that produced and consumed it, without resorting to naïve Marxist notions of the class consciousness of the author, or of characters as representatives of social classes. It was also no longer necessary to explain epistolarity's rise and fall simply as an "exhaustion of the literary device." The union of form and content, as in the letter novel, for example, was explainable through the doctrine of publicizing the private.

In this theory, the entrance of literature, art, and philosophy into processes of marketing and reification is what allows them to function within the public sphere:

> Inasmuch as philosophical and literary works, artworks in general, are produced for the market and distributed through the market, they come to resemble information in general: as commodities they are in principle accessible to all. They no longer remain elements in the representation of the public sphere of church and court. . . . The private persons who have access to the work as a commodity profane it, in that they autonomously, in the way of rational conversation, search out its meaning, discuss and therefore make known what as long as it was ineffable had been able to develop authoritative power.

> In dem Maße aber, in dem die philosophischen und die literarischen Werke, Kunstwerke überhaupt, für den Markt hergestellt und durch ihn vermittelt werden ähneln sich diese Kulturgüter jener Art Informationen an: als Waren werden sie im Prinzip allgemein zugänglich. Sie bleiben nicht länger Bestandteile der Repräsentation kirchlicher wie höfischer Öffentlichkeit. . . . Die Privatleute, denen das Werk als Ware zugänglich wird, profanieren es, indem sie autonom, auf dem Wege der rationalen Verständigung untereinander, seinen Sinn suchen, bereden und damit aussprechen müssen, was eben in der Unausgesprocheheit solange autoritative Kraft hatte entfalten können. (*SdÖ* 97–98)

Without acknowledging Walter Benjamin's notion of reproducibility as destructive of the artwork's *aura,* Habermas here uses it to describe an historical transformation which, though it seems to reduce the aesthetic qualities which we identify with art, brings the work into our life-world for the first time and allows it to function as public discourse. From a literary-historical point of view, however, something rather different happens as well in the early modern period, namely the "invention" of new forms such as the essay and literary criticism, along with the increasing production of novels and other realistic and open-ended forms. Adorno, it is well known, took Benjamin to task for his views on the potential political benefits of eliminating the magical element of art, a viewpoint which Adorno saw as coming from Brecht.[14] Thus, one can see that Habermas's aesthetic theory diverges significantly from Adorno's, which posits the truth of the work of art as inhering in its not giving up its meaning to rational analysis. For Habermas, the discourse of artworks is specialized like that of law or technology. The difference is the high degree of emotional content and subjectivity, which are nevertheless communicative. It is perhaps not coincidental that Habermas, unlike Benjamin and Adorno, never published significant analyses of artworks or literature.

Habermas's *Öffentlichkeit* can thus be seen as the space of dialogic interchange that mediates between private concerns of the "sphere of intimacy" and commercial, bureaucratic, and political modes of discourse, preventing the "I" from collapsing beneath the onslaught of instrumental reason and mass culture. Adorno's relentless dialectic cannot explain the concrete historical transformation Habermas documents in the public sphere, which for one moment in history at least, enabled historical change through communicative action rather than through instrumental reason.

Though Habermas was critical of the conditions in the Federal Republic of Germany in the late 1950s and early 1960s, his emphasis on *Öffentlichkeit* seems optimistic in comparison with Adorno's depiction of a totally reified society. It is also less self-contradictory—how does Adorno account for his own critical thought with his theory? Adorno's writing is philosophically rich, but empirically poor. That Adorno can declare class conflict—the very engine of dereification capitalism provides itself—at an end in a totally consumerist society is perhaps explainable from Adorno's situation, but not from what we see and hear around us, despite the intervention of mass media and state bureaucracy. Nevertheless, Habermas's self-critique, published in the 1990 edition of *Strukturwandel,* finds his original analysis of the disappearance of the public sphere under the onslaught of media an excessively gloomy prognosis, where "the strong influence of Adorno's theory of mass culture is not difficult to discern" (*SdÖ* 29; "der starke Einfluß von Adornos Theorie der Massenkultur unschwer zu erkennen").

SdÖ demonstrated that at one point in European history, instrumental rationality had helped produce a discursive rationality that could mediate subjectivity and the dominating societal structures of appellation, into which, in Adorno's view, subjectivity collapses. More specifically, *SdÖ* depicted the nascent forms of mass consumption and of the culture industry as having provided the material conditions for a public sphere, when it identified, for example, the coffee-house and the early newspaper as new sites for the public exchange of information and for the use of reason. The prerequisite for entering the public sphere, according to Habermas, is an ability to reason and to debate based on literacy, provided through the technological developments of print media which render increased access to books and newspapers.

The Polysemy of *Öffentlichkeit*

Öffentlichkeit is not a coined term, nor was Habermas the first to write an extensive essay on it. Indeed, the word appears in article 42 of the the *Grundgesetz* (Basic Law) of the Federal Republic of Germany, which guarantees the openness of parliament and of court trials. It is listed in Grimms' *Wörterbuch* as a coinage of the eighteenth century, a nominalization of the adjective *öffentlich*. The relatively recent coinage of the noun, which seems deliberately formed on the French term, *publicité*, bears out Habermas's point that the bourgeois public sphere only fully came into existence in the eighteenth century. Furthermore, the term's antonym, "*Innerlichkeit*," dates from the same period. Habermas's originality lies not in coining a new, obscurantist theoretical term, but in unveiling the history and maximally exploiting the multivalence of an existing, everyday German word, *Öffentlichkeit*.

Following the lead of Hannah Arendt in works such as *The Human Condition* (1958), Habermas's study revived the Kantian idea of a public sphere, where genuine, reasoned political debate takes place—though never on the terms of equality or unhindered access theorized by the bourgeoisie. Perhaps the most straightforward definition of this sphere given in the *SdÖ* is as

> the sphere of private people gathered together as a public. Against the public powers [*öffentliche Gewalt*] these private people claim for themselves the public sphere regulated from above [*die obrigkeitlich reglementierte Öffentlichkeit*], in order to engage such powers in a debate over the general rules governing relations in the basically privatized but publicly relevant sphere of commodity exchange and social labor. The medium of this political confrontation was peculiar and without historical precedent: people's public use of their reason [*das öffentliche Räsonnement*].

> die Sphäre der zum Publikum versammelten Privatleute . . . [D]iese beanspruchen die obrigkeitlich reglementierte Öffentlichkeit alsbald gegen die öffentliche Gewalt selbst, um sich mit dieser über die allgemeinen Regeln des Verkehrs in der grundsätzlich privatisierten, aber öffentlich relevanten Sphäre des Warenverkehrs und der gesellschaftlichen Arbeit auseinanderzusetzen. Eigentümlich und geschichtlich ohne vorbild ist das Medium dieser politischen Auseinandersetzung: das öffentliche Räsonnement. (*SdÖ* 86)

This passage makes clear that Habermas constructs his notion on Kant's definition of *öffentliches Räsonnement* given in the essay *"Was ist Aufklärung?"* (What is Enlightenment?). There, Kant limits public reason to the use a "Gelehrter" makes of his knowledge in public. The concept of *Öffentlichkeit* is thus not a mass democratic *"volonté de tous."* It requires the existence of a cultural elite whose work represents the public use of reason. In this sense, by painting a positive picture of the relatively short window of opportunity enjoyed by German thinkers and academics in the late eighteenth and early nineteenth centuries, culminating in their important contributions to the Frankfurt constitutional convention of 1849, Habermas's book critiqued the subsequent marginalization or coopting of German intellectuals during the nineteenth and twentieth centuries. At the same time, it laid the foundation for Habermas's own sphere of action: As Oskar Negt points out, Habermas himself is one of the very few German thinkers in whom intellectual achievement has not stood at odds with concrete political intervention.[15] With his *Doktorvater* Abendroth, for example, Habermas founded the Socialist Alliance as an "older man's" version of the SDS.

As the English translator of *SdÖ*, Thomas Burger, has pointed out, *"Öffentlichkeit"* has at least three distinct meanings: "'(the) public,' 'public sphere,' or 'publicity.'"[16] It refers both to a set of relationships and structurations we call in English "the public," and also to a quality that may inhere in discourse, artworks, or social relationships, which we might call "publicness," since the culture industry has coopted and emptied "publicity" of any political content. What Habermas does with *Öffentlichkeit*, then, parallels what Plato did with the word *mimesis* as used in fifth century Athens. Plato combined several disparate meanings of the term, and through its dialogic usage by Socrates in a number of contexts forged it into a new term linking the role of art in society with art's epistemology. Europeans have paid homage to the complexity of *mimesis* by adopting the word into other European languages rather than translating it. *Öffentlichkeit,* on the other hand, has not been so lucky.

One can trace the multivalence of the term by comparing some of its translations. The French translators have chosen as the title of Habermas's book: *L'espace public: Archéologie de la Publicité comme dimension constitutive de la société bourgeoise.*[17] In addition to the two terms—*L'espace public* and *publicité*—used in the title, the translator also adduces terms such as *sphère publique,* and *domaine publique,* in the text itself. In fact, the title is rather misleading, since the book immediately turns to *sphère publique* and its synonym, *domaine publique,* as its master terms for translating *Öffentlichkeit.* Only once, in section §22, does the text of the translation substitute *publicité* for *Öffentlichkeit.* The German title of this section is "Hergestellte Öffentlichkeit und nicht-öffentliche Meinung" (*SdÖ* 312) which in French appears as "«publicité» fabriquée et opinion non-publique" (219), a substitution that is maintained throughout the section. In choosing the title he does, the French translator places his emphasis not on a group of people, organizations, or bureaucratic structures, but on an arena or space where certain transactions occur. Is that equivalent to the notion of *publicité* given later in the title? Only the narrowest definition of French *publicité* comes close to Habermas's *Öffentlichkeit:* "ce qui n'est pas tenu secret. *Publicité des débats en justice. Publicité des régistres des hypoteques*" (*Robert,* 2nd ed.). As Habermas notes, the public sphere began as a space conceded by the government for open discussion of issues. "Bourgeois individuals are private individuals. As such, they do not 'rule' [in the early modern period] . . . To the principle of the existing power, the bourgeois public opposed the principle of supervision—that very principle which demands that proceedings be made public (Publizität)."[18] The loss of this original meaning of "publicity" from European languages points to one of the significant transformations in publicity, from the granting of openness to the use of opinion polls and plebiscites to demonstrate the solidarity of the public with measures taken through the cooperation of large organizations and the state.

The Spanish translation runs the risk of readers' mistaking this form of coerced public opinion as the object of Habermas's inquiry, for the title *SdÖ* becomes simply *Historia y crítica de la opinion pública*.[19] One notes that this translation was carried out and published in Mexico, where the nonexistence of a public sphere under years of paternalistic, one-party rule constitutes a serious political issue, and where the original idea of publicity, discussed above, has not been widely established. The translators deliberately chose the term most recognizable to their readers. Public opinion forms only part of *Öffentlichkeit*, as can be seen from separate sections of *SdÖ*—§12 and §24—which are devoted to this particular aspect of publicity (*SdÖ* 161–78, Burger 343–52). Not only does the German term include much more than "public opinion," but the latter idea is more associated with nineteenth- and twentieth-century phenomena such as plebiscites and polling mechanisms than with public discussions based on reason. Public opinion on legislative issues, for example, can be a powerful motivating factor in the way they are adjudicated, without necessarily being based upon reason. From the other direction, literature, for example, forms invented and patronized by the middle classes, such as the *drame larmoyante* or the epistolary novel, are important instruments of *Öffentlichkeit*, forms of publicity, without constituting public opinion *strictu sensu*.

Habermas is right: in the course of the early modern period there was a gradual giving up of secrecy, a turning outward of governmental function. Secretaries, whose very name derives from the antitype of publicness, began giving out information rather than keeping it secret as they were supposed to do. With the advent of mass media, on the other hand, the publicity offered by secretaries, open court proceedings, and other practices was superseded by advertising, in which as Habermas points out the meaning of publicity is now to attract public attention to something rather than subject it to public scrutiny. This difference is what the French subtitle encapsulates in its term *Archéologie de la Publicité*. The French subtitle greatly inflates Habermas's original claims in German to have written Investigations on a Category of Bourgeois Subjectivity ("Untersuchungen zu einer Kategorie bürgerlicher Gesellschaft.") The subtitle seems chosen less as a translation of the original than as an allusion to Michel Foucault's *Archéologie du savoir* (1969), which had appeared three years earlier. Habermas plus Foucault? The former's strictures on the latter in the *Philosophical Discourse of Modernity* make that marriage unlikely.[20]

Thus, wherever Habermas uses the term *Öffentlichkeit* to refer to people rather than to procedures or institutions, the French translation must find another term. For example, Habermas devotes many pages to delineating the institutions of public reason developed in the eighteenth century. He notes that the coffehouses, salons, and the press and its growing institution of criticism all "form the publicness of a literary use of reason" (*SdÖ* 116; "bilden die Öffentlichkeit eines literarischen Räsonnements"). The French version of this notes that "les couches bourgeoises incarnent la conscience publique (*Öffentlichkeit*) qui correspond à un usage littéraire de la raison" (61). Suddenly the more abstract, passive notions of a public sphere or of publicity are no longer adequate translations for *Öffentlichkeit*. Instead, the translator uses the more active term "public consciousness," which corresponds to the notion of litera- ture as one of the most important carriers of *Öffentlichkeit*, a making conscious of bourgeois subjectivity. *Conscience publique, sphère publique*, and *domaine publique* are all neologisms in French, indicating the dynamism of Habermasian thinking when applied to the French situation. What is interesting in this translation is the question of whether it represents an expansion of the meanings of the French term *publicité* as a result of the theoretical twist Habermas's theory gives it.

English translators face similar difficulties with the term "publicity." The En- glish translation, *The Structural Transformation of the Public Sphere*, also substitutes two terms for one. Though "sphere" is not in the German title, Habermas uses it consistently in his text. The addition of this word is absolutely necessary in order to avoid stilted or nonsensical English sentences. For example, the sentence "Die pol- itische Öffentlichkeit geht aus der literarischen hervor" (*SdÖ* 90) would be mislead- ing if rendered, "The political public derives from the literary one," or perhaps worse, "Political publicity derives from literary publicity." Burger translates it thus: "The public sphere in the political realm evolved from the public sphere in the world of letters" (30–31). On the other hand, as pointed out above, the use of "sphere" makes the English term sound far more concrete than the German. "The problem with the term 'public sphere,'" writes Julia Koivisto, "is . . . that it renders as a separate 'sphere' something that could also be understood as an 'aspect' or 'quality' of various practices in the sense of 'openness' or 'public access.'"[21] Similarly the subtitle, "an inquiry into a category of bourgeois society," makes the obvious choice of "bourgeois" for "bür- gerlich," but the term fails to capture the double meaning of the German.

Early in his treatise, Habermas clarifies the relationship between publicity and *Öffentlichkeit:*

> The subject of this publicness is the public as carrier of public opinion; public- ness, for example the public nature of court proceedings, relates to the critical function of public opinion. In the context of the mass media, publicness has of course changed its meaning. It leaves off being public opinion, and becomes an attribute of whoever attracts public opinion to himself: public relations efforts, which recently have been called "publicity work," are dedicated to the creation of such publicity.

> Das Subjekt dieser Öffentlichkeit ist das Publikum als Träger der öffentlichen Meinung; auf deren kritische Funktion ist Publizität, etwa die öffentlichkeit bei Gerichtsverhandlungen, bezogen. Im Bereich der Massenmedien hat Publizität freilich ihre Bedeutung geändert. Von einer funktion der öffentlichen Meinung wird sie auch zum Attribut dessen, der die öffentliche Meinung auf sich zieht: public relations, Anstrengungen, die neuerdings »Öffentlichkeitsarbeit« heißen, sind auf die Herstellung solcher publicity gerichtet (*SdÖ* 55).

Here I have used the term "publicness" for *Öffentlichkeit* despite its clumsiness in English. "Public sphere" will not do in the opening sentence, since Habermas emphasizes a process or quality of social life, rather than a separate realm of communicative action. "Publicity" obviously also will not do, since Habermas here invokes precisely the origin of the French term *publicité*, of "making public," which then was taken up into German as *Publizität*. This impossibility of using the English term "publicity" to denote any type of social sphere in the present day provides excellent support for Habermas's historical approach: the transformation of the public sphere can be traced in the semantic shift of the term "publicity" that renders it useless to translators of *Öffentlichkeit*. German, on the other hand, absorbed foreign words like *Reklame* and *Publizität*, allowing *Öffentlichkeit* to keep its full range of meanings.

While the Spanish translator has been conservative, eschewing the invention of new critical terms at the expense of radically delimiting the polysemy of *Öffentlichkeit*, Habermas's French and English translators have used a series of terms to try to capture that multivalence. Some of these terms are new to the target languages, producing the interesting effect of making Habermas a more innovative thinker in English and French than in German: "translation has uwittingly created a new concept, 'the public sphere,' associated with Jürgen Habermas, whereas in the German Habermas reads more clearly as trying to understand a traditional legal principle. . . . 'Public sphere' in English or 'L'espace publique' in French—Habermas's originality grows in translation."[22]

Uses and Abuses of *Öffentlichkeit*

Everyone who reads *SdÖ* notices the interdisciplinarity of Habermas's approach. In the words of Peter Hohendahl, "[Habermas] buttresses his socio-political argumentation with extensive references to other sources. Cultural history, legal history, mass media theory, empirical social science: Habermas draws upon a variety of disciplines in coming to grips with the phenomenon of the public sphere."[23] Scholars and social critics in far-flung fields have thus been able to extract the desired disciplinary valences of the term in adapting it to their own critical practices.

Uses of Habermas's concept, by historians, literary historians, political scientists, cultural critics, and others, are often indistinguishable from critiques of the problematic status of *Öffentlichkeit*, especially when the reality of the public sphere has been shown not to live up to its ideal type. The very depth of historical detail, which I have identified above as having been of great use to historical and literary scholarship, also militates against the construction of an ideal type of this sort. To give an example, the notion of "Veröffentlichung der Innerlichkeit" (publication of the private), which Habermas tells us was instrumental in the construction of a public sphere, does not automatically imply the use of reason, since "Innerlichkeit" also implies both religious belief and irrational emotion. A literary example is Goethe's *Leiden des jungen Werthers* of 1774, in which Werther's personal fate is determined in part by his inability to enter either the sphere of *Gewalt* represented by the aristocracy, nor the middle class realm represented by Albert, who marries Werther's beloved, Charlotte. The domains of poetry and of nature constitute his refuge. Werther is most definitely a *Bürger,* yet his discourse is hardly that of *Räsonnement.* He undermines his acute social and political insights with a morbid self-absorption that leads him to suicide. Yet Werther became a public figure and culture hero to an entire generation, a focus of public discourse, and a symbol of the negative consequences of feudal structures hindering the full development of *Öffentlichkeit* in Germany. Habermas chooses to analyze instead Goethe's classical *Bildungsroman, Wilhelm Meister,* as indicative of the "afterglow" (Abglanz) of representative *Öffentlichkeit* (*SdÖ* 68). Habermas's willingness to accept literature as an important vehicle of the public sphere seems to have been purchased with a repression of the former's emotional and irrational aspects, making it appear just another form of rational discourse. Literature gives up its "aura" in order to become a form of political communication.

Habermas's ideal type too closely resembles the public sphere's own self-image—as if Habermas were an apologist for, rather than a critic of bourgeois ideology. *SdÖ* tells us how bourgeois intellectuals thought the public sphere operated, rather than how it really did. In other words, "Habermas largely replaces the historical analysis of the forms of public sphere by the history of ideas on the public sphere."[24] One might quibble with the word *replaces* here, as there do not seem to be any large-scale historical studies that Habermas could have used. On the contrary, the controversy surrounding his model of the public sphere has provoked scholars such as Joan Landes, Patricia Roberts, Michael Schudson, and many others to examine more closely how the public sphere actually operated in early modern France and in Puritan New England.[25] One can envision the study of "comparative public spheres" as a propadeutic to comparative literature or comparative cultural studies.

Investigations such as Schudson's provide evidence that lead to another objection to the Habermasian model: *SdÖ* fails to emphasize properly, as Alexander Kluge, Rainer Nägele, J. F. Lyotard, and a host of feminist scholars have pointed out, the extent to which the pubic sphere, like any other social category, defines itself by principles of exclusion. The rationality that Habermas sees as the only conceivable medium of public debate limits *Öffentlichkeit* in terms of genre, class, and gender. Issues not capable of rational resolution—such as religious conviction—are simply banished to the private sphere. Indeed, the English and French translations that use the term "sphere" become almost accusatory in this context. German radicals of the 1960s and 1970s spoke of the need for the creation of an "oppositional public sphere," a concept that spawned a number of varieties. Author and filmmaker Alexander Kluge has developed an entire approach to creative writing and filmmaking based on the need for creating a nonreductive public sphere. In Kluge's view, neither the classical public sphere of the eighteenth century, nor the privately owned, "pseudo-public" sphere of postwar Germany, is capable of producing true democracy.[26] Kluge sees his oppositional public sphere as a necessary expansion of the existing ones. With Oskar Negt, he has elaborated the notion of a proletarian public sphere that uses not reason but physical action related to seizure of the means of production. Sit-down strikes, for example, which cannot be fit into Habermas's model of reasoned debate, may constitute a worker's only means of entrance into the public sphere. Negt and Kluge's *Öffentlichkeit und Erfahrung* argues that "a plant where there is a strike or a factory that is being occupied is to be understood . . . as the essential core of a conception of public sphere that is rooted in the production process."[27]

Above all, and most visibly in the early modern period, as Marie Fleming, Nancy Fraser, Cindy Griffin, and Joan Landes have shown, despite the common feeling of humanity that is developed in the "intimate sphere" of the family, and hence presumably co-constructed by both genders, the public sphere's apparent neutrality is in fact masculine—Kant's "Gelehrter."[28] As in Kant's apparently innocent choice of the masculine form of the German word for "scholar," most often the exclusion of women from the public sphere is covert: women are the "unthought" of public discourse. The emphasis on rationality, for example, as the privileged discourse of the public sphere, excludes women indirectly, both on the pragmatic grounds of educational differences, and on the long-standing dichotomy in Western thought between "masculine" rationality and "feminine" emotion. John Peters has called this feminist scholarship the "foremost challenge to Habermas's account of the rise of the public sphere."[29] However, the exact force of that challenge is unclear, if for no other reason than that it must use *Öffentlichkeit*'s own self-definition in order to challenge its realization. In his 1990 reassessment of *SdÖ*, Habermas acknowleges the *lapsus* of not addressing the issue of gender. Yet he notes, with some justification, that critiques of women's problematic status vis à vis the public sphere can be made only on the basis of the principles of *Öffentlichkeit,* that such critique "does not contradict the rights to unrestricted access and equality inherent to the self-understanding of liberal *Öffentlichkeit,* but rather makes its own claims on them (*SdÖ* 20; ". . . dementiert . . . nicht die ins Selbstverständnis der liberalen Öffentlichkeit eingebauten Rechte auf uneingeschränkte Inklusion und Gleichheit, sondern nimmt sie in Anspruch"). Indeed, so often have feminists taken up the concept of *Öffentlichkeit,* that one can say that it has been at least as much of a contribution to feminist scholarship as an overlooking of its claims.

As an example of identity politics, the feminist critique of Habermas raises the question of whether a concept of public sphere can be made compatible with the forms of cultural analysis and ethnic studies based on such politics. For Jean-François Lyotard, Habermas's emphasis on reason rather than on the positionality and *différence* that characterize the "postmodern condition" makes his public sphere a totalizing meta-discourse: "what Habermas requires from the arts and the experiences they provide is . . . to bridge the gap between cognitive, ethical and political discourses, thus opening the way to a unity of experience."[30] Such unity can be provided only by a meta-language that all who enter the public sphere would have competence in. In literary studies, structuralism and semiotics were the last attempts at providing a meta-language. The subsequent proliferation of critical discourses and subspecializations points to the impossibility of such a meta-language. Comparative literature's attempts to extract universals from the multiplicity of cultural traditions has largely given way to a questioning of the unity of such traditions. Rainer Nägele points out that even Kant had framed the possibility of the public use of reason as but one discursive practice among many:

Kant's ear hears the voice of reason among other registers of discourse such as telling stories (*Erzählen*) and joking (*Scherzen*), and it almost seems as if reasoning finds its place among these other registers as a latecomer. In any case, it finds its place, but it does not take over. It is part of a conversational chorus. In commenting on this passage of Kant, Habermas casually silences the other voices and hears only the reasoning which seems to have occupied all the places. Although we can no longer hear the voices speaking to Kant, we can still read the texts of the Enlightenment. We can also read its obsession with jokes, wit, comedy, tears, ghosts and ghostbusters, *Schwärmer* and *Geisterseher,* criminals, clowns, and *Hanswürste.*[31]

Habermas might respond that all of these other voices were present before the Enlightenment, and therefore recounting their presence can do nothing to help our historical analysis of how the Enlightenment gave Western history a new direction. At the same time, he has at least acknowledged, as Adorno did not, the importance of popular genres as true resistance to the pseudocultural sphere. In addition, one might say that Habermas's goal was precisely to reify the public sphere—as an antidote to the almost complete collapse of subjectivity into mere publicity.

Habermas fails to analyze the possibility of counterpublic spheres, half-public spheres, proletarian public spheres, and the like. His concept of the public sphere is a totalizing one. In fact, two critiques that seem to oppose each other can be viewed as one. On the one hand, we can certainly ask, with Michael Schudson, "Was There Ever a Public Sphere?" On the other hand, several scholars have questioned Habermas's implication that there has ever been only one public sphere—and that this "belonged" to the educated bourgeoisie. In their book *The Public Sphere and Experience,* Oskar Negt and Alexander Kluge have provided a monumental supplement to Habermas, correcting above all his bracketing of the proletarian public sphere as having been suppressed within the historical process.

Much of the reception of Habermas's work in general takes place in the university, and for professors in the humanities there is undoubtedly a utopian element to his analysis. Habermas, like Adorno, attributes the impoverishment of culture to the inner dynamics of capitalist society. A cause of such impoverishment is the depoliticization of the public sphere that accompanies the welfare state's involvement in a capitalist economy: society is now administered by bureaucracies and agencies rather than negotiated by political factions. Negotiations of the public sphere give way to client-consumer relations. Another example of impoverishment corresponds roughly to Karl Marx's idea of alienation in the field of knowledge production. One reason why the eighteenth century might have been a "golden age" of the public sphere was the balance in that age between too much and too little information. Beginning with the nineteenth century and the rise of technical disciplines, an ever-increasing overload of information led to the fragmenting of the public sphere through the development of specializations and expert cultures. Less and less can there be any common language or knowledge base for cultural elites to talk with one another. The various expert cultures housed in the university are largely split off both from society as a whole, and from one another.

It seems clear that one result of expert culture and specialization has been the politicization of literary studies. Literary texts, unlike philosophical or legal texts, are usually understandable by a broad spectrum of the public, and they engage issues on an emotional and nontechnical level that provides a commonplace from which different parties may enter the debate. From cultural studies to the law and literature movement, politicized literary criticism seeks to reconstitute the missing nexus of shared concerns that allowed eighteenth-century texts such as Schiller's *Ästhetische Briefe* to function simultaneously as literary and as political theory. From gay issues to incarceration, any issue seems a likely subject for debate through the prism of literary studies. The genre of "theory" has proven to be a flexible tool that can be brought to bear on nearly any discursive practice. Indeed, this may be one reason for the renewed interest in the Frankfurt School during the last decades of the twentieth century. Habermas's ideal of reason is upheld, as nonprofessional politicians use literature to debate politics. However, in general these debates have hardly been accessible even to the general learned public, as institutional affiliation and peer-review mechanisms continue to be used in exclusionary fashion.

The Internet: A Global Public Sphere?

In his 1990 introduction to the reedition of his work, Habermas addresses the issue of whether technological developments might furnish once again the basis for a renewed, postbourgeois sphere. He notes the work of Joshua Meyrowitz, who argues that the simultaneity of events created by media such as television has increasingly weakened the boundaries of class and nation, returning us to a nomadic situation, where there is, we might say, only a public sphere and no private sphere.[32] The role of the media in collapsing public and private spheres in the cases of O. J. Simpson and Clinton and Lewinsky, as well as in "reality" TV programming, seemed to bear out Meyrowitz's thesis. George Landow has made the argument that hypertext and Internet communication technology foster the public sphere: "the use of communications technology is also a concretization of certain political assumptions. In particular, hypertext embodies . . . assumptions of the necessity for nonhierarchical, multicentered, open-ended forms of politics and government."[33] Internet chat rooms and electronic discussion groups approach the disembodied subjectivity and instantaneous communication required for an effective public sphere—screen names can block out or confuse the filters that gender, race, class, and nationality place on the exchange of ideas. As in the early modern period, there has taken place a revolution in the publicizing of the private, implying a need to renegotiate the boundaries between the two domains.

    Andrew Ó Baoill's analysis of the Slashdot website as a public sphere phenomenon is instructive.[34] Slashdot is a moderated, hierarchically organized bulletin board where interested parties comment on news stories related to the Internet and to communications technology. Baoill finds three criteria in this virtual public space that identify it as a public sphere: universal access; rational debate; and disregard of rank. On the latter point, Baoill uses Habermas to refute Mark Poster's claim that the

Internet cannot function as a public sphere, simply because "without embodied co-presence the charisma and status of individuals have no force."[35] Disembodiment allows the removal of signals of rank and status irrelevant to the issues being discussed, and thus causes participants to focus on the force of the argument. Baoill admits that rationality only inheres in portions of the discussion list. Elsewhere, the discussion threads are examples of the polyphony of voices identified by Nägele and Lyotard. Universal access is still more problematic. Baoill cites a discussion on Slashdot concerning extending Internet access to Sub-Saharan Africa: "The fact that a large part of the spectrum [of economic and social backgrounds] are not only lacking from the debate, but lack any reasonable possibility of access, must cast serious doubt on the ability of Slashdot, and the Internet in general, to act as a public sphere for the discussion of questions of this nature." The construction of a global public sphere is hindered by lack of capital and infrastructure. At the same time, the dominance of English as the language of the Internet suggests that it has become the "meta-language" of the global public sphere, such as one exists. Naturally, this situation also hinders both access and the possibility of a level playing field.

The Internet proved entirely feckless in the political struggles surrounding the presidential elections of 2000, which were decided by elite institutions such as the Supreme Court. Voting on the Internet, which could provide an alternative to using aging mechanical voting machines, seems years away and may never materialize. Interestingly, the failure of the Internet to rise to the occasion in 2000 coincided with the collapse of so-called dot-communism, concerted efforts by corporations to stop peer-to-peer distribution systems such as Napster, and the public's gradual realization that the truly profitable Internet companies are Old Economy giants trying out new media. One can see this transition played out in the fortunes of Slashdot: formerly operated by students, and then ex-students, it was then acquired by VA Linux. This annexation of public space by a for-profit corporation raises both troubling questions about the capability of that space to embody *Öffentlichkeit,* and the possibility that we are seeing again, in miniature, a *Strukturwandel* similar to the one analyzed by Habermas, in which client-consumer relations replace free and rational exchange of ideas.

One can reduce the complexities of these events neither—pessimistically—to "just another product of the culture industry" nor—optimistically—to the emergence of a new, global public sphere. As Habermas points out in response to Meyrowitz's own reductionism: "There is considerable evidence which speaks for the ambivalence of the democratic potential of a public sphere whose infrastructure is determined by the increasing compulsion to choose offered by mass communications" (*SdÖ* 49; "Vieles spricht dafür, daß das demokratische Potential einer Öffentlichkeit, deren Infrastruktur von den wachsenden Selektionszwängen der elektronischen Massenkommunikation geprägt ist, ambivalent ist"). Habermas wrote this before the explosion of the Internet in the mid-1990s, but the oxymoronic idea of "Selektionszwang" (compulsion to choose) seems entirely applicable to the Internet, whose driving force is increasingly the compulsion to press buttons and click on links, rather than to actually read or write any material. Adorno would have found the claim of the free Internet service provider Netzero to be the "Defenders of the Free World" particularly apt for dialectical analysis, combining as it does an allusion to the Cold War and to consumer paradise. Besides the pun on the word "free" for this no-cost ISP, it's staying free also depends on the user's continually clicking on ads. If there is a new, technology-based structural transformation of the public sphere operating today, then, it is an extremely messy one in which it is difficult to distinguish compulsion from freedom, impotence from power, thus making the methodology of critical theory more needful than ever before. As anyone who has looked behind Habermas's ideal type to the actual complexities and conflicts of public discourse in the early modern period will attest, however, this messy *Öffentlichkeit* may be all we have ever had to work with.

Notes

1. Jürgen Habermas, 1990, *Strukturwandel der Öffentlichkeit. Untersuchungen zu einer Kategorie der bürgerlichen Gesellschaft*, 2nd ed. (Frankfurt am Main: Suhrkamp), Thomas Burger and Frederick Lawrence, trans., 1989, *Structural Transformations of the Public Sphere: An Inquiry into a Category of Bourgeois Society* (Cambridge, Mass.: MIT Press). All English translations in this essay, except where noted, and including ones from *SdÖ*, are mine.

2. I will not attempt in this essay to show how *SdÖ* functioned as a preliminary study for Habermas's more elaborate theoretical concept of communicative action. For a brief overview of the totality of Habermas's work, see Detlef Horster and Willem van Reijen, 1992, *Habermas: An Introduction*, trans. Heidi Thompson (Philadelphia: Pennbridge).

3. Jürgen Habermas, 1993, "Remarks on the Development of Horkheimer's Work," trans. Kenneth Baynes and John McCole, in *On Max Horkheimer: New Perspective*, ed. Seyla Benhabib, Wolfgang Bonß, and John McCole (Cambridge, Mass.: MIT Press), 62.

4. Jürgen Habermas, Fall 1974, "The Public Sphere (1964)," trans. Sara Lennox and Frank Lennox, *New German Critique* 3: 42.

5. Arthur Strum, Winter 1994, "Bibliography of *Öffentlichkeit*," *New German Critique* 61: 161–202.

6. Josef Früchtl and Jürgen Habermas, 1991, "Eine Generation von Adorno getrennt," in *Geist gegen den Zeitgeist: Erinnern an Adorno*, ed. Josef Früchtl and Maria Calloni (Frankfurt am Main: Suhrkamp), 50.

7. Indeed, Habermas points out that empirical analysis ran counter to Critical Theory as conceived by Adorno: "I don't think it is possible for Critical Theory in its strictest form to refer to any form of empirical or even discursive analysis of social conditions." Jürgen Habermas, 1986, *Autonomy and Solidarity: Interviews*, ed. Peter Dews (London: Verso), 108.

8. William Outhwaite, 1992, *Habermas: A Critical Introduction* (Cambridge: Blackwell), 9–10.

9. Theodor Adorno, *Briefwechsel Alfred Sohn-Rethel*, ed. Christoph Gödde (Munich: Edition text + kritik, 1991), 158.

10. For details, such as Habermas's critique of the leader of the student movement, Rudi Dutschke, see Oskar Negt, "Autonomie und Eingriff: Ein deutscher intellektueller mit

politischem Urteilsvermögen," in 1986, *Theorie und Praxis Heute. Ein Kolloquium zur Theorie und olitischen Wirksamkeit von Jürgen Habermas,* ed. Oskar Negt, Diskussionsbeiträge Institut für Politische Wissenschaft an der Universität Hannover, 14 (Frankfurt am Main: Materialis Verlag), 14–15.

11.   Jürgen Habermas, 1992, "Interview with Detlef Horster and Willem van Reijen," in Detlef Horster and Willem van Reijen, *Habermas: An Introduction,* trans. Heidi Thompson (Philadelphia: Pennbridge), 83.

12.   Jürgen Habermas, 1987, "The Entwinement of Myth and Enlightenment," in *The Philosophical Discourse of Modernity,* trans. Frederick Lawrence (Cambridge, Mass.: MIT Press), 113.

13.   Theodor Adorno, "Benjamin der Briefschreiber," in *Schriften 11: Noten zur Literatur* (Frankfurt am Main: Suhrkamp), 585–86.

14.   Adorno to Benjamin, 18 March 1936: "I now find it somewhat disturbing — and here I can see a sublimated remnant of certain Brechtian themes — that you have now rather casually transferred the concept of the magical aura to the 'autonomous work of art' and flatly assigned a counter-revolutionary function to the latter. . . . [I]t seems to me that the heart of the autonomous work of art . . . is inherently dialectical, that is, compounds within itself the magical element with the sign of freedom." Henry Lonitz, ed., 1999, *The Complete Correspondence 1928–1940,* (Cambridge, Mass.: Harvard University Press), 128.

15.   Negt, *Theorie und Praxis Heute,* 7–8.

16.   Burger, *Transformations,* xv.

17.   Marc B. de Launay, trans. 1978, *L'espace public: archéologie de la publicité comme dimension constitutive de la société bourgeoise,* by Jürgen Habermas (Paris: Payot).

18.   Habermas, "The Public Sphere," 52.

19.   Antonio Domenech, trans. 1994, *Historia y crítica de la opinion pública,* by Jürgen Habermas (Naucalpan, Mexico: Gustavo Gili).

20.   Jürgen Habermas, "The Critique of Reason as an Unmasking of the Human Sciences: Michel Foucault," and "Questions Concerning the Theory of Power: Foucault Again," in *The Philosophical Discourse,* 238–93.

21.   Julia Koivisto, and Esa Valiverronen, Fall 1996, "The Resurgence of Critical Theories of the Public Sphere," *Journal of Communication Inquiry* 20, 2:18.

22.   John D. Peters, October 1993, "Distrust of Representation: Habermas on the Public Sphere," *Media, Culture and Society* 15, 1: 543–34.

23.   Peter U. Hohendahl, Fall 1974, "Jürgen Habermas, 'The Public Sphere,'" *New German Critique* 3: 45.

24.   Koivisto and Valiverronen, 22.

25.   Joan Landes, 1988, *Women and the Public Sphere in the Age of the French Revolution* (Ithaca: Cornell UP); Patricia Roberts, Winter 1996 "Habermas, *Philosophes,* and Puritans: Rationality and Exclusion in the Dialectical Public Sphere," *Rhetoric Society Quarterly* 26, #1: 47–68; Michael Schudson, 1992, "Was There Ever a Public Sphere?" in *Habermas and the Public Sphere,* ed. Craig Calhoun (Cambridge, MA: MIT Press), 143–63.

26.   Alexander Kluge, Fall–Winer 1981, "Film and the Public Sphere," *New German Critique* 24–25: 213.

27.   Oskar Negt and Alexnder Kluge, 1993, *Public Sphere and Experience: Toward an Analysis of the Bourgeois and Proletarian Public Sphere,* trans. Peter Labanyi, Jamie Owen Daniel, and Assenka Oksiloff (Minneapolis: University of Minnesota Press, 1993), xliv.

28.   Marie Fleming, "Intimacy," *Emancipation and Illusion* (University Park, Penna.: Penn State Press, 1997), 197–216; Nancy Fraser, Spring–Summer 1985, "What's Critical About Critical Theory? The Case of Habermas and Gender," *New German Critique* 35: 97–131; Cindy L. Griffin, Winter 1996, "The Essentialist Roots of the Public Sphere: A Feminist Critique," *Western Journal of Communication* 60, #1, 21–39; Landes, *Women and the Public Sphere,* see n. 21.

29.   John D. Peters, October 1993, "Distrust of Representation: Habermas on the Public Sphere," *Media, Culture and Society* 15, 1: 553.

30.   Jean-François Lyotard, 1984, *The Post-Modern Condition,* trans. Geoff Bennington and Brian Massumi (Minneapolis: University of Minnesota Press), 72.

31.   Rainer Nägele, 1987, "Public Voice and Private Voice: Freud, Habermas, and the Dialectic of Enlightenment," in *Reading After Freud: Essays on Goethe, Hölderlin, Habermas, Nietzsche, Brecht, Celan, and Freud* (New York: Columbia University Press), 72.

32.   Joshua Meyrowitz, 1985, *No Sense of Place: The Impact of Electronic Media on Social Behavior* (New York: Oxford University Press).

33.   George Landow, 1992, *Hypertext: The Convergence of Contemporary Critical Theory and Technology* (Baltimore: Johns Hopkins University Press), 182. Cf. the direct application of Habermas to hypertext in Charles Ess, 1994 "The Political Computer: Hypertext, Democracy, and Habermas," in *Hyper/Text/Theory,* ed. George P. Landow (Baltimore: Johns Hopkins University Press), 225–267.

34.   Baoill, Andrew Ó, September 2000, "Slashdot and the Public Sphere," *firstmonday* 5, 9: http://www.firstmonday.dk/issues/issue5—9/baoill. Unpaginated.

35.   Mark Poster, 1999, *Comunication in History,* 3rd. ed. (London: Longman), 336.

IV

CONCLUSION

13

The Frankfurt School

Agnes Heller

Dedicated to Gyorgy Markus on the occasion of his sixty-fifth birthday, in friendship.

The Frankfurt School was a school. It is unimportant that the name "Frankfurt School" was invented only in the sixties and that the members of this school identified themselves rather with the Institute of Social Sciences, with the *Journal of Social Sciences,* or described themselves as the group of thinkers committed to the so-called critical theory. For the name "Frankfurt School" describes properly the relationship of the men who once belonged to it, the character of their friendships, their solidarity with one another, as also their eventual disloyalty and falling out with one another, the reasons for their commitment to each other and also their disappointments and gratifications. Adorno reflected several times on the intrinsic ties between school and friendship, yet perhaps never so graphically as in an essay written about the private correspondence between Stefan George and Hugo von Hofmannsthal. Adorno speaks of the "Georgesche Schule" (the George school), the friendship between George and Hofmannsthal, and about the constantly recurring and never solved conflicts and tensions within this friendship. Then he proceeds: "Die Freundschaft der beiden ist im Zerfall, ehe sie jemals sich verwircklichte. Damals war Freundschaft selbt unter Menschen der aussderordentlichsten Produktivkraft nicht mehr aus blosser Sympathie und blossem Geschmack möglich, sondern einzig auf dem Grunde bindend gemeinsamer Erkenntnis: Freundschaft aus Solidarität, welche die Theorie als Element ihrer Praxis einschliesst."[1] One could read this also as a confession. The friendship between Horkheimer and Adorno, and also the friendship among other members of the school could not have survived, perhaps not even developed, on the basis of personal sympathy or taste alone. What was needed in addition was the cement of solidarity. But what is the cement of solidarity, what motivates solidarity? Adorno's answer is, To share theory as the element of their praxis.

The statement is strong because of its historicizing and generalizing character. Adorno does not speak only about George and Hofmannsthal. He says that friendship between two persons, between two extremely productive persons, is no longer possible on the ground of mutual sympathy and taste alone; in fact it was already impossible in the times of the George school, and this has remained true since. In the twentieth century only those friendships prevail, particularly between two men of highly creative powers, where the men have a common cause. And he also specified the common cause. What kind of common cause should it be that calls for solidarity and makes friendship possible? It cannot be merely theoretical, neither can it be only practical. It must be based on a theory rooted in the practical and returning to it. If two men share a theory of their praxis or a theory of practical intent, furthermore, if sharing such a theory and practice calls for solidarity, then, and only then, can modern friendships among highly creative men overcome personal schisms, tensions, and conflicts; only then can friendship also endure censure, insensitivity, and occasionally also spite, yet still prevail. Friendship prevails in modern times if it is more than friendship, or at least also something else. Three elements are thus connected: that of personal friendship, that of a common cause, and that of high productivity. Modern friendship is cemented by elements that are normally contingent to friendship.

Adorno expresses himself in too categorical a manner. In the twentieth century, and already in times of George and Hofmannsthal, friendships are no longer possible without a common cause, at least they have not endured time or survived conflicts without it. Adorno simply takes the situation and the experience of the Frankfurt School for granted. What has happened among them could not have happened otherwise. He had a central experience in life, and thus he generalized and extrapolated this experience.

When I term Adorno's statements "categorical" I do not mean it metaphorically. Adorno's statement was a generalized statement, and he also extrapolated it. Adorno said that although hitherto—that is until the twentieth century—there have been other kinds of friendships, since our age this is no longer possible. We who—here and now—are living in the future of Adorno's present, will remark that he was wrong. If there is something one hardly encounters in our own times it is exactly a friendship based upon a common cause. There are no common causes, at least not the kinds that are significant enough to cement the friendships of men of high creativity, to make them endure censure, occasional injustice, and constant interference. Yet there are still friendships, and since they exist, they are also possible. Our friendships are now, by and large, based again on sympathy and taste, as they can also be cemented by common interests and shared ideas. As far as friendships are concerned, the so-called highly productive—and also less productive but still concerned intellectuals on the broadly conceived left or liberal space of culture, politics, and everyday life—seem to be closer to Nietzsche's age than to the twenties, the thirties or even the sixties of our century. Yet I would not like to be categorical. Who knows what kind of new friendships will develop around possible or impossible new causes tomorrow or a century from now?

Adorno was categorical, yet I was not, as no one would be in my place. The difference is mainly historical. On my part, I am at the present moment not committed to any school whatsoever (as I once was). Adorno, however, when composing his essay on George and Hofmannsthal, in fact was, or believed that he still was, committed to the Frankfurt School, or at least to Horkheimer, its symbol. If one is committed to a cause and a school, one develops the tendency to talk categorically, to indulge in hasty generalizations and extrapolations. This is not a personal character trait, neither is it a forte or a weakness. If one has faith in a cause—and as long as one has—one will utter such and similar categorical statements. A person who just asks questions without even experimenting with answering them, an inconsistent skeptic who understands everything or almost everything or nothing, a person who is curious but withholds judgment at all costs, will not be affiliated with a school. In contrast, even the most sophisticated creative intellect such as Adorno will become highly judgmental and in this respect narrow-minded through and because of his commitment to his school. But this narrow-mindedness is not at all self-serving. It is narrow-mindedness emerging from a purpose and serving a purpose. And it is a kind of narrow-mindedness that can, although not necessarily will, also enhance—to speak with Adorno—high productivity.

A whole library has been written about the Frankfurt School's relation to Walter Benjamin. Adorno and Horkheimer stand here accused—among others by Hannah Arendt and Hans Jonas—for having been partly responsible for Benjamin's death. First, because they did not offer enough financial support for Benjamin to survive and were not fast enough to secure his affidavit. This issue I put aside, because I cannot judge it. The other is the accusation of censorship. Both Horkheimer and Adorno asked Benjamin to change certain things in articles he sent for publication in their journal: they asked him to change his wording, they also replaced certain expressions with others and so on. Yet one does not need to attribute exclusively lowly motives to Adorno and Horkheimer because of this. They might have been jealous, envious, stingy, and self serving, I do not know. But had they not been any of them, they would have still done the same. As long as men believe in their cause they will speak and act in the first person plural and not in the first person singular. They will ask also the outsiders or semi-outsiders to adjust to their conceptions. It will matter for them and matter very much whether the essay or the study published in their journal furthers the common cause or hinders it. Nowadays, articles sent to journals are also turned down unless rewritten, or they are outright rejected, even if they are splendid and original, and frequently precisely because of it, for motives no more noble than the alleged motives of Adorno and Horkheimer, and yet without any other cause but preference for mediocrity. Academic censorship is not lighter than the censorship of the *Journal of Social Sciences,* but its yield is significantly less original and interesting.

Being categorical, having a common cause, and exercising a kind of censorship (which was perceived as censorship only by the outsiders), all these are just different aspects of the same. Namely that the Frankfurt School was a school. Yet it was also tied by friendships. Not everyone one now enumerates as members of the school were personal friends. Among the earlier generation of the Institute, under the leadership of Gurnberg, only a few remained in contact with Horkheimer's group. Yet even within this group, Fromm was only Leo Löwenthal's friend, not the friend of Horkheimer, Pollock, or Adorno, and he left the school, which strongly disapproved of his theoretical work, relatively early. Horkheimer and Pollock, Horkheimer and Adorno, Adorno and Löwenthal, were also personal friends, and they were the also most enthusiastic carriers of the common cause. Sometimes Marcuse too belonged to the inner circle, sometimes, and finally, he also parted ways.

To be the carrier of the common cause meant to speak in plural. To speak in plural meant to interfere with each other's work. I mentioned that the members of hard core never considered this constant interference as a censorship. They have been committed, they regarded criticism by their peers as something that contributes to the common cause and also to the properness of their own writing. Interestingly, however, Horkheimer was almost always spared. Moreover, with the exception of the last issue, his articles were always leading articles in the *Journal for Social Sciences.* He had a special standing. He was the measure of correctness, so he could hardly be criticized because of his incorrectness. To Horkheimer's special standing I will yet return.

The combination of cause and friendship is a very sensitive connection. On the one hand, if one is a friend, one is more ready to accept criticism, sometimes even abuse. And if one is committed to the cause one has duties additional to the duties of friendship. For example when Horkheimer renewed his contact with Adorno from the United States, he writes him the following: "If it is possible at all for there to be productive relations between people working on theory at the moment, regular collaboration between yourself and the Institute is part of that . . . *It was simply your duty to remain in touch with us . . .*" Let me now quote from Adorno's answer: "I was . . . part and parcel of the Institute itself, just like yourself, Pollock and Löwenthal. You would not have seen as a *betrayal* of *our* friends for the Institute to ensure that these three were materially provided for first of all, since they are its innermost productive forces. . . . My own case was no different."[2] When Adorno sends Horkheimer his work on modern music, then, he likes it, but simultaneously also warns Adorno that his criticism should be directed against society itself. Adorno answers: "whether *we* should really continue . . . to . . ."[3] When Marcuse sends them both *Eros and Civilization* to read, Horkheimer reacts to it in the following way in a letter written to Adorno: "By the way, Herbert's work seems to be quite decent . . . although the psychological approach does not really appeal to *us*, there are so many things that *we* should accept it completely." The subject of the "we" is constantly shifting. *We* can stand for those committed to critical theory, but it can also stand for the friends Horkheimer and Adorno, or to the broader hard core of the school, Pollock and perhaps even Löwenthal included. Yet even if the "we" stands only for the closest friends it also stands for the cause, for the personal relation is substituted for the cause, since it *is* the cause, since even personal friendship is meant to serve the cause. Löwenthal rightly said that the "hard core" determined the Institute's theoretical orientation.[4]

At the end of the story the cause was gone, friendship remained where it remained, within the trio Adorno/Horkheimer/Pollock. Yet the golden days, where friendships and cause were inflated and merged, were gone, and there remained a feeling of loss and nostalgia. As Löwenthal remembers: "My first years at the Institute were a sort of anticipated utopia; we were different and we knew the world better."[5] Here Löwenthal describes perfectly what a school is all about. It is about the self-consciousness that we are different and we know the world better.

But what was the difference between the Frankfurt School and a traditional kind of a theoretical/philosophical school? And what was still held in common among them? What was the historical locus of this school? What was the so frequently mentioned common cause of this school?

Philosophical schools are as old as philosophy itself. They consist normally of thinkers of different ages/groups who remain learners even after becoming teachers, as long as they remain members of the school. At the center point of a school sits the master/ philosopher, the man of perfect wisdom, the repository of truth. Even the skeptics are repositories of the truth of skepticism. Their master needs to wield personal authority, he is not just supposed to be wiser, but he is mostly also a charismatic personality. The members of a school are committed to the master and this is roughly tantamount to being committed to Truth. The school is an institution, although mostly self-instituted. It is also a community, sometimes tightly, sometimes loosely knit. It is relatively insular; admittance in a school is formally or informally restricted, sometimes even regulated. A school is frequently conceived of as an alien body, as marginal both in its thinking and in its way of life. For the members of the school their marginality means their superiority. There is solidarity among the members, solidarity in the name of Truth. That is, members of the school believe exactly what was, according to Löwenthal's testimony, the Frankfurt School's conviction during their finest hours: "We are different and we know the world better." Since the members of a school consider themselves both different and superior in knowledge to all others, they assume a strongly polemical attitude against the truths of other schools or against mere opinions. If only because of this, they practice criticism.

There are great differences among schools. Some are characterized by a common and strict way of life, others not. Some display a special style of thinking, others not. Some are as closed as a sect, some others not. Yet they share the previously enumerated features: relative isolation, opposition, sense of superiority, knowing things better or entirely differently from the rest, being the repository of truth. It is in this conviction that they surround the master, the head of the school.

Traditional schools of philosophy have lost momentum at the dawn of modernity. Descartes had no school, neither had Leibniz or Spinoza. Modern philosophers became loners, philosophical communities were withering. There were substitutes for schools, first and foremost in the universities, the emerging institutions of academic learning. But the relationship between the university professor and his pupils is entirely different from the relation between the master and his disciples, although the two roles coalesce sometimes. What is new is the dynamism of the relationship. Whereas disciples of old times did their best to preserve the Truth of the master and to pass it on to the next generation of disciples, unless they established a new school of their own, in modern times the critique of the work of the master and sometimes also its destruction will be—wittingly or unwittingly—the pupil's eminent task. True, there are also "intermediary" phenomena. One need only to think of the students of the University of Berlin and the Hegelian school. The pupils' relationship to the professor resembled the relationship of the disciples to the old master. Their humble work at the publication of the master's lectures and books kept close to the traditional devotion. Yet schools concerned with the interpretation of old masters, as the Kantian schools of Marburg and Heidelberg, respectively, offered shared knowledge, interest, approach, sometimes loyalty, yet nothing else. Groups of theoretical friends like the Vienna Circle can hardly be termed a school, either in the old sense or in the modern sense. Where there is no central master there is no ancient kind of school, and where there is no common cause other than the pursuing of a certain kind of philosophy or science there is no modern school.

In the nineteenth century schools had been mostly replaced by "isms." Marxism was not a school. Marx had no school, and he hastened also to declare that he was no Marxist either. Perhaps the common feature among schools and isms is that both acknowledge a common source, and both claim to interpret this common source. Isms can also be presented and represented by movements. The "ists" in general consider themselves repositories of truth, yet since the source is interpreted differently, the common source does not satisfy the criterion of truth. Those affiliated with an ism are not friends because of their common theoretical ancestry; they can be even, as they frequently are, bitter and deadly enemies. They do not form communities, or if they do, for another reason, they do not read each other's manuscripts, even if they write some; they perhaps do not even know one another. Besides the master/figure of origin (Marx) the Marxists surround many different master/figures of interpretations.

To repeat: Marx had no school. Yet Freud had. But Freudianism is not identical with Freud's school. Neither is the latter identical with the psychoanalytical movement. Freudianism is an ism just like Marxism. But Freud's school—and here I come to my point—was the first *modern school.* A modern school that already manifested all the basic features characteristic of the later Frankfurt School. In Freud's school the members of the school were friends, and they had a common cause. Psychoanalysis was a common cause. Many times did they repress their feelings of personal hurt and disappointment for the sake of the common cause. They knew that they were different from the rest, and that they knew everything better. They were a small group of people, relatively isolated and marginal. They were the rebels of science. They rebelled also against the prejudices of the society that surrounded them. They were also involved in a theory related to practice. They also believed in loyalty, they despised treason (e.g., they considered Carl Jung's change of mind in psychoanalytical theory as treason). They read one another's manuscripts, and they expressed their disappointment if something they read did not met their expectations. They spoke the language of "we." And they had a master, the charismatic repository of truth in the center of the school.

What is new in such a school? First and foremost its relationship to the surrounding world. The Freud school was subversive, as all the twentieth century schools are. If they cease to be subversive they will soon decompose as schools. Modern schools—and this is one of their practical elements—are in a way self-contradictory. For they are a relatively closed world of a group of friends, and this is precisely the utopia Löwenthal spoke about in his recollections. Yet their cause is to make their truth be acknowledged, their vision accepted, their thoughts widespread in practice. They seek for more and more general recognition. They need not only books to write but also journals to publish, for they want their ideas to be disseminated in wide circles all around the world. They are an informal and self-institutionalized institution but their cause includes also that their thought, theories, ideas be admitted into all institutions of import and significance. They are subversive and desire to be accepted and embraced.

Was Existentialism a school? Certainly not. But Sartre had his school gathered around a café table and the journal *Les Temps Modernes,* a school shared with Simone de Beauvoir, Maurice Merleau-Ponty, Albert Camus and a few other friends. Sartre had also his traitor, his "Jung" in the person of Serge Mallet. The Sartre school was also rebellious and subversive; it considered itself marginal even if it initiated one of the most popular movements after World War II, as it was also a philosophy with practical/political intent. The school as school collapsed finally in 1968 when its subversive character became questioned. Old friends remained friends, new friends joined, the journal remained: they still had something in common, but they ceased to be a school.

The Frankfurt School was in fact the second representative school in our century (after Freud and before the Sartre school), and also the *first authentically modern philosophical school in our century.* The Freud group had not seen itself as a philosophical school. They understood psychoanalysis as a science. As we know, this was at first also the self-understanding of the Frankfurt School. At the beginning, they wanted to present the true, and practically relevant, modern social science. Both the name of the institute and of the journal advertises this approach. Only later, in the United States, and particularly at the end of the thirties, did they start to identify themselves also or even mainly as a philosophical school, and of course as a philosophical school that first and foremost must thematize society. They were also affiliated with sociology.

I emphasize that this is, again, an innovation. Modern philosophers had, as a rule, no schools. Neither had sociologists. There is no Weber school, and as we know from Arendt's recollection, Heidegger positively loathed the thought of having disciples and of establishing a school. Wittgenstein's circle in Cambridge was a philosophical community of thinking, but not a school. Marcuse studied with Heidegger yet he became a member of the Frankfurt School. Other members of the Frankfurt School (like Horkheimer) came from a Marxian (if not Marxist) tradition or inspiration.

There is a blatantly new feature in the schools of the twentieth century. In spite of school solidarity and the frequent employment of the first person plural, despite the self-censorship practiced for the sake of the cause, the members of modern schools were from the beginning of their history as thinkers up to the end of their creative life independent scholars. By being an independent scholar I do not mean only that they had their own style of thinking, but also that they had their own interests, they were involved in entirely different philosophical or theoretical projects. This change, which was in fact ushered in first by the Frankfurt School, and was put into practice later also by the Sartre school, and even later in the Budapest School (which I know from the inside), was intimately related to one very important matter. This matter I could sum up with the following: *the cause was substituted for truth.* Sure, the cause has to do something with truth, because the conviction "we know it better" can be also read in a way that we are the ones who know the truth. Yet not quite. For in a modern school the *truth is not something what we receive from the hand or the mouth of the master, but is understood as the avenue whereon we need to tread in order to arrive at the truest insights.* If one reads attentively Horkheimer's manifestos (I will return to them later) one realizes that they normally show the way to truth, they present guideposts, offer indications, tell the faithful ones which avenue they should tread to take the right direction, but they do not present the truth pure and simple, with the exception of time/diagnoses. Perhaps this is why Horkheimer's manifesto style is now so irritating. He utters mostly not even very well-hidden commands addressed to his friends, to do this rather than that in the future, and warns them to behave better theoretically. Yet even this clumsy manifesto style discloses the new secret, that the avenue to truth and not truth received or discovered is what the cause is meant to be.

Members, or the most productive members, of the school were all supposed to do something different, or to contribute on different fields to the common cause. Horkheimer obviously shared Lukács's position that in a good household everything can be made use of. He also made the point that different fields of scholarship needed to be covered by the journal, particularly in the review section, given that the books reviewed in this section do not need to be politically correct. Löwenthal, who edited the review section, contributed thereby—according to Habermas—to the essence of the journal.⁶ Horkheimer, who wrote the guidelines for the book review policy—and all policies—expressed himself as follows: "Because the existing intellectual confusion makes the undaunted pursuit of certain ideas in the various fields of social theory particularly necessary, it is the best interest of each and every philosophical thinking to keep track of work done within individual disciplines . . . In this case, differences in theoretical attitude play a far lesser role than the clarification of particular content." It was obvious for Horkheimer that every written text—with the exception of the *Journal for Social Sciences*—manifests just intellectual confusion; alas, in a good household everything can be useful if one is able to put things into their right place.

The hard-core members of the school and sometimes also those on the periphery felt that they had a cause, that this cause was eminently important, that it consisted— among others—in putting intellectual confusion into order, something that only they could do, precisely because they knew "everything better," who had remained because of this an *ecclesia pressa*. It is far from my intent to unmask these convictions as self-delusion. The Frankfurt School really had a cause, and even if this cause did not have the world historical importance they attributed to it, it was still important. They were, indeed, an *ecclesia pressa*, not primarily because they knew everything better or because they and they alone could put the intellectual confusion into order, but for other reasons. Yet among them one reason was certain, that they were thinking differently, and also better, than the theorists of leftist political movements and the academic mainstream. Without the conviction that they knew everything better and without the conviction that they were *ecclesia pressa* first and foremost because of their supreme insights, without the belief that this conviction enhances creativity, the school would have never been established. Löwenthal tells in one of his interviews that he was always a rebel, he loved everything oppositional, he meant to be (together with Benjamin!) always at the side of the losers in world history.⁷ Hostility against the status quo everywhere and at any time, was the fuel of enthusiasm. They did not only know everything better but they *were* also better than anyone else, because they were not opportunists, because their ambition reached higher than snatching good positions, achieving official recognition, earning much money, or living simply in peace. There was something of the Nietzschean feeling of superiority in the hard core of the Frankfurt School. They were the patricians who stood far above the multitude and the crowd both in Germany and in America.

Without a kind of elitism there is no school. Yet it does not need to be this kind of elitism. The style of the elitism of the Frankfurt School, not, albeit, its content, had something to do with the social background of the hard core of the school. Elitism was shared for a while, but later on it took very different shapes in the thought of different members. One could say that the radical cultural pessimism of Horkheimer, Adorno, and Marcuse of the *One-Dimensional Man,* was intimately connected to elitism. This does not tell anything, of course, about the *content* of the works, which manifested different branches of cultural pessimism, even less does it justify or call into question the cultural diagnosis itself.

I already pointed at the inner tension in the life of the Frankfurt School. The school members were marginals, or at least considered themselves an *ecclesia pressa,* yet at the same time they longed for institutions, institutionalization; they wanted their ideas to move closer to the center, to be recognized. But what is interesting in the story is *that the center in the oppositions to which the marginals determined their own identity was also shifting.* It did not remain the same center. Briefly, at first they were marginals as against the centers of leftist/socialist practical theory, later they became marginals as against the centers of academic sociology and philosophy.

When Horkheimer took over the directorship of the Institute for Social Sciences, he took the directorship of an institute within the Frankfurt University. He was very young at that time. By no means could he have rightly considered himself then as an academic marginal. His was a very early and very successful career, which went together with a secure income guaranteed by the donation of a millionaire friend, Felix Weil. I mention on the side that according to my view, this career at the time was by all academic standards entirely undeserved. But why did Horkheimer feel himself still a rebel, still a marginal? *Where the margin is depends on where the center is.*

Horkheimer's dream (which became true when he no longer had it) was at that time to make an essential contribution to Marxian social theory. I do not say Marxist, but Marxian, for Horkheimer was first and foremost inspired by Marx himself, as were other members of the institute, some of whom became, at least for a while, also affiliated with the Frankfurt hard core, as Marcuse, who turned from Heidegger to the young Marx after the publication of the *Paris Manuscripts,* which also influenced the work of Fromm. As is well-known, Karl Wittfogel and Franz Neumann were at that time Marxists pure and simple, and the pre-Horkheimerian institute under Grunberg was a Marxist institute. The influences of Lukács and Karl Korsch were at that time significant.

Horkheimer's conviction was not self-delusory. The Frankfurt School was indeed marginal, and also rebellious, in relation to a center that was then its point of orientation: Marxian, revolutionary, socialist, leftist thinking. At that time, just as before and also in the following decade, the Marxian legacy was identified with Marxisms. There was Leninist Marxism, Social-Democratic Marxism, a little later Trotskyite Marxism, Stalinist Marxism, and all the other kinds of Marxism. Yet all of them were isms, and all isms where embedded in, or expressed by, parties and movements—to put it bluntly, by political organizations or power machines. Even the intellectuals expelled from parties or leaving them because of deep disappointment, developed their own ideas as recommendations for parties and for movements.

They wanted to influence another communist party or another social-democratic party, yet they always wanted to influence a party. Now, the Institute of Social Sciences and the *Journal of Social Sciences* under Horkheimer was, or rather became, different. Even when Horkheimer regarded the work of Marx as the main source of inspiration, he was not committed to any party or movement, he wanted an institute where the chief organization remains theoretical, where it becomes possible to think about society, to offer a diagnosis of society, independently from the concrete conflicts and even concrete objectives of political parties. To remain political without theorizing for short-term political targets, this was Horkheimer's dream. At the time when Horkheimer became the director of the institute, very few on the socialist left were raising questions in this light. And on the left/socialist side of the political spectrum even fewer believed that personal creativity grows out of relatively independent thinking, or that the enhancement of personal creativity is important, or that one can yet serve a cause without becoming absolutely subservient to a political machine. Horkheimer and his friends wanted theory with practical intent, but no political machine. And practical intent meant a free intent. We work on our critical theory, we busy ourselves to give a diagnosis of the present world, any movement or institution can (and had better!) accept our diagnosis, and if it does it will act in a superior way. This conception was not just marginal, but in a way ridiculously so. Kings never listen to philosophers. As Gyorgy Markus pointed out to me, there were still moments in Horkheimer's life when he experimented with the idea (e.g., in his paper "Impotence of the German Working Class") to offer a theory for a new party constituted by the best elements of Communism and Social-Democracy. But these moments remained episodical.

The Frankfurt School was frequently attacked (among others by Phil Slater) for having abandoned praxis. Löwenthal answered to this accusation with a *bon mot:* "It was not we who abandoned praxis, but praxis has abandoned us." I see things in a little different light. At the beginning, the school conceived theory with practical intent, at first Marxian, later less and less so. Simultaneously with the development of a penchant toward radical cultural criticisms and cultural pessimism, the core of the Frankfurt School seemed to abandon the so-called practical agenda. This only meant that they lost hope in the affectivity of intervention. Yet—with the exception of Horkheimer—none of them lost faith entirely in a certain kind of this-worldly redemption. Except for Horkheimer, there was a deeply Jewish stream in the radical cultural pessimism of Adorno and Marcuse. The Messiah can come at anytime, but he comes rather in darkest times. Horkheimer abandoned the dreams of his youth, and Adorno, although he always yearned for salvation and reconciliation, remained under the influence of Horkheimer, whose faithful knight he was. But as always, radical pessimism easily jumps into radical hope. Look at Marcuse in 1968 and after.

There was another factor—besides the distance from the then socialist left—in the marginality of the early Frankfurt School. All of their members were Jewish. True, they did not realize that this too conditioned their rebellious attitudes, or that their Jewishness might present a problem, even in a Germany that was at that time ready to embrace Nazism. Furthermore, although they came from different family backgrounds, they were all bourgeois youth, and in contrast to Benjamin, pampered by their parents. And even when they rebelled against their fathers, they were very easily reaccepted by them, owing to the fathers' high respect for intellectual achievements. Thus the energies of the generation conflict (which were too successfully settled soon) also became vested in the rebellious attitude of the common cause.

In times of emigration, from the first moment that they settled in New York, the cause began to shift. The center against which the Frankfurt School identified itself as marginal was less and less Marxism or leftist social theory. This was left behind in the Old World and swept away by Hitler's seizure of power. In addition, some old conditions of marginality were reinforced and new experiences of marginality were added. According to Löwenthal, they experienced anti-Semitism first in the United States. Moreover, they had to discover that their cultural style and thinking was entirely alien to their new milieu. In Germany they were Jews, in America they became Germans. Yet in a way, this dual alienation spurred their theoretical activity. They could work out their culture shock, and in and through the fact that they also *shifted the center in relation to which they maintained the self-consciousness of marginality.*

I mention only at the sideline that it was not just for opportunistic reasons and for securing a relatively independent livelihood for a few members, that the institute participated in empirical sociological research projects such as the project on family, the radio project or the project on authoritarian personality and prejudice. This was also a way to link their theory to praxis, even if the latter meant something other than before. Besides, those researches were undertakings where a collectivity, t*he school as such* could participate, or at least might have participated.

In an already quoted letter from Horkheimer to Adorno—who came to America only in 1938—we read the following passage: "We are the only group whose existence does not depend on gradual assimilation, the only group which can maintain the relatively advanced state of theory which has been achieved in Germany and advance it even further."[8] By gradual assimilation Horkheimer means assimilation into the American academy and particularly into American positivism. It is at this stage that the cause shifted. In the center to the opposition of which the Frankfurt School, or more precisely critical theory, has now to prevail and develop, are *academic theories.* Both positivism and metaphysics. After the war, fundamental ontology was also added to the list. Fundamental ontology, so Adorno says, agrees with positivism in their fight against metaphysics. Yet fundamental ontology is as uncritical as positivism. "So wenig der Geist das Absolute ist, so wenig geht er auf im Seienden. Nur dann wird er erkennen was ist, wenn er sich nicht durchstreicht. Die Kraft solchen Widerstandes ist das Einzige Mass der Philosophie heute." And then he adds that philosophy should be absolutely modern.[9] The quotation is telling, for in critical theory being absolutely modern equals being absolutely critical, and resisting.

Critical theory (philosophy) is meant now to be *die Philosophie des Widerstandes.* The cause is and remains *resistance.* The *what* and the *how* of the resistance changes, yet resistance remains. (Again with the exception of the old Horkheimer.) I mention in brackets that this "*Widerstand*" was not associated with the resistance against Nazism, or as they called it those times, fascism. At first, the members of the

Frankfurt School regarded fascism as a necessary or contingent outgrowth of capitalism. Yet even after changing their understanding and agenda, the hard core of the Frankfurt School has never a acknowledged resistance against Nazism as their central cause or issue. They would have regarded this as an issue of special interest (Jewish) in contrast to the war efforts of the United States. Still, they made some theoretical efforts to understand the phenomenon of fascism, first and foremost in general terms, that is historically and psychologically, as in the "Anti-Semitism" chapter of the *Dialectic of Enlightenment* and the studies on authoritarian personality. (Neumann at the time of *Behemot* was no more considered a school member.) True, the mythical/diabolical dimensions of the Holocaust were at that time not known. Adorno's later declaration that one cannot write poetry after Auschwitz can also be seen as a belated tribute to the awareness of having been impotent face to face with the demonic. Yet at any rate: since *Widerstand* was not meant as *Widerstand* against Nazism—even if three members of the school worked for American agencies during the war—the members of the school did not experience the Allied victory as the victory of their own cause and did not feel they had any obligations for the European future.

Critical theory was not meant to be just a critical social theory, except in the beginning. Everything had to be subjected to critique. Yet Horkheimer emphasized the "immanent" character of critique. This was a new approach in leftist theory, which normally operated with the hermeneutics of suspicion and with the procedure of unmasking. It was also a new approach in the then positivistically inclined academic philosophy and sociology. The broadening of the scope and objects of criticism, as much as their family background and previous interests, made the members of the Frankfurt School deeply interested in psychoanalysis and the works of Freud in particular, especially of the later Freud, also critically. In fact, one could observe a similar tendency in the development of the Sartre school. After a strong rejection of Freud, psychoanalysis of a special branch became admitted into the philosophy of existence. If one wants to be absolutely modern, one can hardly avoid taking this step.

Let me return to the beginning. The slow demise of the Frankfurt School begins after Horkheimer and Adorno return to Frankfurt. What is lost is the cause. Since Adorno and Horkheimer cannot shift their cause again as they once did, their resistance becomes objectless. The conviction that one knows things better than others does not preserve a school on its own, if the conviction that this knowledge makes a difference in the world is missing. Adorno could still remain true to some of his causes, such as the critique of positivism, of fundamental ontology, metaphysics, and cultural criticism. Yet, even if he continued to speak in plural, he philosophized in the singular. So did Marcuse in America. Horkheimer on his part became a university professor, and soon the rector (the president) of the Frankfurt University. According to the testimonies of his former students (Thomas Leithauser for one) he gave well-ordered and wonderful seminars, e.g., on French materialists. He was also mistrustful not just toward rebels but also toward critical minds. It is well-known that he prevented Habermas's habilitation in Frankfurt. To put it bluntly, after 1948 there was no more Frankfurt school except in name. Professors and their disciples remained. Among Adorno's disciples many became distinguished scholars like Habermas, Wellmer, Offe, Negt, and others. But as there was no Heidegger school (in spite of the imposing list of names who studied under Heidegger), there is no Adorno school either. Perhaps only the early Habermas did, and Alfred Schmidt still does, something that reminds us of the old, traditional issues of the institute and the *Journal for Social Sciences*. Adorno's former students might have remained friends or not, they might have influenced one another or not, yet they were not assembled in a school. Perhaps—with the exception of a living organism—it is always difficult to determine how long the identity of a subject (*hypokeimenon*) is preserved through several changes and when it is no more, for neither generation nor destruction can be pinned down exactly. I choose as the point of destruction of the Frankfurt School the time when the former core of the school ceased to have a common cause, and the younger generation was understood as heirs or followers yet not as members, and even then not by Horkheimer, not by the master of the school

The greatest puzzle of the Frankfurt School is not its cause but its center. Normally, in a philosophical school the most significant and most creative member occupies the center, or at least a creative person who used to be original and significant. This was also the case in the Budapest School with Lukács in the center. But this was not the case in the Frankfurt School. Horkheimer was the center of this school. Yet he was not particularly creative, original, or significant. Not even "productive." Helmut Dubiel, in his interview with Leo Löwenthal, refers, among others, to Horkheimer's project of conceiving an all-embracing theory of social life. Löwenthal answers with noticeable irritation: "Now listen. Horkheimer never wrote such a book. This is not an accident. You may, if you wish, collect essays, as has been done, choose a title for publication purposes, and call it Critical Theory. And yet, this will not provide a systematic theory."[10] The question is, however, not that Horkheimer wrote only essays or aphorisms. I would be reluctant to say "only" in this case, since Nietzsche did the same, and in the Frankfurt School almost all of Adorno's works were exercises in aphoristic style or essay style. The problem is rather that Horkheimer was—in matters of theoretical creativity—not particularly significant. In the main, he wrote programs and manifestos in which he prescribed to others what paths they should take. True, in the given historical context these writings—such as the one on the difference between traditional and critical theory—could serve as theoretical signposts, but they are no longer sources of inspiration. Not only is *Dialectic of Enlightenment* Adorno's book, but the *Eclipse of Reason* (although it was published in Horkheimer's name alone) was also inspired and perhaps even worked out by Adorno. To put it bluntly: Horkheimer had meager talent for social theory and philosophy, whereas some members of his school had much talent. Especially Adorno, who was highly creative, who lived constantly in a state of feverish creativity. True, not everything Adorno wrote is now of interest, but many things still are. Adorno can be read and reread, and after each reading one gets something new and surprising out of his works, even if the work is a mess, as in the case of *Negative Dialectics*. Horkheimer, however, does not say anything new for the contemporary reader. Even Fromm with his anthropological humanism can surprise us sometimes (for example in his comparison between Stalin's and Hitler's psychological character) and Marcuse's *Eros and Civilization* still has its freshness and can be illuminating. Even Löwenthal's sociology of literature offers some points of departure. Only Horkheimer's work does not offer the contemporary reader anything, or anything new. Besides, his apodictic and schoolmasterly style annoys them. It seems to be a puzzle why Adorno was constantly subservient to Horkheimer. Why did he flatter him (because he did), why did he look up to him and ask his guidance, for what he never needed? Having a conflict with Horkheimer meant to be ousted from the school, of course. But why? He was the director of the institute. He was also in control of the money. He had solid financial means of livelihood even in exile. He was always better provided for than any other member of the school. This can explain something, yet not the whole thing. For example, Horkheimer was not even very generous or loyal. Adorno had to wait for his Frankfurt chair until 1957, because Horkheimer, a professor from the beginning, decided not to raise the issue of his professorship for political reasons. And Adorno did not even complain. Why?

Perhaps the master was in possession of charisma. This is difficult to judge by persons who never met him. He also had class, he behaved like class. Thomas Leithauser described him as a "grand segnieur." But I think that something else was decisive. It was Horkheimer who represented the spirit of the school. It was Horkheimer for whom it was of the greatest importance that they should be a real group with a common cause and not just a bunch of friends of creative powers. It was Horkheimer who stuck to the cause. It was to him that the cause was more important than anything else. This is why he issued his commands, programs, manifestoes. This is why he behaved as a schoolmaster scolding his fellows as little children. He had the passion of the master, he had the conviction that he, and he alone, knew where the path toward the Truth led. He showed the way. Those who followed him remained, those who resented him left. But as long as he had a cause there was a cause. The cause of the Frankfurt School was the cause of Horkheimer. He represented it. Without him they would have been just another group of radical or romantic intellectuals, like the Positano group of Ernst Bloch, Benjamin, Siegfried Kracauer, Sohn-Rethel, and occasionally also of Adorno, described by John Ely as a bunch of *philia*-laden romantic intellectuals from Goethe's novel of *Elective Affinities*. Horkheimer's strong presence made the Frankfurt School different. And in this why he was a real master in the ancient style.

This also explains the loss of the identity of the Frankfurt School. It was Horkheimer who lost his cause after returning to Germany. And, to pay him sincere tribute, this is why he did not issue any more commands or manifestoes. This is why—although he still exercised authority in matters concerning Frankfurt University's Department of Philosophy—he ceased to claim authority in matters of a cause. He remained in fact silent; he withdrew. There was something elegant in this withdrawal where friends became friends again after having lost their significance as allies and as co-workers in the service of something higher than themselves.

The old Horkheimer disliked the young Horkheimer; he disliked the Horkheimer of a cause. Particularly his own leftist writings, his strongly critical writings, irritated him. Leftist radical rhetoric became alien from the spirit of those times, at least in Germany. There was no historical cause left, and for the Frankfurt School only a world historical cause was a real cause. To defend the status quo can sometimes be a sober political choice. But a cause it is not.

Adorno (and to a lesser degree Horkheimer) have continuously influenced a few outstanding young thinkers in Germany and beyond; they initiated a tendency in philosophy that was neither positivistic nor Heideggerian. Yet the resurrection of the Frankfurt School as a school came in the sixties, with the reemergence of a cause, or rather of several causes. It was in the sixties that the name "the Frankfurt School" was invented, first in America. A new generation, being fed up with positivism and annoyed by conservative politics, discovered the writings of the Frankfurt intellectuals, together with their spirit of resistance. These were the times of the resurrection of the Frankfurt School. Among the young Americans, Martin Jay played the pivotal role in presenting the first biography of the Frankfurt School in his *Dialectical Imagination*. He did the research necessary to unearth works already forgotten and to establish the identity of the subject (*hypokeimenon*), whose story he told. There was nostalgia in this story, yet also promise.

The times of the resurrection of the Frankfurt School are gone again; the story became history again to be explored by academic dissertations. Thus I return to the beginning of this essay. Schools are no more. If someone tried to establish one, she would look rather ridiculous. Still, I on my part—and perhaps not just I—*look back not in anger but in a paradoxical nostalgia to a world where something that we do not now wish for ourselves was still possible.*

Notes

1. Theodor Adorno, 1997, *Gesammelte Schriften*, 10-1 (Frankfurt am Main: Suhrkamp), 218.
2. Rolf Wiggershaus, 1994, *The Frankfurt School: Its History, Theories, and Political Significance,* trans. Michael Robertson (Cambridge: MIT Press), 156–57.
3. Ibid., 302.
4. Ibid., 77.
5. Leo Löwenthal, 1987, *An Unmastered Past: The Autobiographical Reflections of Leo Löwenthal,* ed. Martin Jay (Berkeley: University of California Press). 11. Quote of Habermas, taken from Jay's Introduction.
6. Judith Marcus, and Zoltan Tarr, eds. *Foundations of the Frankfurt School of Social Sciences,* "The Frankfurt School in New York" 59.
7. Leo Löwenthal, *Unmastered.*
8. Rolf Wiggershaus, *Frankfurt School.*
9. Theodor Adorno, *Gesammelte,* 10–2, 463.
10. Leo Löwenthal, *Unmastered,* 75.

CONTRIBUTORS

Thomas O. Beebee, Professor of Comparative Literature and German at the Pennsylvania State University, publishes on the literatures of Europe, South America, and North America, specializing in the early-modern period, epistolary fiction, translation issues, genre theory, and millennial studies. His most recent published volume (1999) is entitled *Epistolary Fiction in Europe 1500–1850,* and his recently completed book, *True Imaginary Places,* examines literary landscapes in modern European and American fiction. Beebee is the editor of the journal *Comparative Literature Studies.*

Ronald V. Bettig is Associate Professor of Communications at the Pennsylvania State University. He has published a number of articles and book chapters on the political economy of the culture industries. He is the author of *Copyrighting Culture: The Political Economy of Intellectual Property* (Westview, 1996) and co-author of *Beat the Press: Media Texts in Context* (Rowman & Littlefield, 2002).

Kevin DeLuca is Assistant Professor in the Department of Speech Communication at the University of Georgia. He is the author of *Image Politics: The New Rhetoric of Environmental Activism* (1999) and several articles on environmentalism and rhetorical theory.

Agnes Heller is Hannah Arendt Professor of Philosophy at the New School for Social Research Graduate Faculty. Her most recent publications include *The Time Is Out of Joint: Shakespeare as Philosopher of History* (Rowman and Littlefield) and *Concept of the Beautiful* (Routledge).

Andreas Huyssen is Villard Professor of German and Comparative Literature at Columbia University and an editor of *New German Critique.* He is the author of *After the Great Divide: Modernism, Mass Culture, Postmodernism* (1986) and *Twilight Memories: Marking Time in a Culture of Amnesia* (1995) and he co-edited, with David Bathrick, *Modernity and the Text: Revisions of German Modernism* (1989).

Caren Irr teaches American Literature at Brandeis University. Her book *Suburb of Dissent: Cultural Politics in the United States and Canada* appeared in 1998, and she is currently researching issues concerning gender and intellectual property.

Fredric Jameson is William A. Lane Jr. Professor of Comparative Literature, Professor of Romance Studies (French), and Chair of the Literature Program at Duke University. His most recent books include *Postmodernism, or, The Cultural Logic of Late Capitalism* (1991, winner of the MLA Lowell Award), *Seeds of Time* (1994), *Brecht and Method* (1998), and *The Cultural Turn* (1998).

Douglas Kellner is George Kneller Chair in the Philosophy of Education at UCLA and is author of many books on social theory, politics, history, and culture, including *Critical Theory, Marxism, and Modernity* and *Jean Baudrillard: From Marxism to Postmodernism and Beyond.* He has just published a book on the 2000 presidential election, *Grand Theft 2000: Media Spectacle and the Theft of an Election* and *The Postmodern Adventure. Science, Technology, and Cultural Studies at the Third Millennium* (co-authored with Steve Best).

Richard A. Lee Jr. is Associate Professor of Philosophy at DePaul University. He is the author of *Science, the Singular, and the Question of Theology* (Palgrave-St. Martin's, 2002) and articles on medieval philosophy, early modern philosophy, and critical theory.

Nancy Love is Associate Professor of Political Science and Speech Communication at Pennsylvania State University. Her research interests include critical theory, democratic theory, and feminist theory. She is the author of *Marx, Nietzsche, and Modernity* (Columbia 1986; reissued 1996), "'Singing For Our Lives': Women's Music and Democratic Politics," *Hypatia: A Journal of Feminist Philosophy* (forthcoming), and "Disembodying Democracy: Habermas's Legalistic Turn," in *Confronting Mass Democracy and Industrial Technology: German Political and Social Thought from Nietzsche to Habermas,* ed. John McCormick (Duke, forthcoming). She is currently working on a book tentatively entitled, *Musical Democracy.*

Jeffrey T. Nealon teaches in the English Department at the Pennsylvania State University. He is author of *Double Reading: Postmodernism after Deconstruction* (1993) and *Alterity Politics: Ethics and Performative Subjectivity* (1998). He is presently at work on a book concerning contemporary culture and finance capital.

Imre Szeman is Assistant Professor of English and Cultural Studies and Associate Director of the Institute on Globalization at McMaster University (Hamilton, Canada). He is co-editor of *Pierre Bourdieu: Fieldwork in Literature* and author of *Zones of Instability: Literature, Postcolonialism and the Nation* (forthcoming). His current research focuses of globalization and visuality, and on the concept of mediation in Marxist cultural theory.

Evan Watkins is Professor of English at the University of California, Davis. He publishes in cultural studies, literacy studies, American studies, and composition theory. His recent books include *Everyday Exchanges: Marketwork and Capitalist Common Sense, Throwaways: Work Culture and Consumer Education,* and *Work Time: English Departments and the Circulation of Cultural Value.*

INDEX